Females, Males, and Sexuality

SUNY Series in Sexual Behavior
Donn Byrne and Kathryn Kelley, EDITORS

Edited by KATHRYN KELLEY

Females, Males, and Sexuality
THEORIES AND RESEARCH

State University of New York Press
ALBANY

Published by
State University of New York Press, Albany

© 1987 State University of New York

Printed in the United States of America

For information, address State University of New York
Press, State University Plaza, Albany, N.Y., 12246

Library of Congress Cataloging in Publication Data

Females, males, and sexuality.

  (SUNY series in sexual behavior)
  Includes bibliographies and index.
  1. Sex.   2. Sex differences (Psychology)   I. Kelley,
Kathryn.   II. Series.   [DNLM: 1. Sex Behavior.
HQ 21 F329]
HQ21.F39   1987   155.3   87-6423
ISBN 0-88706-309-8
ISBN 0-88706-308-1 (pbk.)

10   9   8   7   6   5   4   3   2   1

Contents

List of Tables

List of Figures

Biographical Sketches

c

John DeLamater has been at the University of Wisconsin-Madison since receiving his doctoral degree in social psychology at the University of Michigan in 1969. His research interests are in human sexuality; his current research includes work on the determinants of contraceptive use and choice of contraceptive method by single women. He has just completed a textbook entitled *Social Psychology* which will be published in January, 1986.

Meg Gerrard received her Ph.D., and completed her first study of contraceptive use, at the University of Texas at Austin in 1974. Her primary research interest over the last 10 years has been the relationship between attitudes toward sexuality, sexual activity, and contraceptive use. She has taught and conducted research at the University of Texas and the University of Kansas and currently is at Iowa State University.

William Griffitt is currently a Professor of Psychology at Kansas State University. His major research interests are concerned with the personality and social psychological factors involved in interpersonal sexual functioning.

Kathryn Kelley, the editor of this volume, received her doctorate in social-personality psychology at Purdue University. She has held faculty positions at Marquette University, the University of Wisconsin, and the State University of New York at Albany where she is Associate Professor of Psychology. Her theoretical, research, and teaching interests focus on human sexual behavior and attitudes.

Douglas T. Kenrick is Associate Professor in the social and environmental psychology programs at Arizona State University. His main research interests are in the areas of interpersonal attraction and person-environment interactions. His main theoretical interests involve the integration of sociobiological approaches with social learning and social cognition models.

Craig Kinsley received his Ph.D. from SUNY-Albany in 1985 and is currently an NIH Postdoctoral Fellow in the Laboratory of Human Reproduction and Reproductive Biology at Harvard Medical School. His major research interest is behavioral endocrinology.

Bernice Lott is Professor of Psychology and Women's Studies at the University of Rhode Island with a Ph.D. from the University of California, Los Angeles. Major research interests in social psychology have been interpersonal attraction, social learning/socialization, and women's issues. She is the author of *Women's Lives: Themes and Variations in Gender* (second edition in progress) and winner of a Distinguished Publication Award in 1982 from the Association for Women in Psychology.

Beverly Rolker-Dolinsky received her Master's degree at the California State University in Sacramento and is currently working towards her Ph.D. in social-personality psychology at the State University of New York at Albany. She has focused most of her studies and research in the general areas of health psychology, sex roles, and attraction. She is currently a Visiting Instructor of Psychology at Skidmore College.

Bruce Svare received his Ph.D. from Rutgers in 1976 and was an NIH Post-doctoral Fellow for 3 years at the Worcester Foundation for Experimental Biology. He is currently Associate Professor at SUNY-Albany. His major research interest is behavioral endocrinology.

Melanie R. Trost is a doctoral student in social psychology at Arizona State University. Her research interests include interpersonal attraction, divorce mediation, and decision-making regarding international disputes.

CHAPTER 1

Perspectives on Females, Males, and Sexuality

KATHRYN KELLEY

The topic of this volume is the relative contributions of femaleness and maleness to sexuality. Long a subject guaranteed to provoke controversy, the difference between the sexes remains a source of unanswered questions and interesting debates. Whether differences in sexual responses are the result of biological sex differences alone or in combination with attributed characteristics of gender are examined here by authors with competing as well as complementary approaches.

The biological components form the topic of the first two chapters. The first chapter, by Svare and Kinsley, is an empirical account of the potential, although necessarily limited, contribution of data from infrahuman species. The second, by Kenrick and Trost, proposes a sociobiological perspective on sex differences in sexuality. The third chapter combines endrocrinology with psychological approaches to this area, in a comprehensive summary by Rolker-Dolinsky of current knowledge on the premenstrual syndrome. Next, the volume includes some distinctly sociological theorizing by DeLamater, supporting the idea that many components of sexual identity and emotional orientation stem from sexual scripting or scenarios. In a thorough review by Griffitt of similarities and differences attributed to sex, the observable variables of sexual arousal, affect-evaluation, cognition, and selected behaviors are examined, and only some of these variables provide consistent evidence of differences. A feminist perspective is included from Lott in order to broaden the views taken here and to suggest that the subjective can also yield understanding about a controversial issue. A chapter by Gerrard on contraceptive attitudes and behavior follows, using data from females as a theoretical model for males.

As an addition to the series of volumes on human sexual behavior, these combined chapters will make an important contribution. This book pulls together theories and research from a diverse sample of behavioral scientists, who comment on the roles of sex and gender in sexuality. Other volumes have discussed physical attractiveness, sexual coercion, including exposure to erotica and violent pornography, sex education, dysfunctions, and therapy. The present volume contains evidence that we are beginning to understand the interplay between one's sex and sexuality.

Approaches in This Volume: Brief Summaries

After a brief review of basic neuroendrocrinological concepts, Svare and Kinsley examine the hormonal control of sex-related behaviors in infrahuman animals. The three activities, copulation, aggression, and parental care, are seen as the arenas in which hormonal variations are most likely to be contributors to sexually dimorphic behavior. Analogies are sometimes drawn by other authors between these infrahuman activities and human sexual behaviors, but Svare and Kinsley point out the difficulties and limitations of that strategy. Whalen (1985) echoes this caveat, saying that, except for the few exceptions of hormone levels falling below threshold levels, human sexual behavior is predominantly under "specific and powerful stimulus control" (1985:288). The authors mention the low probability of separating social from prenatal endocrine factors in determining gender identity and sexual orientation. They review some evidence for a link between hormonal organizational effects and cognitive or personality traits. The potential roles of gonadal hormones in sexual arousability and rare cases of sex role reversal are also discussed. The evidence for the contribution of postnatal testosterone levels to aggression and social dominance they characterize as conflicting and tentative at best. Svare and Kinsley recommend scepticism in evaluating animal models of interactions between hormones and behavior and descibe hormones in human sex-related behaviors as having a "minor modulatory role." Hormones play increasingly minor roles in the control of behavior, including the sexual component, as species at higher levels of the phylogenetic scale are considered.

Kenrick and Trost propose a biosocial model for sexuality and concentrate on the roles biological foundations might play in differences between males and females. They argue that complex social behaviors in humans (Bleier 1984) are, in part, naturally selected by the forces and pressures of evolution and by procreative needs. At each stage of the developing relationship between a couple, this push for eventual reproductive success shapes their interactions.

The premenstrual syndrome has attracted wide attention as a significant component of female sexuality and psychology, perhaps because neither its definition nor causes have as yet been precisely described. Rolker-Dolinsky first tackles the premenstrual syndorme on definitional grounds, pointing out the lack of agreement about a general identification. Perhaps a variety of subtypes can be assessed, with different antecedents, correlates, and even treatments. If estrogen, progesterone, or prolactin are not the culprits that lead many women to experience significant premenstrual distress, perhaps more and better evidence can someday be martialed to support the renin-angiotensen-aldosterone system as a factor. Despite attitudes to the contrary, no convincing evidence exists to support strong relationship between premenstrual symptomatology and neurotic, psychiatric, or affective disorders. Psychodynamic theorists have also expressed biases about the maladaptive personalities of premenstrual sufferers, but the data indicate that the latter express very specific attitudinal adaptations, including negative sexual attitudes and sexual dissatisfaction, rather than general psychopathology. The more traditional the sex role, the greater the likelihood of significant premenstrual distress, although the evidence does not always support this notion. The author also reviews the contribution of expectations and stereotypes about the premenstrual syndrome and concludes that it consists of more than psychological manifestation alone. Despite extensive research, enough questions remain to classify the premenstrual syndrome as a significant area for additional study.

DeLamater outlines a number of important differences between the sexes using a developmental scheme. For DeLamater, sex differences are large and well established enough to justify the use of the term "sexual scripts," coined by Simon and Gagnon. In preadolescence, differences occur with respect to males' greater experience with and enjoyment of masturbation, and puberty is conceptualized as having primarily reproductive significance for females and as promoting sexual gratification among males. Young females and males also differ in the sources of their socialization about sexuality in Western cultures, the mother being the main educator of females and peers or books being the information source for males. With the advent of heterosexual experience, more sex differences appear, including females' more negative reactions to first intercourse and the contrasting reactions of their partners to the first sexual intimacy. Adult sexuality continues to be characterized by differences consistent with scripting, or sexual scenarios. Male initiation and dominance and female general lack of interest in external sexual cues are easily learned as outgrowths of their different socialization experiences. Males' greater interest in unconventional sexuality completes the scenario of differences, rather than major similarities, between the sexes for the phenomena reviewed in this chapter.

Both similarities and differences between the sexes can be found, however, when a broader range of attitudes, physical responses, and behaviors are examined. Griffitt finds this picture compelling rather than confusing, mainly because the inconsistencies become understandable when closely scrutinized. Sexual responsiveness includes arousal, affective-evaluative, cognitive-informational, and behavioral aspects. The sexes respond similarly throughout the response cycle, with a few minor exceptions, and males and females usually report their arousal in a veridical, psychophysiological manner. Griffitt distinguishes between trait and state components of the process, in order to demonstrate the overlap between personality and social factors in the response. Males typically indicate more positive affective state reactions to sexual stimuli of a wide variety, but both sex role stereotypes and individual personality factors temper this result. Cognitive responses occur in two broad classes, sex dreams and waking sexual fantasies, both of which can be taken to the point of orgasm in females and males. The informational component consists of education and other socialization that may result in misinformation and a type of sexual scripting that is seen as appropriate for each sex. Perhaps the greater encouragement young males receive for the appetitive aspect of sexuality contributes to their stronger expectancies for sexual stimulation to result from exposure to sexual cues. Each of the previous aspects of sexual responding affects the resultant sexual behavior, but sex differences appear to be more attitudinal and cognitive than behavioral.

Lott takes a feminist perspective on the role of sex and gender in sexuality, stating that the sexes demonstrate their basic similarity at several points. In fact, the similarities exist primarily at the two end points of the process of sexual responding described by Griffitt. Sexual arousal and behavior patterns reveal much overlap between females and males, but the differences occur at the points of psychological mediation, namely the affective-evaluative and cognitive-informational levels. Lott's thesis that sex differences in sexuality are more traceable and attributable to socialization experiences rather than sociobiological input, thus receives support from this distinction. Lott also describes the techniques of recasting sexual behavior for the fulfillment of other goals including commodity, sport, and status symbol. Some will use sex to satisfy sensation-seeking or communicative needs, and these uses may agree with cultural stereotypes of appropriate female and male sexuality.

An important area in human sexuality, the study of contraceptive attitudes and behavior, has been focused mainly on females. Gerrard uses the comprehensive research on females as a model for studying male contraception. A negative orientation to sexuality can indeed interfere with effective contraceptive behavior, to the point of making it easier to use certain contraceptives rather than others (Kelley 1979). The deciding factor is the degree to which the technique involves genital touching (Kelley 1985a). Negative sexual attitudes do not necessarily interfere with engaging in heterosexual intercourse unprotected from unwanted pregnancy, however. In examining the necessary contraceptive steps that Byrne (1983) outlines, Gerrard agrees that a negative orientation may contribute to success or failure at each behavioral choice point. Within relationships, a passive, traditionally oriented female may succumb to the predilections of her male partner, either for taking action to prevent pregnancy or for playing the dangerous game of pregnancy roulette. Male contraceptive use is more predictably reliable and more highly related to initial attitudinal orientations to sexuality than is the case among females. Whether this difference is indeed attributable to some females' greater subservience to male preference or to the more effective measurement of psychological characteristics among males than females (Deaux 1976) remains to be tested. The author uses a quasi-experimental design to compare sexual attitudes with contraceptive behavior among university females over a ten-year span and documents a period of cultural behavior change in this relationship.

THE PROBABILITY OF OBSERVING SEX DIFFERENCES IN SEXUAL RESPONSES

Predicting whether sex differences will occur in a particular realm of attitudes or behavior is a difficult task. One strategy is to extrapolate from a favored theory what the probability is that sex differences would exist. Sexual scripting, for example, could be applied to the responses to pornography observed in the laboratory or living room. This theory might indicate at the descriptive level what variables contribute to this data set. A different strategy is to begin with the available data, then determine which concepts could adequately describe the dynamic determinants of sex differences, and generalize from there.

Figures 1 and 2 depict the second strategy. Two major sets of constructs seem to encompass the variables involved in the resultant sex differences. One component is the degree of external versus internal stimulation, which consists of the situational exposure to sexual cues at one end and the individual's personality or biological resources at the other. The second major component includes distinguishing between those variables or responses that have a strong

affective basis and those that have a nonaffective basis in their
development or socialization. The expression of sex guilt on the one
hand and the development of secondary sexual characteristics on the
other would qualify here, respectively. Figure 1 outlines a schema
for evaluating whether a given set of variables can be associated
with sex differences in responses. Figure 2 amplifies this conceptualization by postulating the relative frequencies with which sex
differences might then occur.

A fair test of these distinctions could use the information currently
available and reviewed in this volume. Externally stimulated, affective
aspects of sexual responses would be associated with a number of
sizable sex differences. Such differences include socialization experiences surrounding masturbation and first intercourse, the attraction
to and physical attractiveness of potential partners, and the effects
of exposure to erotica including violent pornography. Internally stimulated but still affective components lead to some sex differences as
well, but with only moderate probability. Contraceptive attitudes and
behavior, for example, are greatly influenced by sexual attitudes,
which in young females are slightly more negative than in young
males. The developmental milestones of sexuality—puberty, pregnancy, parenting, and aging—are, of course, internally stimulated
but elicit powerful affective reactions that theoretically can influence
sexual responses and some sex differences (Byrne 1983).

Comparatively fewer sex differences occur in nonaffective responses. An externally stimulated, nonaffectively based phenomenon
has definite, cognitive information conveyed about it, such as the
cultural expectation that females will display more selectivity and
males will exhibit more promiscuity (Kelley and Musialowski 1986).
These inputs seem to have comparatively less impact in contrast to
affective components, but they potentially exert a strong influence
on affect in the long run. Finally, internally stimulated, nonaffectively
based behavior contains limited hormonal and biogenetic influences,
which account for relatively little in the total variance of human
sexual responses.

As theorized in Figures 1 and 2, sex differences occur among some
attitudinal or behavioral dimensions and not among others. Differential socialization is apparently responsible for sex differences in
evaluative and affective responses to sexually explicit stimuli. College
males also report greater subjective sexual arousal than females in
response to some explicitly sexual but not personally threatening
scenes (Kelley 1985a, 1985c). With the use of an objective assessment
like thermography, however, that can be applied similarly to both
sexes (Rosen and Beck 1986), only differences due to sexual attitudes
within sexes and not sex variations alone appear (Abramson et al.

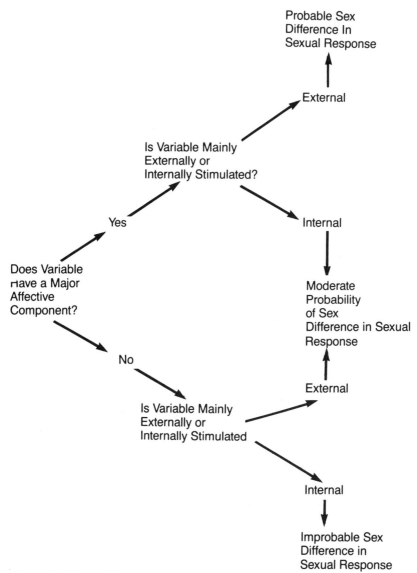

Figure 1. A complementary conceptualization of the decision process for describing human sexual responses in terms of the probability they would lead to observable sex differnces.

1981). The message of this general area of research on sex differences and similarities in the psychophysiology of sexual response becomes clear. Subjective variables to sexual stimuli have a greater likelihood of resulting in sex differences in sexual response than do objective ones.

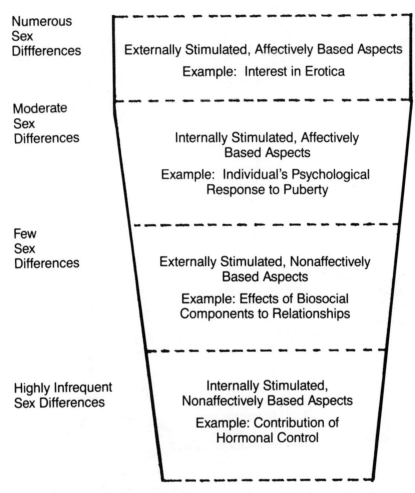

Numerous
Sex
Diffferences

Externally Stimulated, Affectively Based Aspects

Example: Interest in Erotica

Moderate
Sex
Differences

**Internally Stimulated, Affectively
Based Aspects**

**Example: Individual's Psychological
Response to Puberty**

Few
Sex
Differences

**Externally Stimulated, Nonaffectively
Based Aspects**

**Example: Effects of Biosocial
Components to Relationships**

Highly Infrequent
Sex Differences

**Internally Stimulated,
Nonaffectively Based Aspects**

**Example: Contribution of
Hormonal Control**

Figure 2. Comparison of the hypothesized frequency of sex differences in human sexual responses. The figure describes externally stimulated aspects with a major affective basis as being associated with more numerous sex differnces than internally stimulated, nonaffectively based aspects.

INDIVIDUAL PERSONALITY TRAITS: WHERE DO THEY FIT IN?

Information about the role of personality traits in individual experience comes from two major sources. Personality tests of various kinds assess one's tendency to respond in a particular way in various situations. Both sex similarities and differences are found with respect to the operation of personality variables. Responses to certain situational manipulations also provide evidence for differing perceptions of situations, depending on the personality trait being measured. The latter argument comes from experimental personality psychologists, who, for example, have discovered that persons with positive sexual attitudes find erotic stimulation a motivational influence on their subsequent performance (Kelley 1985b). After viewing an erotic film, such individuals subsequently performed more effectively on a paired-associates learning task if it was noncompetitive and thus easier; but their performance was impaired on a more difficult, competitive task compared to the performance of those who viewed a nonsexual, control film. The expression of negative sexual attitudes was associated with avoidant behavior in similar circumstances; these persons simply performed better on the easier task than on the difficult one, regardless of the type of film they had just seen. This study thus demonstrated that the expression of positive or negative sexual attitudes affects how an individual responds to an erotic film.

As Lott suggests in this volume, by using well-defined personality variables, investigations can illuminate the impact of biological sex per se on personality. Socialization experiences apparently channel the development of these personality traits, which culminate in personality differences rather than simply in major sex differences. In the study described above (Kelley 1985b), no sex differences occurred in performance levels; rather, the results were attributed to how positive the individual's sexual attitudes were, regardless of sex.

Sexual attitudes are composed of a strong affective component, but, of course, content determines that affect. Information must be conveyed in order to build up a primarily positive or negative orientation to sexuality. Even the naming of genitalia in childhood conforms to the expectation for reduced attention to this aspect of socialization among females. Gartrell and Mosbacher (1984) described the deficiencies in females' learning, for example, their education about genital naming lagged considerably behind that of males. By adolescence, females have a less comprehensive sexual vocabulary than males, after having had fewer names for genitalia in childhood. Upon this sort of foundation rests the affective differences between the sexes in sexual response.

Our current knowledge about psychosexuality includes the realization that males and females express sex roles. Individuals vary in the degree to which they agree that stereotyped conceptions of masculinity and femininity apply to themselves. Sex roles have been shown to influence a variety of aspects of sexuality. On the attitudinal level, androgynous husbands indicate greater tolerance for male contraceptive pill usage (Marsiglio 1985). Behaviorally, more adaptive coping with the problem of reproductive infertility occurs among females and males who express either the masculine or androgynous sex role (Adler and Boxley 1985).

Other research has expanded this basic association between sex roles and coping styles or mental health. Androgyny may produce beneficial coping with marital disruption, for example (Felton, Brown, Lehmann, and Liberatos 1980). Kelley et al. (1985) have developed a scale to assess chronic self-destructiveness, defined as the tendency to engage in behaviors that result in negative consequences for the individual, as well as the tendency to avoid performing behaviors that lead to positive consequences for the individual. (The Appendix to this book contains the items included in the scale of chronic self-destructiveness.) Affective responses theoretically mediate this tendency, which has been found to be related to externality in three languages and four cultures (Kelley, Cheung, Rodriguez-Carrillo, Singh and Wan 1986) in college and middle-aged samples. Chronic self-destructives also tend to perform counterproductively in their intimate relationships, where they report more hostility and shorter duration in their liaisons compared to those low in chronic self-destructiveness. Their sexual health also shows evidence of chronic self-destructiveness, as shown by the tendency of middle-aged women to delay obtaining a Pap smear test for cervical cancer significantly longer if they reported chronic self-destructiveness. With respect to sex roles, chronic self-destructiveness tends not to be androgynous but rather sex-typed on the Bem sex role inventory (Bem 1974). On the Spence, Helmreich, and Holahan (1979) indicators of sex roles, college female chronic self-destructives displayed tendencies toward negative, masculine qualities (e.g., arrogance) and verbal aggressiveness, but lacked the positive masculine (e.g., dominant) and feminine (e.g., sensitive) characteristics that might have helped avoid these chronic, self-destructive tendencies. College males lacked the same positive characteristics in their self-descriptions if they tended toward chronic self-destructiveness. Such findings suggest that problems in coping and behavioral difficulties are influenced somewhat similarly in males and females, but that females possess additional negative components such as negative masculinity that may interfere with their potentially successful functioning. The work on chronic self-destructiveness has only begun to elucidate the contribution of personality variables to understanding and predicting human sexual response. This research has, however, demonstrated how a nonsexual but affective personality trait relates to a variety of important issues in sexuality.

Even vastly different perspectives on the roles of sex and gender in sexuality can illuminate the variety of existent interrelationships. Sex differences as well as similarities can reveal much about our psychosexuality. This volume examines the area of psychosexology using a representative sampling of varying accounts, both theoretical and empirical in orientation. Some insights into this complicated subject would be useful, especially if we can then foresee the most productive directions for researchers to take.

REFERENCES

Abramson, P. R., Perry, L. B., Rothblatt, A., Seeley, T. T., and Seeley, D. M. (1981). Negative attitudes toward masturbation and pelvic vasocongestion: A thermographic analysis. *Journal of Research in Personality,* 15, 497–509.

Adler, J. D. and Boxley, R. L. (1985). The psychological reactions to infertility: Sex roles and coping styles. *Sex Roles,* 12, 271–279.

Bem, S. L. (1974). The measurement of psychological androgyny. *Journal of Consulting and Clinical Psychology,* 46, 648–659.

Bleier, R. (1984). *Science and gender: A critique of biology and its theories on women.* New York: Pergamon Press.

Byrne, D. (1983). Sex without contraception. In D. Byrne and W. A. Fisher (eds.), *Adolescents, sex, and contraception* (pp. 3–32). Hillsdale, NJ: Lawrence Erlbaum Associates.

Deaux, K. (1976). *The behavior of women and men.* Monterey, CA: Brooks-Cole.

Felton, B., Brown, P., Lehmann, S., and Liberatos, P. (1980). The coping function of sex-role attitudes during marital disruption. *Journal of Health and Social Behavior,* 21, 240–248.

Gartrell, N. and Mosbacher, D. (1984). Sex differences in the naming of children's genitalia. *Sex Roles,* 10, 869–876.

Kelley, K. (1979). Socialization factors in contraceptive attitudes: Roles of affective responses, parental attitudes, and sexual experience. *Journal of Sex Research,* 15, 6–20.

Kelley, K. (1985a). Sex, sex guilt, and authoritarianism: Differences in responses to explicit heterosexual and masturbatory slides. *Journal of Sex Research,* 21, 68–85.

Kelley, K (1985b). Sexual attitudes as determinants of the motivational properties of exposure to erotica. *Personality and Individual Differences,* 6, 391–393.

Kelley, K. (1985c). Sexual fantasy and attitudes as functions of sex of subject and content of erotica. *Imagination, Cognition, and Personality,* 4, 339–347.

Kelley, K., Byrne, D., Przybyla, D. P. J., Eberly, C., Eberly, B., Greendlinger, V., Wan, C. K., and Gorsky, J. (1985). Chronic self-destructiveness: Theory, conceptualization, and intial validation of the construct. *Motivation and Emotion,* 9(2), 135–151.

Kelley, K., Cheung, F., Rodriguez-Carrillo, P., Singh, R., and Wan, C. K. (1986). Cross-cultural generality of chronic self-destructiveness. *Journal of Social Psychology,* in press.

Kelley, K. and Musialowski, D. (1986). Repeated exposure to sexually explicit stimuli: Novelty, sex, and sexual attitudes. *Archives of Sexual Behavior,* in press.

Marsiglio, W. (1985). Husband's sex-role preferences and contraceptive intentions: The case of the male pill. *Sex Roles, 12,* 655–663.

Rosen, R. C. and Beck, J. G. (1986). In D. Byrne and K. Kelley (eds.), *Alternative approaches to sexual behavior* (pp. 43–86). Hillsdale, NJ: Lawrence Erlbaum Associates.

Spence, J. T., Helmreich, R. L., & Holahan, C. K. (1979). Negative and positive components of psychological masculinity and femininity and their relationship to neurotic and acting out behaviors. *Journal of Personality and Social Psychology, 37,* 1673–1682.

Whalen, R. E. (1985). Sex and aggression. [Review of *Connections between sex and aggression.*] *Contemporary Psychology, 30,* 288–289.

CHAPTER 2

Hormones and Sex-Related Behavior: A Comparative Analysis

BRUCE SVARE AND CRAIG H. KINSLEY

Reproductive behaviors of most mammalian males and females are governed by hormones secreted by the gonads. In this paper, we will examine the relationship between gonadal hormones and the exhibition of sex-related behaviors in laboratory rodents, infrahuman primates, and humans. Because our analysis cannot be exhaustive of the available literature, we have focused this review on those aspects of sexually dimorphic behavior that have been most frequently studied by behavioral endocrinologists. Specifically, in the case of lower animals, we will address the issue of gonadal hormone involvement in copulatory and aggressive behavior; for the human, we will explore gonadal hormone involvement in gender identity, sexuality, and sexual orientation (in particular the question of homosexuality), sex role reversal, aggression, mood and the menstrual cycle, and cognition.

As Beach (1974) pointed out, hormones can act on at least three different levels to influence sex-related behavioral responses. First, they can act at the effector level (e.g., muscle tissue) to either increase or decrease the capacity to perform certain responses. Second, they can act at the sensory or perceptual level to modify the reception of sitimuli. Third, they can act at the central or neural level to modify how incoming stimuli are interpreted by the organism. Because the scope of this review is limited to gonadal hormone effects on the central or neural level and their importance for sex-related behavior, the reader is referred to a review by Gandelman (1983) for an excellent discussion of the other areas of hormone action listed above.

Our review is divided into three main sections. We first briefly review basic neuroendocrine concepts essential for understanding research in behavioral endocrinology. This review includes an analysis of hypothalamic-pituitary relationships, putuitary-testicular regulation in the male, and pituitary-ovarian function in the female. Also included in this overview is a primer on mammalian sexual differentiation. The second section of this review examines the hormonal control of copulatory behavior and aggression in laboratory animals. The examination explores the behavioral effects of gonadal hormone exposure during early, critical periods of development (referred to as organizational effects) as well as the effects of continued hormone exposure during adult life (referred to as activational effects). The third section explores the relationship between gonadal hormones and sex-related behavior in humans. Specifically, we examine the effects of perinatal gonadal hormone exposure (e.g., organizational effects) on gender identity, sexually dimorphic behavior, sexual orientation (homosexuality), aggression, and cognition. We then look at the influence of postnatal gonadal hormone exposure (e.g., activational effects) on mood and the menstrual cycle, sexuality, sex role reversal in pseudohermaphrodites, and aggression. Several recent books provide comprehensive reviews of the literature in behavioral endocrinology, and the reader is referred to Leshner (1978), Adler (1981), and Svare (1983) for more in-depth coverage of the material presented here.

BASIC NEUROENDOCRINE CONCEPTS

The Hypothalamic-Pituitary-Gonadal System

Figure 1 illustrates the basic neuroendocrine relationships involved in ovarian and testicular hormone release in mammals. Although a detailed examination of these relationships is beyond the scope of this presentation (see Turner and Bagnara [1976] for a more extensive analysis), a brief review of reproductive biology in the male and female is necessary.

Gonadal hormone secretion is controlled by hormone secretions from the pituitary gland, which, in turn, are controlled by the production and release of hormones from the hypothalamus. The coordination of these physiological changes is essential for production of sperm in the male and ova in the female, for the growth of reproductive organs, and, most importantly, for the timing of sex-related behaviors.

For the male, the hormonal sequence of events involved in reproductive competence is a relatively simple process. Luteinizing hormone-releasing hormone (LHRH) from the hypothalamus stimulates the anterior pituitary to secrete the gonadotropins, follicle

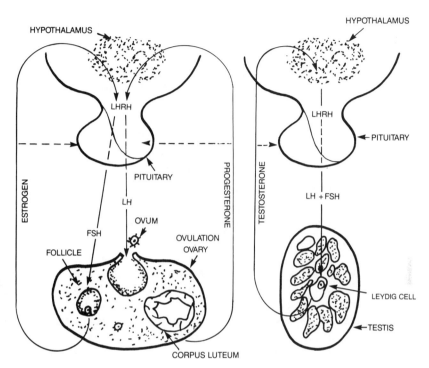

Figure 1. Hypothalamic-pituitary-gonadal relationships in females (left) and males (right) (Adapted from Levine 1972).

stimulating hormone (FSH), and luteinizing hormone (LH). Once these hormones enter general circulation, they act on the testes to promote the production of testosterone as well as the growth of sperm. In turn, testosterone can act back on the hypothalamus in a negative feedback loop to reduce the secretion of LHRH. As a result, testosterone secretion is relatively stable, and the reproductive endocrinology of the male has been classified as acyclic.

In contrast to the simple chain of events involved in male reproductive physiology, neuroendocrine control in the female is much more complex. The female exhibits a cyclic pattern of hormonal release, with the end point being ovulation, or the production of a mature egg. The duration of these cyclic changes is species-dependent, with ovulation occurring in the human female about every 28 days, the guinea pig every 15 days, and the rat every 4 or 5 days. The process is initiated by FSH, which stimulates the growth of the Graafian follicles and induces the ovary to produce estrogen. Estrogen then acts back on the hypothalamus and the pituitary to inhibit further release of FSH and to promote the release of LH. The first surge of LH stimulates ovulation. It also is involved in the formation of the corpus luteum, as well as in the production of progesterone by the ovary. Progesterone then feeds back on the hypothalamus and the pituitary to inhibit LH secretion, thereby marking the end of the cycle. If fertilization does not occur, a new cycle will begin as outlined above. If, however, the egg is fertilized and is subsequently implanted in the uterine lining, the cyclic nature of neuroendocrine secretion ends and a new set of hormonal events ensues.

Mammalian Sexual Differentiation

The foregoing principles show that the pattern of gonadotropin secretion in the male is acyclic (e.g., tonic) while that of the female is cyclic (e.g., regular variation). To understand the development of this sexual dimorphism in reproductive physiology, a brief examination of the sexual differentiation process is essential (see Money and Ehrhardt 1972).

Until about the sixth to seventh week of intrauterine life, the gonadal tissues in the human fetus have not diffferentiated into testes or ovaries. The gonad until this point is capable of developing in either a male or female fashion. The ovary and the testes have their common beginning in a primitive, bipotential structure. If the genetic code is XX (female), the primordial gonads develop into ovaries, and the mullerian duct system begins to emerge. These tissues will later develop into female internal reproductive organs including the uterus, fallopian tubes, and upper vagina. Concurrently, the male reproductive tissues, referred to as the wolffian duct system, begin to regress. On the other hand, if the genetic code is XY (male), the primordial gonads develop into testes, testosterone begins to circulate, and the wolffian duct system begins to elaborate. The vas deferens, seminal vesicles, and ejaculatory ducts of the male develop from this duct system, while the mullerian (female) tissues simultaneously begin to regress. External genitalia for both sexes develop from the same structure, referred to as the genital tubercle. In the male, the penis and the scrotum develop, while in the female the clitoris and labia differentiate.

It is important to note that the ovaries and their secretory products do not have a role in the differentiation process. Instead, the critical determinant of internal and external sexual differentiation is the presence or absence of testosterone secreted by the testes. For example, in the case of Turner's syndrome, in which there is only one X chromosome (XO), the internal and external anatomy of the human develops as female in spite of the fact that the ovaries never fully develop. Therefore, mullerian duct differentiation (female) is not dependent upon the presence of estrogen and progesterone. In contrast, a great deal of experimental work in laboratory animals as well as clinical research with developmental accidents in humans show that females exposed to abnormally high levels of testosterone during early, critical periods of differentiation (e.g., adrenogenital syndrome in the human female) develop external anatomy and reproductive organs that are male-like.

To summarize, then, the presence of testosterone, regardless of genetic sex, results in wolffian duct differentiation, mullerian duct regression, and male external genitalia, while the opposite is true when the steroid hormone is absent (i.e., mullerian duct development, wolffian duct regression, and female external anatomy). Put another way, the female appears to develop by default (i.e., absence of testosterone) since the ovaries apparently play no role in the differentiation process.

The principles elucidated above regarding the differentiation of internal and external anatomy also seem to hold for the determination of reproductive cyclicity. Numerous elegant experiments with laboratory animals support the proposition that the presence or absence of testosterone during early life determines whether or not gonadotropin secretion in the organism will be cyclic (female) or tonic (male). Some of the earliest work, however, consisted of the casual and sometimes anecdotal observations of cattle breeders. They noted that when opposite-sexed twins were born, the female was sterile. These females, which were referred to as "freemartins," were apparently "contaminated" by testosterone from the adjacent male twin. Not until the work of Pfeiffer (1936), however, was it definitively shown that secretions from the neonatal testis have a suppressive effect on ovulation. Using rats, Pfeiffer demonstrated that transplanting testes from newborn males into neonatal females prevented the latter from ovulating. Conversely, males castrated as adults and given an ovary do not ovulate. However, ovulation can be induced in the male who receives an ovary transplant in adulthood if castration is performed early in life (e.g., within a few days of birth) (see also Harris and Levine 1965). Subsequent work by Barraclough (1967) showed that sterility could be produced in females by a single injection of testosterone during neonatal life. The virilizing effects of this exposure were age dependent, since testosterone injections at ten days of age did not produce sterility while those at five days of age were intermediate in their effectiveness.

Although Pfeiffer accurately identified testicular secretions as the main source of masculinization (promotion of tonic gonadotropin secretion in the male) and defeminization (suppression of cyclic gonadotropin secretion in the female), he incorrectly identified the pituitary as the brain area testosterone acted upon to produce these effects. In a classic experiment, Harris and Jacobsohn (1952) interchanged the putuitaries of adult males and females and found no effects on the inherent pattern of gonadotropin secretion in each sex. This work led to the notion that an extrapituitary brain area, in particular the hypothalamus, was the site of action for the virilizing effects of testosterone. Anatomical, biochemical, and morphological data now show that this brain area is the true site for the action of testosterone on the central nervous system. Anovulatory sterility can be produced in female rats when they are given intracranial testosterone implants in the hypothalamus soon after birth (e.g., Nadler 1968), and autoradiography studies show that testosterone normally accumulates in high concentrations in this area (e.g., Sheridan, Sar, and Stumpf 1974). Testosterone exposure during early life also brings about a host of hypothalamic biochemical changes, the most important of which appear to be alterations in protein synthesis and monoamine transmission.

Indeed, the course of CNS sexual differentiation can be altered by manipulating these physiological systems (e.g., Kobayashi and Gorski 1970; Arai and Gorski 1968). The most compelling evidence, however, for hypothalamic involvement in sexual differentiation comes from studies examining morphological differences in the brains of males and females. Males and females differ with respect to the size and number of neurons in certain hypothalamic areas, most prominently in the preoptic area (Gorski, Gordon, Shryne, and Southam 1978; Jacobson and Gorski 1981), as well as in the structure of the dendrites in this brain area (Greenough, Carter, Steerman, and DeVoogd 1977; Raisman and Field 1973). More recently, some researchers (Toran-Allerand 1980) have even demonstrated that testosterone stimulates neuritic growth patterns in cultured preoptic area tissue taken from neonatal mice. Clearly, these studies provide very persuasive evidence that the locus for brain sexual differentiation is in the hypothalamus.

Four recent developments in the field of behavioral endocrinology suggest that the sexual differentiation process outlined above may require significant modification in the future. First, because some researchers have shown in rodents that testosterone circulates in females as well as in males during early, critical periods of differentiation (e.g., Weisz and Ward 1980), the theory has been advanced that some level of testosterone imprinting may be necessary for feminine differentiation (e.g., Goy and McEwen 1980). Unfortunately, empirical support for this position is lacking at the present time. Second, the observation that neonatal estrogen treatment is as effective as testosterone in producing sterility in female rats (e.g., Whalen and Nadler 1963) has suggested to many researchers that the metabolic conversion of testosterone to estrogen (referred to as aromatization) may be obligatory for masculine differentiation. Additional support for this proposition is derived from work with the testicular feminized (Tfm) rodent, a genetic mutation in which testosterone receptors in the central nervous system are severely reduced but in which estrogen receptors are spared. Interestingly, Tfm males undergo normal masculine brain differentiation, indicating that estrogen alone or testosterone to estrogen conversion may be essential (Shapiro, Levine, Adler 1980). Third, female fetuses are apparently protected from the masculinizing and defeminizing action of ovarian and maternal estrogen by binding proteins (FEBP-fetoneonatal estrogen binding protein) that inactivate the steroid (e.g., Plapinger, McEwen, and Clemens 1973). In an elegant proof of this hypothesis, Mizejewski, Vonnegut, and Simon (1980) recently reported that treatment of female rats with antibodies that antagonize FEBP results in the suppression of cyclicity (defeminization). Finally, behavioral endocrinologists now agree that masculinization and defeminization are independent processes (e.g., Baum 1979). In rodents, experimental evidence shows that masculinization occurs during prenatal life, while defeminization occurs during early postnatal life. The importance of the prenatal environment was recently established by vom Saal and colleagues (vom Saal and Bronson 1978, 1980; vom Saal, Grant, McMullen, and Laves 1983). They found that developing in utero between fetuses of the opposite sex dramatically influences fetal and amniotic hormone titers as well as masculine behavior potential in male and female mice. Also, McEwen and his colleagues (Davis, Chaptal, and McEwen 1979; McEwen, Lieberburg, Chaptal, and Krey 1977) were able to elevate feminine behavior potentials in male rats by postnatal treatment with aromatization inhibitors. Importantly, however, they reported that the ability to exhibit masculine behavior was not impaired.

HORMONAL CONTROL OF SEX-RELATED BEHAVIOR IN INFRAHUMAN MAMMALS

Behavioral endocrinologists have focused most of their attention on gonadal hormone involvement in aggressive and copulatory responses of rodents (rats, mice, hamsters, and guinea pigs) and to a lesser extent of infrahuman primates. The purpose of this section is to review these findings in the context of organizational and activational hormone influences. (See Beatty [1979] and Balthazart, Prove, and Gilles [1983] for reviews of endocrine involvement in other behavioral responses.)

As previously stated, perinatal exposure to hormones induces irreversible changes in the central nervous system (CNS). These "organizational" effects of hormones also underlie the capacity of the animal to exhibit appropriate behavioral responses in adulthood and dictate the manner in which such behaviors develop. Another aspect of endocrine involvement in behavior concerns the effects of gonadal hormone exposure during adult life. Such hormonal effects are referred to as "activational" influences. Unlike organizational hormone effects, activational hormone influences produce transient, temporary changes in behavior. In mammals, hormonal stimulation during adulthood is necessary for the exhibition of copulatory and aggressive behaviors. Removal of these hormones (by gonadectomy) usually results in the eventual decline of such behaviors. Thus, the full expression of sex-related behaviors is dependent upon the presence or absence of hormone exposure during adult life in combination with the permanent structural changes produced by hormone alterations during perinatal life.

Perinatal Hormones and the Development of Sexually Dimorphic Behavior

The realization that hormonal stimulation during prenatal and/or early postnatal life was responsible for sex differences in reproductive physiology prompted behavioral endocrinologists to ask similar questions for sexually dimorphic behaviors. Indeed, after literally thousands of research articles on the topic, it can be said quite definitively that dimorphisms in sex and aggression follow the same basic rules. Thus, in most rodent species studied, the presence of testicular hormones during early life increases the capacity to exhibit male-like behaviors (e.g., masculinization) and decreases the capacity to exhibit female-like behaviors (e.g., defeminization). Conversely, the absence of testicular hormones during early critical periods of development lowers the capability to exhibit masculine behaviors and elevates the capacity to exhibit feminine behaviors. Let us examine some of the findings contributing to this conclusion.

Copulatory Behavior The repertoire of behaviors that produce the copulatory sequence in rodents consists of a number of highly stereotyped behavior patterns. After a short sequence of courtship activity involving mutual anogenital sniffing, the male approaches the receptive female from behind and begins mounting. Although intromission (insertion of the penis into the vaginal area) is not usually obtained on the initial mounting sequence, it soon follows after a series of priming mounts by the male. Once intromission is obtained, the characteristic shallow pelvic thrusts of the male change to more vigorous thrusts. After about eight to fifteen intromissions, each separated by short intercopulatory intervals, the male exhibits ejaculation. In this sequence, the male mounts, continues to exhibit vigorous pelvic thrusting, and then maintains a final deep intromission during which seminal emission occurs. At this time, the male tightens the muscles of its hindquarters and forelegs. Following ejaculation, the male slowly dismounts and pauses for four to five minutes before initiating another intromission. The time between ejaculation and a subsequent copulatory series lengthens with each subsequent ejaculation. Thus, the behaviors typically assessed for the male are mounts, intromissions, ejaculations, post-ejaculatory interval, and the latencies to engage in each of these behaviors.

The receptive female rodent shows a characteristic hop-and-dart reaction upon being approached by a male. This reaction is followed by crouching behavior, in which the female remains motionless with the spine parallel to the ground. The most prominent feature of female sexual responsiveness is the lordosis response. This reaction is characterized by flexion of the legs, the pelvis tilted upward, the tail distinctly elevated and deviated to one side, and the head raised. The behaviors typically assessed for the female are the lordosis response, as well as the latency to engage in this behavior. In addition, behavioral endocrinologists frequently calculate the lordosis ratio— the number of times the female exhibits lordosis over the number of times the male mounts the female.

Two seminal papers laid the groundwork for almost all investigations that followed in the area of hormonal organization of copulatory behavior. The first, by Phoenix, Goy, Gerall, and Young (1959), examined the sexual responses of female guinea pigs that were administered testosterone propionate (a long-acting androgen) during prenatal life. When ovariectomized and administered testosterone in adulthood, these females exhibited copulatory behavior identical to that of normal males. Phoenix et. al. therefore concluded that the central nervous system of these females had been masculinized by the early testosterone treatment. In addition to this research, Phoenix and his colleagues also explored the feminine responses of the androgenized females when they were administered priming injections of estrogen and progesterone in adulthood. These females failed to exhibit the lordotic responses typically displayed by normal females when given ovarian hormone stimulation, thus indicating that their central nervous system had also been defeminized.

The logical next step for behavioral endocrinologists was to deprive genotypic males of testosterone during early life and then examine feminine and masculine behavior potentials. Because guinea pigs are fully differentiated at birth and, therefore, castration during fetal life is not feasible, researchers examined this question in rodents, who are not fully differentiated at birth. In a now classic report, Grady,

Phoenix, and Young (1965) castrated male rats during the first few days of life and, in adulthood, examined their masculine behavior when given testosterone and their feminine responses when given estrogen and progesterone. The findings of Grady et al. were consistent with the earlier Phoenix et al. report. The males exhibited very little copulatory behavior in response to adult testosterone treatment, although their feminine behavior following ovarian hormone stimulation was equivalent to that of normal females. These findings clearly show that testicular hormones are the primary agents for masculinizing and defeminizing the organism with respect to copulatory behavior. In contrast, the presence or absence of the ovaries does not play a significant role in mammalian organizational processes (e.g., Gerall, Dunlap, and Hendricks 1973).

Recent work on rats and mice has provided another means for examining the influence of prenatal gonadal hormone exposure on the development of sexual behavior. This method, which utilizes the naturally occurring phenomena of fetuses developing in the uterus adjacent to other fetuses of the same and opposite sex, has been termed the "intrauterine position effect." In some respects, it bears a strong similarity to the aforementioned "freemartin effect" in cattle. For females, developing next to males in utero results in elevated fetal levels of testosterone, elevated masculine sex behavior in response to adult testosterone, and reduced feminine behavior in response to adult estrogen and progesterone (e.g., Clemens, Gladue, and Coniglio 1978; vom Saal and Bronson 1980). For males, developing next to females in utero results in elevated fetal levels of estradiol and elevated masculine sexual behavior in adulthood (vom Saal, Grant, McMullen, and Laves 1983).

The critical period for the organizing effects of early gonadal hormone exposure is species-dependent. For example, masculinization and defeminization of sexual behavior can be produced with prenatal testosterone treatment in guinea pigs (e.g., Phoenix, Goy, Gerall, and Young 1959), sheep (e.g., Short 1974), and rhesus monkeys (e.g., Goy 1970). In dogs, some combination of pre- and postnatal treatment is effective (e.g., Beach and Kuehn 1970). In species with shorter gestation lengths, the requirements appear to be predominantly postnatal. These include the rat (e.g., Gerall, Hendricks, Johnson, and Bounds 1967), hamster (e.g., Carter, Clemens, and Hoekema 1972), mouse (Edwards and Burge 1971), and ferret (Baum 1979).

There is considerable evidence indicating that testosterone acts as a prohormone and that its metabolites are the actual agents responsible for early organizational effects. In the central nervous system and in peripheral tissue, testosterone can be metabolically converted (aromatized) to estrogen as well as reduced enzymatically to dihydrotestosterone. Numerous studies have reported that perinatally administered estrogens or aromatizable hormones (testosterone, androstenedione) are effective in masculinizing and defeminizing rodents, while hormones that are not aromatizable (dihydrotestosterone) are ineffective (e.g., Whalen and Nadler 1963). Recent studies, however, indicate that the requisite hormonal stimulus for producing organization may be more complex than just a straight aromatization process. For example, some studies indicate that dihydrotestosterone alone is effective in masculinizing the behavior of female guinea pigs and ferrets when it is administered prenatally (Goldfoot and van der Werff ten Bosch 1975; Baum, Gallagher, Martin, and Damassa 1982), while other studies show that dihydrotestosterone combined with estrogen is effective (e.g., Booth 1977).

Behavioral endocrinologists have specified, with some precision, the areas of the brain in which hormones produce their organizing effects on copulatory behavior. In particular, the preoptic area and the ventromedial nucleus of the rodent hypothalamus have been singled out as key areas linked to masculinization and defeminization of sex behavior by testicular hormones (e.g., Dorner and Staudt 1969). As previously reviewed (see previous section on sexual differentiation), numerous hormone-induced morphological changes take place in these hypothalamic areas. In addition, more recent data show that areas of the rat spinal cord are also sexually dimorphic and androgen dependent (Breedlove and Arnold 1980).

How do gonadal hormones produce such profound behavioral and morphological changes in the developing organism? Researchers in this area have provided some exciting answers to this question over the last few years. It is thought that hormones act on the cell in one of two ways. They can interact with cell surface receptors, or they can interact with receptors in the cytoplasm of the cell. Steroid hormones act in the latter fashion and exert their effects by way of the genome (i.e., the chromosomes) to alter protein synthesis. In support of this theory of hormone influence on the organizational process, researchers have identified intracellular receptors for testosterone and estrogen in the rodent brain during prenatal and early neonatal life (e.g., Vito and Fox 1982; Lieberburg, MacLusky, and McEwen 1980). Additionally, protein synthesis inhibitors have been reported to ameliorate the defeminizing effects of perinatal testosterone administration (e.g., Gorski 1979). Finally, there is growing interest in the possibility that hormone-induced alterations in monoamine transmission may be implicated in the organizing effects of gonadal steroids (Dorner 1980).

Aggressive Behavior   The aggressive behavior most often studied by behavioral endocrinologists is intermale aggression in rodents. Mice have been most frequently studied in this context because they display an easily quantifiable repertoire of aggressive responses that reliably occur when two adult males confront each other for the first time. The topography of this type of aggression in male mice consists of a series of initial anogenital investigations, followed by episodes of rough grooming. After several minutes, the behavior escalates into attacks (severe biting and wrestling), with retaliation by each upon the other. The attacks are usually directed at the back and flank area of the male and will continue until one or the other assumes a submissive posture.

Females have long been considered nonaggressive. Indeed, if similarly tested against an adult male intruder, most females will simply investigate the opponent and groom it. Thus, there appears to be a marked sex difference in this behavior, with males being much more aggressive than females. The main thrust of the research on aggressive behavior has, therefore, concentrated on males. It has recently become apparent, however, that the female is as aggressive, if not more aggressive, than the male during certain reproductive stages. Maternal aggression, observed during pregnancy and lactation, consists of lunges and threats during gestation and intense attacks during the postpartum period. This behavior can be directed toward other males and females. Aggression related to the estrous cycle (sometimes referred to an interfemale aggression), consisting of attacks, lunges, and hip throws, is generally less intense than maternal aggression. Both forms of female aggression can be elicited by adult males and females, although there is some evidence to suggest that attacks are directed more vigorously toward males. We will examine both forms of female aggression for possible gonadal hormone involvement.

For the male mouse, the organizational effects necessary for the adult expression of intermale aggressive behavior apparently parallel those for sexual behavior. This hypothesis has been explored by examining the aggressive behavior of male mice castrated on the day of birth and of female mice treated neonatally with testosterone. In two classic experiments, Edwards (1969) and Bronson and Desjardins (1970) found that neonatally androgenized female mice readily exhibited intermale aggression in response to adult testosterone exposure. Female mice injected with testosterone beyond day 10 of postnatal life were much less aggressive than neonatally androgenized females. Conversely, male mice castrated after day 6 exhibited intense aggression in adulthood when administered testosterone, while those castrated prior to day 6 seldom fought (Peters, Bronson, and Whitsett 1972). The realization that neonatally castrated male mice and nonandrogenized female mice will exhibit intermale aggressive behavior if given chronic high doses of testosterone in adulthood (e.g., Svare, Davis, and Gandelman 1974; vom Saal, Gandelman, and Svare 1976) has suggested to some (e.g., Gandelman 1980) that sensitization rather than organization is a more appropriate description of early testosterone effects on intermale aggression.

Behavioral endocrinologists have also explored the effects of prenatal androgen exposure on intermale aggression. When female mice are exposed to testosterone during prenatal life, they are much more aggressive in response to adult testosterone exposure than are nontreated controls (vom Saal 1979). Once again, the aforementioned intrauterine position effect has been especially helpful in documenting prenatal steroid hormone influences. When compared to female mice surrounded by other females during intrauterine life, females contiguous to males (i.e., high fetal testosterone) are much more likely to exhibit intermale aggressive behavior when challenged with testosterone in adulthood (Gandelman, vom Saal, and Reinisch 1977). Interestingly, residing in utero betwen two females renders male mice (exposed to high fetal estrogen) less sensitive to the aggression-activating effects of adult testosterone compared to males surrounded by two males (vom Saal et al. 1983). The latter findings on aggression in male mice has prompted at least one investigator to suggest that prenatal estrogen may serve as an anti-testosterone agent during fetal life (vom Saal et al. 1983). (However, see below for data supporting a facilitative role for estrogen.)

As noted earlier, testosterone may not be the only hormone responsible for orgnizing the brain during life. Exposing neonatal female mice to estrogen or aromatizable androgens (androstenedione) promotes aggressive responses when animals are subsequently administered testosterone in adulthood (e.g., Edwards and Herndon 1970; Simon and Gandelman 1978). Also, treatment of neonatal female mice with MER-25, an anti-estrogen, prevents the masculinizing effects of early estrogen or testosterone exposure on androgen-activated aggression in adulthood (Gandelman 1980). These findings suggest that aromatization of testosterone to estrogen may be an important step in organizing neural systems for aggressive behavior. This interpretation must be considered preliminary, however, since many of the studies have used pharmacological dosages of estrogen. Also, no one to our knowledge has examined the aggression-potentiating effects of the nonaromatizable androgen, dihydrotestosterone.

A tactic recently used by some researchers has been to explore the effects of perinatally administered progestins. For example, exposure of neonatal female mice to NET, an androgen-based progestin, facilitates fighting behavior in response to adult testosterone stimulation (Gandelman, Howard, and Reinisch 1981). This finding is especially provocative since NET was used in the 1950s and 1960s for maintaining at-risk pregnancies in humans.

As previously noted for copulatory behavior, gonadal hormones act at specific hypothalamic areas to organize the neural substrate for later activation by steroid hormones. At present, there is no data examining the important brain sites involved in the effects of perinatal hormones on intermale aggression. Studies of the biochemical mechanism responsible for the effects of early hormonal stimulation on aggressive behavior have also not appeared in the literature. However, it would be very surprising if future research did not verify that the same brain areas and biochemical process were involved in both sexual and aggressive responding.

Our knowledge of perinatal gonadal hormone involvement in female aggressive behavior is limited to a few recent reports. Female mice residing between two males in utero (high fetal testosterone levels) exhibit higher levels of postpartum aggressive behavior and interfemale aggression than females residing between two females (vom Saal and Bronson 1978). Also, the injection of female mice with very low levels of testosterone during prenatal life elevates postpartum aggressive behavior (Mann and Svare 1983). These findings would therefore suggest that female aggressive behavior, like intermale aggression, is sensitive to, and promoted by, early testosterone exposure.

Conclusion   The findings reviewed above give clear and compelling evidence that perinatal gonadal hormones dramatically influence both sexual and aggressive behavior in laboratory animals. The presence of testicular hormones during early life masculinizes copulatory and aggressive behavior and defeminizes feminine sexual behavior, while the reverse is true in the absence of virilizing hormones. Hypothalamic sites and steroid hormone receptors within those areas play a critical role in the organizational process stimulated by testosterone and its metabolites. Early hormone exposure apparently masculinizes behavior by altering genomic processes such as the pattern of protein synthesis.

Postnatal Hormones and the Activation of Sexually-Dimorphic Behavior

Copulatory Behavior   The onset of puberty in male rodents corresponds to increased levels of circulating testosterone and elevated sexual interest (e.g., Beach 1942). Also, in seasonally breeding animals, increases in circulating testosterone are correlated with increased sexual activity (e.g., Gordon, Rose, and Bernstein 1976, for data on rhesus monkeys). Numerous studies in a variety of different mammalian species show that adult castration and the resulting loss of testicular hormones reduces copulatory behavior in the male (see Hart 1974 for a review). However, there is wide individual and species variation in postcastration copulatory behavior. For example, some castrated male cats continue to exhibit vigorous copulatory behavior many months following castration, while other males show a relatively rapid decline (Rosenblatt and Aronson 1958). Sexual experience modulates the reduction, in that sexually naive animals exhibit a more rapid decline than do experienced studs (e.g., Rosenblatt and Aronson 1958). Interestingly, some reports indicate that sexual behavior in male rhesus monkeys is not affected by castration (e.g., Phoenix 1974). Attempts to correlate individual variation in male copulatory behavior with variation in circulating testosterone have been generally unsuccessful (for data on male guinea pigs, see Harding and Feder 1976). This failure appears to be due in part to the fact that there is considerably more testosterone produced in rodents than is actually needed for the performance of sexual behavior (Damassa, Smith, and Davidson 1977).

The administration of testosterone to castrated male rodents results in reinstatement of sexual behavior in a dose-dependent fashion (e.g., Beach and Holz-Tucker 1949; Davidson 1966). It is not possible however to elevate copulatory behavior beyond precastration levels, no matter how much testosterone is administered (Grunt and Young 1953; Larsson 1966). Replacement therapy experiments have shown that aromatization of testosterone to estrogen, as well as reduction of the steroid to dihydrotestosterone, may be essential for the maintenance of copulatory behavior. It is important to note that this requirement may be species-dependent. Estrogen activates sexual behavior in castrated male rats, while dihydrotestosterone has no stimulatory effects (McDonald, Beyer, Newton, Brien, and Baker 1970). However, a synergistic relationship between estrogen and dihydrotestosterone has been proposed for the rat, since replacement therapy with the hormone combination restores the sex behavior of castrated animals (Baum and Vreeburg 1973). In other species such as the guinea pig, dihydrotestosterone alone restores copulatory behavior following castration (Alsum and Goy 1974).

The major brain area coordinating hormonal effects on male copulatory behavior is the anterior hypothalamus-preoptic area (e.g., Davidson 1966), although the penis (Beach and Westbrook 1968) and the spinal cord (Hart 1979) are also behaviorally relevant sites. Lesions in the anterior hypothalamus-preoptic area reduce copulatory behavior in male rats (Heimer and Larsson 1966/1967), while implants of testosterone in this region stimulate copulatory behavior in castrated males (Davidson 1966). The biochemical mechanism responsible for testosterone modulation of copulatory behavior may be related to intracellular testosterone receptors in the anterior hypothalamus-preoptic area as well as in the spinal cord. These areas are known to contain a high concentration of androgen receptors (e.g., Stumpf and Sar 1979). Recently, behavioral endocrinologists have turned to the possibility that testicular hormones interact with dopamine and serotonin as well as with the endogenous opioids to modulate copulatory behavior in male rodents (e.g., Crowley and Zemlan 1981; Gessa, Paglietti, and Quarantotti 1979).

Female rodents, in marked contrast to males, exhibit a cyclic pattern of sexual responsiveness, with high levels of receptivity observed during the periovulatory period and low levels accompanied by rejection behavior during the postovulatory period. In primates, such as the rhesus monkey, this relationship is also evident, although the timing of receptivity appears to be less rigidly controlled by ovulation (e.g., Goldfoot, Kravetz, Goy, and Freeman 1976). Ovulation in rodents is accompanied by declining estrogen titers juxtaposed against increasing plasma progesterone. Numerous studies in a variety of different species show that overiectomy results in the complete loss of sexual receptivity (e.g., Young 1961), although the behavior can be reinstated with a regimen consisting of estrogen priming followed a short time later by progesterone stimulation (e.g., Young 1961). Progesterone itself seems to have biphasic effects on female sexual receptivity in that it initially promotes the behavior, but continued stimulation can supress sexual responsiveness (Zucker 1966). Estrogen alone has been found to stimulate copulatory receptivity in ovariectomized female rats (Davidson, Rodgers, Smith, and Block 1968), although it is generally agreed that combined estrogen and progesterone stimulation is probably responsible for normal behavioral estrous.

The ventromedial nucleus of the hypothalamus is the most important area for coordinating female sexual receptivity. Lesions of this area produce deficits in the sexual responsiveness of rats (e.g., Singer 1968), while intracerebral implants of estrogen and progesterone in this brain area restore copulatory behvior in rats and guinea pigs (e.g., Morin and Feder 1974; Davis and Barfield 1979; Rubin and Barfield 1983). One way in which steroid hormones might facilitate female sexual behavior is suggested by the work of Blaustein and Feder (1979). They found that estradiol treatment elevated the number of progesterone receptors in a variety of brain areas, including the hypothalamus. Other work by Schwartz, Blaustein, and Wade (1979) showed that continued high levels of progesterone can cause depletion of progesterone receptors in the brain. It is thus theorized that estradiol induces progesterone receptors that, in turn, facilitate behavioral estrous. The continued presence of progesterone reduces progesterone receptors and thus terminates receptivity.

Recent studies indicate that simple estrogen-progesterone synergism in the brain may not be the only hormonal interactions required for normal female sexual responsiveness. In rodents, steroid induction of behavioral estrous has been linked to ovarian hormone synergism with neurotransmitter function (Nock and Feder 1981; Zemlin, Ward, Crowley, and Margules 1973), prolactin (Harlan, Shivers, and Pfaff 1983), and luteinizing hormone releasing factor (Moss and McCann 1973).

Aggressive Behavior In male mice, the development of aggressive behavior corresponds to the increase in circulating testosterone around the time of puberty (e.g., McKinney and Desjardins 1973). In seasonally breeding animals, such as the rhesus monkey, heightened plasma testosterone levels and aggression are associated with breeding activity (e.g., Bernstein, Gordon, and Rose 1983). Castration in adulthood reduces intermale aggression behavior in mice, rats, and hamsters (e.g., Beeman 1947). The postcastration decline in the behavior is modulated by previous fighting and copulatory experience; male mice with considerable pre-gonadectomy fighting or sexual experience persist in their aggressive behavior following castration much longer than niave animals (Schecter and Gandelman 1981; Palmer, Hauser, and Gandelman 1984). In rodents, attempts to correlate level of aggressive behavior with plasma testosterone have generally been unsuccessful (e.g., Selmanoff, Goldman, and Ginsburg 1977). However, in mice, genetic variation in the propensity to exhibit intermale aggression has been linked to variation in circulating testosterone during pubertal stages of development (e.g., Maxson, Shrenker, and Vigue 1983).

Testosterone replacement therapy restores aggression in male rodents in a dose-dependent way, with high doses more effective than low doses (e.g., Beeman 1947). It is unclear, however, as to the exact hormonal requirements for intermale aggression. Some reports suggest that aromatization of testosterone to estrogen may be important for the maintenance of aggressive behavior. For example, the hormones estrogen and androstenedione (an aromatizable steroid) have been found to maintain fighting behavior in mice (Luttge 1972; Luttge and Hall 1973). Also, administration of antiandrogens does not block testosterone-maintained aggression (e.g., Clark and Nowell 1980), although systemic administration of aromatase blockers does attenuate testosterone-maintained aggression (Bowden and Brain 1978). In contrast, other reports suggest that the reduction of testosterone to dihydrotestosterone may be more important. This theory follows from findings showing that dihydrotestosterone alone can maintain aggression (Schecter, Howard, and Gandelman 1981) and that antiestrogens are ineffective in suppressing testosterone-maintained fighting behavior (Simon, Gandelman, and Howard 1981). At least one report shows that the combined treatment of dihydrotestosterone and estrogen is effective in maintaining intermale aggression (Finney and Erpino, 1976), suggesting of course that both aromatization and reduction may be important for maintaining aggression. The reasons for these discrepancies are uncertain at this time, but genotype may be a major factor (see Simon 1983).

The neural areas implicated in the hormonal modulation of intermale aggressive behavior are the septum and the hypothalamus. Slotnick and Mullen (1972) reported that septal lesions reduced intermale aggressive behavior in mice, and Owen, Peters, and Bronson (1974) were able to restore fighting in castrated males by testosterone implants in this area. Also, Bean and Conner (1978) restored the aggressive behavior of castrated male rats by placement of testosterone in the preoptic area of the hypothalamus.

In contrast to our understanding of the biochemical mechanisms involved in the hormonal modulation of copulatory behavior, we know very little about how gonadal hormones influence brain neurochemistry and aggression. Recently, however, a report by Simon and Whalen (in press) showed that steroid receptors in the brain may be modulating aggression in a manner similar to that reported for copulatory behavior. These investigators found that genetic differences in the aggression-promoting effects of estrogen and testosterone are related to functional characteristics (affinity and binding) of estrogen receptors in the hypthalamic-preoptic-septal region of mice. If confirmed, these results would provide some interesting parallels to the elegant work already conducted on steroid receptor mechanisms and sexual behavior in rodents.

Finally, with the exception of work showing that the pituitary hormone, adrenocorticotropin (ACTH), inhibits intermale aggression (Leshner, Walker, Johnson, Kelling, Kreisler, and Svare 1973), there has been no work exploring gonadal hormone interactions with peptide hormones or neurotransmitters. This deficit is especially unfortunate in the case of neurotransmitters, which have repeatedly been implicated in intermale aggression (e.g., Miczek and Krsiak 1981).

In comparison to the systematic work on gonadal hormones and intermale aggression, the study of endocrine influences on female aggressive behavior is still in its infancy. We will first examine influences on aggression related to the estrous cycle, followed by an investigation of endocrine influences on maternal aggression.

Aggressive behavior during the estrous cycle has been examined in a variety of different mammalian species, but systematic investigations of hormonal involvement have appeared for only a few species (see Floody 1983, for a review). Additionally, there is considerable inconsistency in reports on cyclic changes in female aggressive behavior. In fact, the lack of uniformity makes general conclusions about hormonal involvement difficult, if not impossible.

One tentative observation that can be made for rodents, however, is that aggression, when observed, typically occurs during nonestrous periods (proestrous, metestrous, and diestrous). For mice, Hyde and Sawyer (1977) reported that aggression fluctuated with the four-to-five day cycle, with aggression highest during metestrous and lowest at estrous. For hamsters, Payne and Swanson (1970) reported that aggression was highest during diestrous and proestrous and lowest at estrous. In contrast, for primates the evidence indicates that estrous periods are associated with elevated aggressiveness. For rhesus monkeys, Rowell (1963) and Mallow (1979) reported that females were more likely to engage in fighting behavior during estrous than at any other point in their cycle. Cyclic changes in aggression have not been observed, however, in other primates (e.g., chimpanzees and baboons) (Rowell 1967; Yerkes 1940).

A confusing array of results is obtained when the effects of ovariectomy are considered. For example, ovariectomy has little or no effect on aggression in mice (Barkley and Goldman 1978). In hamsters, some reports indicate that aggression decreases following removal of the ovaries (e.g., Payne and Swanson 1971), while other reports show that the behavior is not altered (e.g., Floody and Pfaff 1977). For rhesus monkeys, aggression diminishes following ovariectomy (Michael and Zumpe 1970). Equally confusing are the results of studies exploring the effects of estrogen and progesterone treatment on female aggressive behavior. In ovariectomized female hamsters, varying reports indicate that aggressive behavior following estrogen treatment is increased (Noble and Alsum 1975), decreased (Ciaccio, Lisk, and Reuter 1979), or unaltered (Floody and Pfaff 1977). In rhesus monkeys, there is some data to show that aggression is reduced following estrogen treatment (Birch and Clark 1946; Zumpe and Michael 1970). According to one report, the aggressive behavior of ovariectomized hamsters treated with progesterone is increased (Payne and Swanson 1971), but several other researchers find no change at all (Floody and Pfaff 1977; Kislak and Beach 1955). For hamsters, combined treatment with estrogen and progesterone has consistently been reported to decrease aggression (Floody and Pfaff 1977; Kislak and Beach 1955). Combined estrogen and progesterone treatments have no effect, however, on the aggressive behavior displayed by rhesus monkeys (Michael and Zumpe 1970).

Two conclusions from the above findings seem warranted. First, behavioral endocrinologists must begin routinely to assay plasma estrogen and progesterone values and relate their studies to cyclic changes in the aggressive behavior of experimental animals. Second, researchers in this area should examine the aggression-promoting effects of sequentially administered hormones that more closely mimic cyclic changes in endocrine status. Until that time, we can tentatively conclude that ovarian hormones are playing a role in the cyclic changes observed in female aggressive behavior; however, the precise nature and degree of that contribution is not clearly established.

Maternal aggression, the defensive behavior seen during pregnancy and lactation, has recently received some attention by behavioral endocrinologists. Increased fighting behavior with advancing pregnancy has been reported in female mice, hamsters, and rhesus monkeys (Mann and Svare 1982; Michael and Zumpe 1970; Wise 1974). In the mouse, a rise in circulating progesterone corresponds to the onset of fighting behavior during midpregnancy, although individual variation in plasma levels of the hormone are not related to variation in the intensity of the behavior (Mann, Konen, and Svare 1984). When virgin female mice are injected with progesterone, they exhibit aggressive behavior similar in some respects to the aggression observed in normal pregnant animals (Mann et al. 1984). The intense maternal aggression seen during the postpartum period, which usually peaks during early lactation and then declines to a low point by the point of weaning, may be related to prolactin in some rodents (for the hamster, see Wise and Pryor 1977); but this relationship is clearly not involved in others (for the mouse, see Svare, Mann, Broida, and Michael 1982; for the rat, see Erskine, Barfield, and Goldman 1980). Importantly, the behavior does not appear to be stimulated by gonadal hormones, since ovariectomized lactating mice do not display a reduction in aggression (Svare 1977). Interestingly, testosterone and estrogen actually suppress the fighting behavior of lactating mice (Svare 1980; Svare and Gandelman 1975).

Conclusions Gonadal hormones are clearly involved in activating sexual and aggressive behavior in lower animals. In the male, the presence of testosterone and its metabolites activates copulatory and aggressive behavior. For the female, the ovarian hormones estrogen and progesterone stimulate sexual receptivity, but their role in aggressive behavior remains controversial. Gonadal hormones apparently activate these behaviors by stimulating hypothalamic structures and by altering steroid receptor function.

HORMONAL CONTROL OF SEX-RELATED BEHAVIOR IN HUMANS

The data reviewed above convincingly show that gonadal hormone exposure during early life (organizational effects) and during adult life (activational effects) dramatically influences copulatory behavior and aggression in laboratory animals. Is it possible to arrive at the same conclusions when we examine the relationship between endocrine function and sex-related behavior in humans? The purpose of this section is to answer that question. Before we do so, however, it is important to briefly touch upon some of the constraints researchers encounter when examining relationships between hormones and behavior in humans.

First, and foremost, it is acknowledged by most behavioral endocrinologists that social learning, culture, and other environmental factors are infinitely more important than are hormonal influences in human sex-related behaviors; however, separating the two historically has been a major problem plaguing much of the work in this area. Second, because of obvious ethical and practical limitations, researchers in this area must rely heavily upon accidents of nature and pathological states for their data base. Clinical disorders of genetic origin provide a major source of information for much of the work, but this research is frequently flawed owing to the inherent inability to separate direct genetic effects on nonhormonal systems from genetically induced endocrine disorder. Third, in most cases the sexually dimorplhic behaviors studied in lower animals have no obvious analogue in the human. The androgen-dependent, biting attack behavior observed in male rodents is qualitatively different from the changes in irritability and dominating behaviors studied in human aggression. Likewise, there is no apparent human parallel for the lordosis behavior observed in female rodents. This dissimilarity makes comparisons across species extremely difficult if not impossible with respect to some behaviors. Notwithstanding these limitations, some exciting work has recently been generated suggesting a linkage between hormones and some sex-related behaviors. We will review this work by first examining those studies dealing with organizational effects of gonadal hormones on gender identity, sexually dimorphic behavior, sexual orientation, aggression, and cognition.

Perinatal Gonadal Hormones and the Development of Gender-Related Behavior

Hormones and Gender Identity   The way in which an individual identifies with one sex or the other is referred to as gender identity. Money and Ehrhardt (e.g., Money and Ehrhardt 1968, 1972; Money 1975) have examined this process extensively and have generally concluded that sex of rearing in contrast to biological factors is the critical determinant of gender identity. For example, in spite of discrepancies between internal and/or external reproductive biology and sex of rearing, gender identity typically develops normally and is not easily reversed. One qualifier, however, is that the physical appearance of the individual must be unambiguously male or female. This appearance, of course, can be achieved through sex-appropriate surgical correction and postnatal hormonal therapy. The strength and permanence of gender identity is especially well illustrated in some unusual cases where pubertal abnormalities result in secondary sex characteristics opposite to patients' sex of assignment and their gender identity (Ehrhardt 1979). While these changes are obviously disturbing to these patients, their gender identity remains true to their assigned sex.

Hormones and Sexually Dimorphic Behavior   Researchers examining endocrine correlates to sex-related behavior have focused much of their research on the sexually dimorphic behavior of patients with a history of abnormal, prenatal hormone exposure. For example, human females exposed prenatally to abnormally high levels of adrenal testosterone (adrenogenital syndrome) or synthetic pregnancy-saving progestins with testosterone-like virilizing qualities (progestin-induced hermaproditism) show identification by self, playmates, and parents as tomboys, demonstrate increased energy expenditure, are oriented toward males during play, show decreased interest in maternalism and playing with dolls, and exhibit increased participation in team sports when compared to normal females not exposed to these altered hormone titers (Ehrhardt and Meyer-Bahlburg 1981). These data are frequently used to provide evidence for a human analogue to the virilization that normally accompanies perinatal testosterone exposure in lower animals. It is important to note, however, that there is no clear evidence indicating that the prenatal hormone exposure was directly acting on the central nervous system to produce the reported behavioral changes; and, as others have pointed out (see Feder 1984), the changes noted in the females are not abnormal and represent a quantitative but not a qualitative shift.

Another condition frequently studied by behavioral endocrinologists exploring prenatal endocrine correlates to sexually dimorphic behavior is the testicular feminization syndrome. This disorder occurs in genetic males and is accompanied by insensitivity of peripheral tissues to testosterone. These individuals are typically raised as females, exhibit a female phenotype, and display female patterns of childhood play behavior (e.g., Ehrhardt and Meyer-Bahlburg 1981). Separating social factors from prenatal endocrine factors is nearly impossible in these studies, and the findings must therefore be cautiously interpreted. Moreover, other studies examining play behavior in males prenatally exposed to synthetic progestins have failed to find differences in childhood play (Meyer-Bahlburg 1977).

Hormones and Sexual Orientation (Homosexuality)   Sexual orientation, erotic responsiveness to one sex or the other, has lately received considerable attention by behavioral endocrinologists. In particular, Dorner (1980) has advanced a neuroendocrine theory of homosexuality based upon experimentation with laboratory rats. When given testosterone during adult life and simultaneously confronted with sexually active adult males and females, male rats deprived of testosterone during early critical periods of development displayed a higher lordosis response/mounting-ejaculatory response ratio than did normal males. In contrast, females treated with testosterone neonatally showed a lower lordosis response/mounting-ejaculatory response ration than did normal females. A number of researchers have objected to the way Dorner uses the term homosexuality in rats, because this usage bears no relationship to the connotation denoted for humans (e.g., Feder 1984). Notwithstanding those criticisms, Dorner's theory postulates that male homosexuals probably experience too little exposure to perinatal testosterone, while female homosexuals (lesbians) receive too much. Earlier work, however, does not support this particular theory. Females exposed to excessive levels of testosterone prenatally (adrenogenital syndrome) do not exhibit abnormal levels of homosexuality in either fantasy or actual experience (Ehrhardt and Meyer-Bahlburg 1981). Also, genotypic males that experience abnormally low levels of testosterone perinatally and are raised as males exhibit a heterosexual orientation (Ehrhardt and Meyer-Bahlburg 1981). However, a recent report by Gladue, Green, and Hellman (1984) supports the existence of a neuroendocrine marker for homosexuality. As previously outlined, the endocrine responsiveness of the hypothalamic-pituitary-gonadal axis is sexually dimorphic, reflecting the organizing influences of testosterone during early stages of differentiation. Gladue et al. found that when challenged with an estrogen preparation called Premarin, male homosexuals exhibited an LH response that was intermediate between men and women declaring a lifelong heterosexual orientation.

It has also been suggested that homosexuality could develop out of the experiences a mother has while she is pregnant. Pregnant female rats exposed to severe stress during the last trimester of pregnancy deliver male offspring that are demasculinized and feminized with respect to copulatory behavior (Ward 1972). The source of this effect apparently is related to perinatal neuroendocrine function, since the stress procedure causes reduced fetal levels of testosterone (Ward and Weisz 1980). After reviewing data on the number of registered homosexuals in Germany, Dorner (1980) concluded that stresses associated with war could decrease fetal testosterone levels and hence elevate the occurrence of homosexuality in males. Though these data are intriguing, they are not compelling by any means. In fact, they have recently been challenged on a number of methodological and empirical grounds by Feder (1984).

An unexplored and potentially important related area of investigation is psychosexual development following prenatal psychotropic drug exposure. Perinatal treatment with phenobarbital, libriu, valium, or methadone reduces sexual behavior in male rats (e.g., Clemens, Popham, and Ruppert 1979).

Hormones and Aggression A number of studies on humans have reported that males are more aggressive than females (Maccoby and Jacklin 1974). These sex differences have held up consistently across cultures, even when very young children (3–6 years of age) who have had little opportunity for role learning were examined (e.g., D'Andrade 1966). It is frequently asserted that this dimorphism in aggressive behavior is attributable to sex differences in activity level, since males are generally more active than females; however, we are unaware of any attempts to systematically examine this important question. The possibility that the presence or absence of perinatal male hormones is responsible in whole or in part for the observed sex differences in aggression is presently still open. When pregnant rhesus monkeys are administered testosterone, their female offspring display threat behavior and rough and tumble play typical of normal males (Goy 1970). However, in several studies of human females with the aforementioned adrenogenital syndrome, aggression as judged by self and others (parents and peers) was identical to that of controls (Ehrhardt and Baker 1974; Money and Schwartz 1976). In a well-controlled study by Reinisch (1981), males and females exposed prenatally to synthetic progestins exhibited a significantly higher potential for exhibiting physical aggression than did unexposed siblings. Clearly, the data are at best ambiguous with respect to perinatal hormone involvement in human aggressive behavior.

Hormones, Cognition, and Cerebral Laterality It is well known that there are sex differences in cognitive abilities, with females excelling in verbal ability while males are better at spatial perception (Maccoby and Jacklin 1974). Unfortunately, these sex differences have not been examined extensively with respect to possible prenatal hormone involvement. Studies examining these parameters of cognition as well as intelligence in adrenogenital syndrome individuals generally do not report prenatal hormone effects (Ehrhardt and Meyer-Bahlburg 1981).

Although prenatal hormones have not been demonstrated to influence sex differences in these aspects of cognitive processing, they may be involved in the phenomena referred to as cerebral laterality. The two hemispheres of the human brain serve quite different functions. In most people (right-handed), the left hemisphere monitors verbal processing, while the right hemisphere is involved in spatial processing. This lateralization of function is stronger in males than it is in females (e.g., McGlone 1980). Recent reports show greatly reduced laterality for auditory stimuli and reversed dominance for verbal stimuli in Turner's syndrome females (Gordon and Galatzer 1980; Netley 1977). In contrast, elevated laterality for verbal stimuli was demonstrated in diethylstilbestrol-exposed (DES) females (Hines 1981). These findings are therefore consistent with the notion that prenatal hormones masculinize and defeminize the organism with respect to some aspects of cognitive function.

A relatively unexplored issue in this area concerns the effects of organizing gonadal hormones on personality development. One recent study by Reinisch (1981) reported that male and female subjects prenatally exposed to progestin or progestin combined with low estrogen were more independent, sensitive, and self-assured than matched, unexposed siblings or individuals exposed prenatally to high doses of estrogen combined with low doses of progestin. Because these attributes are highly correlated with success in academic situations, prenatal hormone involvement in personality traits should receive a great deal of attention in future work.

Conclusions The evidence reviewed above indicates that prenatal gonadal hormone exposure, at best, plays a minor modulatory role in sex-related behaviors in the human. Interestingly, the direction of these effects where they are observed are very similar to what has been reported for organizational effects in laboratory animals. There is no evidence to date indicating that perinatal gonadal hormone status influences gender identity, while the data on adult sexual orientation and homosexual behavior is so preliminary that solid conclusions are precluded. Even in cases where organizational effects of hormones have been implicated, such as in aggression, sexually dimorphic behaviors, and personality, the data do not evidence any direct effect on the CNS of prenatal gonadal hormones.

Postnatal Gonadal Hormones and Gender-Specific Behavior

As reviewed earlier, postnatal gonadal hormones activate reproductive behaviors in lower animals by acting on the CNS. In this section, we review the data on humans regarding sexuality and gonadal hormones, sex role reversal in pseudohermaphrodites, aggression and gonadal hormones, and mood and the menstrual cycle.

Sexuality and Hormones Postnatal gonadal hormone involvement in human sexuality has historically received a great deal of attention by behavioral endocrinologists. In the female, the frequency of sexual intercourse is lowest during menstruation and highest shortly after the period ends (e.g., McCance, Luff, and Widdowson 1952). The low level of sexual intercourse during the period of menstrual flow no doubt represents culturally learned avoidance behavior, while the higher level of sexual activity during other parts of the cycle can be likened to a rebound effect. Regardless, the sexual activity of cycling females is not related to circulating levels of plasma estradiol (Persky, Charney, Leif, O'Brien, Miller, and Strauss 1978). Moreover, the sexual desire of females is generally not reduced during the post-menopausal period, nor is it significantly altered by therapeutic, premenopausal ovariectomy (e.g., Katchadourian and Lunde 1980). These finding apparently suggest that ovarian hormones do not play a deterministic role in the sexual response of the human female. Although ovarian hormones are not essential for any major aspect of female sexuality, they nonetheless may play a modulatory role in arousability. Self-reported frequency of orgasm and degree of sexual arousal in females peaks at midcycle and just before menstruation (e.g., Moos and Lunde 1969; Udry and Morris 1968). These findings seem to provide some basis for a human analogue to cyclic changes in behavioral receptivity in laboratory rodents.

Considerable interest was generated a few years ago by the possibility that adrenal androgens might modulate libido in the female. For example women who underwent adrenalectomy because of cancer were reported to exhibit a general reduction in sexual desire (Waxenberg, Drellick, and Sutherland 1959), a finding that closely paralleled results from work with female rhesus monkeys (Everitt, Herbert, and Hamer 1971). To date, these findings have not been duplicated, but the fact that the patients were seriously ill makes interpretation of the results difficult.

The effects of castration on the sexual behavior of human males are highly variable (e.g., Bremer 1959). Some individuals report a rapid decline in sexual activity, while others report little or no change even years after testes removal. These findings must be interpreted cautiously, however, since many men may be unwilling to admit impotence. Although reliable studies of testosterone level and libido in men are not available (Bancroft 1978), separate reports of testicular function and sexual interest suggest that aging may be accompanied by reductions in both parameters (Vermeulen, Rubens, and Verdonck 1972; Masters and Johnson 1966). In the field of clinical endocrinology, it has been reported that testosterone treatment elevates libido and potency in males classified as hypogonadal (e.g., Davidson, Kwan, and Greenleaf 1982). Also, some studies report success in lowering the libido of sex offenders by treating them with testosterone antagonists, such as medroxyprogesterone acetate and cyproterone acetate (e.g., Laschet 1972; Money 1980). Once again, however, caution is needed in interpreting these results, since the men were simultaneously undergoing other forms of treatment.

Hormones and Sex Role Reversal in Pseudohermaphrodites   Postnatal hormone exposure has recently been implicated in pubertal sex role reveral in pseydohermaphrodites. Imperato-McGinley and colleagues (Imperato-McGinley, Guerrero, Gautier, and Peterson 1974; Imperato-McGinley, Peterson, and Gautier 1976) examined a group of twenty-four girls in two isolated villages in the Dominican Republic who miraculously changed into boys at the time of puberty. These individuals were genetic males, born with ambiguous genitalia that were clitoral-like in appearance. The absence of a normal penis and scrotum in these individuals was due to a genetic defect in their ability to metabolize testosterone to the androgen dihydrotestosterone, a hormone that functions during differentiation to elaborate the genital tubercle in a male fashion. These individuals were assigned and reared as female until the time of puberty when the normal surge of testosterone caused growth of the penis. In spite of their assignment as girls, these individuals changed their gender identity to males. Imperato-McGinley and colleagues have used these data to support the notion that postnatal hormonal factors can override early social learning and sex assignment. Other researchers (e.g., Money 1976; Feder 1984), however, have instead argued that the pubertal external virilization that takes place probably fosters gender identity doubts, which can best be resolved by changing to a male gender identity.

Aggression and Gonadal Hormones   A very active area of research interest in behavioral endocrinology concerns the relationship between postnatal gonadal hormones and aggression. This relationship has been studied by exploring correlations between testosterone levels and aggressive behavior in competitive and noncompetitive situations, by examining men with genetic differences in testosterone production, and by studying the effects on behavior of antitestosterone agents.

Attempts to correlate circulating levels of testosterone in normal males with measures of hostility, aggressive behavior, and social dominance have arrived at inconsistent results, with some investigators reporting a positive relationship (e.g., Persky, Smith, and Basu 1971) and other researchers reporting no association between the hormone and behavior (e.g., Brown and Davis 1975; Doering, Brodie, Kraemer, Moos, Becker, and Mechanic 1975; Meyer-Bahlburg, Boon, Sharma and Edwards 1973). These studies, which have employed assessments of normal volunteers, college men, and athletes, typically rely upon self-report measures, like the fequently used Buss-Durkee Hostility Inventory. Data employing this test must be interpreted cautiously, however, since it has been argued that this test more accurately assesses the immediate, ongoing state of the individual in contrast to more stable, long-term behavior (e.g., Rubin, Reinisch, and Haskett 1981).

Studies examining associations between circulating testosterone and aggressive behavior in prison populations have resulted in more consistent reports of positive relationships. A widely cited study was conducted by Kreuz and Rose (1972)—plasma testosterone was related to observable aggressive behavior in twenty one young male prisoners with records of violent crime. No relationship was found between levels of the hormone, frequency of fighting and verbal aggression in prison, and scores on the Buss-Drukee Hostility Inventory. When the authors examined the ten men with histories of more violent crime during adolescence, however, they found significantly higher levels of plasma testosterone in these individuals compared to prisoners without the same adolescent histories. In view of the fact that plasma testosterone in humans is relatively unstable from month to month (Doering et al. 1975), postulating a causal link between adolescent testosterone levels and adult patterns of violence and aggression is a tenuous process at best.

Another widely cited study in the area of postnatal testosterone and aggression was reported by Ehrenkranz, Bliss, and Sheard (1974). They measured circulating testosterone levels in prison convicts separated into three different categories. One group consisted of men that were socially dominant (i.e., they had asserted themselves into prestigious jobs in the inmate hierarchy) but nonaggressive, a second group consisted of prisoners that were chronically aggressive (i.e., continued acts of aggression and threats while in prison), and a third group consisted of convicts that were neither dominant nor aggressive. The socially dominant but unaggressive group and chronically aggressive group, while not differing from each other in plasma testosterone levels, exhibited significantly higher levels of the hormone than did the nondominant, unaggressive group. Though reports like these are interesting, they do not bear on the issue of causality. An equally viable conclusion could be, of course, that testosterone is a respondent and not a determinant of violent and aggressive behavior in men.

Though the focus of this review is not to examine the hormonal consequences of changes in social status, results from this area may shed some light on relationships between postnatal testosterone and aggression. For example, from the infrahuman primate literature, it is well known that successful attempts to maintain status in the dominance hierarchy increase plasma testosterone, while the opposite (decline in testosterone) occurs following a defeat (e.g., Rose, Bernstein, and Gordon 1975). In an attempt to produce a human analogue to this situation, Mazur and Lamb (1980) rewarded winners in a doubles tennis match by giving them a $100 prize, then measured testosterone one hour after the competition. With few exceptions, winners exhibited a rise in testosterone one hour after the match, while losers exhibited a reduction in circulating levels of the hormone. In a similar study, Elias (1981) reported that winners of college wrestling matches exhibited greater elevations in circulating testosterone than did losers.

Associations between testosterone and a change in status have also been reported. Males receiving their medical degrees exhibited a rise in testosterone within one day of the graduating ceremony (Mazur and Lamb 1980). Also, army recruits during basic training and young men in the initial stages of officer candidate school experience a lowering of plasma testosterone (Rose, Bourne, Poe, Mougey, Collins and Mason 1969; Kreuz, Rose, and Jennings 1972). The degraded status associated with these situations may be responsible for the hormonal changes, but the nonspecific effects of stress might also account for the data. Regardless, it is important to note that there has currently been no empirical work done on the permanence of these changes and whether or not they play any role in the maintenance of future aggressive, violent, or dominating behaviors. This point is not trivial, since work with rodents has already indicated that hormonal changes following defeat have long-lasting effects on the organism's future aggressive responsiveness (e.g., Roche and Leshner 1979).

Another way to examine postnatal testosterone and aggression in the male is to look at genetically based disorders. The XYY condition, or the "supermale" syndrome as it is frequently referred to, stimulated a great deal of attention that, in retrospect, was probably unwarranted. Such individuals were found to be overrepresented in some English prisons that housed criminally insane individuals. It was initially thought that such individuals, by virtue of their extra Y chromosome, might exhibit abnormally high levels of testosterone. However, extensive examination of the testosterone profiles of these individuals did not reveal anything unusual about testicular function (e.g., Borgaonkar and Shah 1974; Witkin, Mednick, Schulsinger, Bakkestrom, Christiansen, Goodenough, Hirschhorn, Lundsteen, Owen, Philip, Rubin, and Stocking 1976). Interestingly, XXY males (Klinefelter's Syndrome) are also overrepresented in prison populations, but such individuals are hypogonadal (e.g., Witkin et al. 1976). The overwhelming evidence in these studies suggests little relation between postnatal testosterone and aggression.

The last category to consider when exploring aggression and gonadal hormones is the effects of castration and antihormone treatments in the control of violent behavior. We have already partially examined this issue in the discussion about hormones and male sexuality (see above). Although castrated sex criminals with records of violent crime are less likely to commit these acts in the future (LeMaire 1956), a direct effect of the loss of testosterone is only one of many possible reasons for their behavior changes. As noted earlier, Bremer (1959) reported that castration does seem to reduce libido, but does not alter aggressiveness per se. Also, progestins and estrogen-like compounds are known to make aggressive individuals and sex offenders placid (e.g., Bell 1978; Money 1980; Laschet 1972), but the simultaneous effects of counseling and psychotherapy make these reports difficult to interpret.

Mood and the Menstrual Cycle   The frequent assertion that women's moods are associated with their menstrual cycle has stimulated behavioral endocrinologists to seek a hormonal explanation. The findings presented here are necessarily controversial ones. This controversy is due, in part, to the many methodological criticisms leveled at this research in the past. A brief examination of these criticisms is needed before we move on to analzing the data.

First, there has been no general agreement by individuals working in this area as to what constitutes negative affect and mood; therefore, there is tremendous variation from study to study in what behaviors are actually measured. Second, because most of the work in this area has focused on unusual populations, including prisoners and patients in psychiatric wards, the extent to which the findings can be generalized to the average, cycling female is limited. Third, much of the older and even some of the more recent work in this area fails to measure plasma hormone levels, thus preventing any reasonable conclusions concerning estrogen and progesterone involvement. Finally, the social expectations of many developing females toward menstruation is rarely considered as a major source of variation and a causal factor by itself.

Notwithstanding the above criticisms, there is a substantial body of evidence showing that women experience relatively negative moods one week prior to, as well as a few days after, menstruation. Perhaps the best study documenting the premenstrual tension syndrome (PMTS) was reported by Rossi and Rossi (1980). Eighty-two college women were studied over a forty-day period. The researchers found that the women exhibited positive moods during the middle (ovulatory) phase of the cycle and negative moods in the seven days prior to menstruation. Negative moods were also reported for the first few days following bleeding. In contrast, women taking birth control pills did not report mood changes, suggesting that the hormonal fluctuations in normally cycling females may have been responsible for the change in affect.

A number of other studies examining cyclic changes in misbehavior, mishap, and morbidity also link the menstrual cycle with mood changes. For example, it is more likely that cycling women will attempt and be successful at suicide during the premenstrual period (e.g., Mandell and Mandell 1967). Cycling women are more likely to exhibit angry outbursts of aggression and to commit violent crimes just before and just after menstruation (e.g., Dalton 1964; Morton, Additon, Addison, Hunt, and Sullivan 1953). Also, older students that are prefects in a girls' school are more likely to punish younger students during the immediate postmenstrual days than at any other time during their cycle (Dalton 1964). In studies of prison populations, women inmates with a history of violent behavior were much more likely to be confined to their rooms for disciplinary reasons during the week prior to menstruation than during any other time of their cycle (Hands, Herbert, and Tennent 1974). Finally, one study of a large sample of cycling female prison inmates found that physical and verbal abuse were much more likely to occur in the perimenstrual days than at any other time (Ellis and Austin 1971).

Estrogen and/or progesterone imbalance is most often cited to explain the above findings; however, no studies to date have reported a relationship between circulating ovarian hormones and PMTDSD (e.g., Dalton 1982). Contraceptives, in particular progesterone-dominated pills, have been used in some cases to ease manifestation of the syndrome, but not all women respond to this hormone treatment (Dalton 1982). Along these lines, it is interesting to note that estrogen treatment has been used with great success in alleviating the depression many women experience during the postmenopausal period (e.g., Klaiber, Broverman, Vogel, and Kobayashi 1976).

Finally, a relatively unexplored and potentially interesting area of hormone-behavior relationships in humans is the well-known changes in mood that accompany the peripartum period (Yalom, Lunde, Moos, and Hamburg 1968). We are aware of only one study in which endocrine correlates for mood changes during the peripartum period were examined. A report by Nott, Franklin, Armitage, and Gelder (1976) showed that the most extreme manifestation of these mood changes, the postpartum "blues" syndrome, was unrelated to estrogen and progesterone levels before, during, or after parturition. Clearly, however, this area is one that requires a great deal more research before we can arrive at any conclusions concerning hormonal involvement.

Conclusions   Our conclusions regarding postnatal gonadal hormone involvement in human sex-related behavior are at best tentative, owing to the relative newness of the field. To date, the data do not permit us to say that postnatal gonadal hormones are playing a direct causal role in any of the behaviors assessed; there are no data to suggest that postnatal hormones are directly working on the CNS to alter any behavior pattern in humans. As was the case for organizational hormone effects, however, the data reveal a minor modulatory role for gonadal hormones. Interestingly, the direction of many of these effects is similar to what has been reported for lower animals. We are uncomfortable, however, even with this statement, since the many qualifiers that go into this conclusion greatly diminish its force. The most promising areas for future research appear to be testosterone influences on aggression and hostility, and gonadal hormone involvement in sexual arousal in males and females. In these two areas, suggestive, positive evidence for gonadal hormone involvement has been reported, thereby justifying more sophisticated examinations. Systematic research in the areas of mood and the menstrual cycle and gonadal hormone involvement in sex role reversal is just beginning to emerge; in neither case is the role of hormones particularly convincing at this early stage.

GENERAL CONCLUSIONS

The findings reviewed in this chapter clearly show that gonadal hormones play a very important role in both aggressive and sexual behavior in laboratory animals. Steroid hormones act during well-defined periods of development to both organize and activate these behaviors by working on specific anatomical structures within the central nervous system. The biochemical alterations produced by steriod hormones and their importance for sexually differentiated behaviors is an emerging resulting field of research. We already know that specific changes in steriod hormone receptors as well as other physiological changes are associated with behavioral changes induced by hormones. Clearly the field of behavioral endocrinology has grown rapidly not only with respect to the number of new findings reported each year but also with respect to the level of sophistication employed by workers specializing in this area.

In spite of the advances made by researchers using animal models of hormone-behavior interactions, a healthy degree of scepticism is necessary when these findings are viewed in toto. In important statements on this issue, Feder (1984) and Beach (1974) have persuasivley argued that findings on lower animals should not be interpreted to mean that hormones play a deterministic, causal role in sex-related behavior, After all, hormonal stimulation of animal behavior has been consistently demonstrated only under highly controlled and specified laboratory conditions.

Do hormones also modulate the sex-related behavior of humans? Strictly speaking, we are not aware of a single study indicating that hormones directly alter behavior in humans by acting on the central nervous system. The findings reviewed here provide some very suggestive evidence that hormones can organize and activate behavior in the human in much the same manner as they do for lower animals. Our considered opinion, however, is that the bulk of the evidence to date shows that hormones, at best, play only a minor modulatory role in the sex-related behaviors studied in humans.

A second, obvious question follows from the above conclusion—did evolution work in such a way to "free" the human being and other "higher" mammals from hormonal control? That is, as one proceeds up the so-called "phylogenetic scale" and neocortical processes are elaborated, do hormones become less important in the control of behavior? Unfortunately, this question might not be a particularly viable one, since it is doubtful that analogous behaviors are being studied across species. Even if we could assume that similar behaviors were being compared in different species, the avilable evidence in a limited number of mammalian species indicates there is little support for the hypothesis (see Hart 1974).

In conclusion, we wish to advance two recommendations for future work in this area, First, there is a need to more accurately define and objectify the behavioral measures being analyzed, Workers examining laboratory animals have done this with great precision, but similar attempts for humans have generally lagged behind. Second, there is a need to expand the scope of the inquiry to other hormones, other behaviors, and other environmental conditions. To a certain extent, this expansion is already being done. For example, endocrine involvement in learning, memory, and attentional processes is being intensively studied in both humans (e.g., Weingartner 1981) and lower animals (e.g., De Wied 1971), and the role of peptide hormones in behavior has emerged as a major area of exploration (e.g., Moss and McCann 1973). Also, recent studies examining hormone-behavior relationships in field studies of freely moving animals promises to give researchers a whole new perspective on endocrine involvement in sex-related behavior (e.g., Harding 1983; Bernstein, Gordon, and Rose 1983). In short, the field of behavioral endocrinolgy is moving in directions that will soon allow us to answer the difficult questions posed in this chapter with more clarity and precision than is currently permitted.

REFERENCES

Adler, N. (Ed.). (1981). *Neuroendocrinology of reproduction.* New York: Plenum.

Alsum, P., and Goy, R. W. (1974). Actions of esters of testosterone, dihydrotestosterone, or estradiol on sexual behavior in castrated male guinea pigs. *Hormones and Behavior, 5,* 207–217.

Arai, Y., and Gorski, R. A. (1968). Effect of anti-estrogens on steroid induced sexual receptivity in ovariectomized rats. *Physiology and Behavior, 3,* 351–353.

Balthazart, J., Prove, E., and Gilles, R. (Eds.). (1983). *Hormones and behavior in higher vertebrates.* New York: Springer-Verlag.

Bancroft, J. (1978). The relationship between hormones and sexual behavior in humans. In J. B. Hutchinson (ed.), *Biological determinants of sexual behavior* (pp. 493–520). New York: Wiley.

Barkley, M. S., and Goldman, B. D. (1978). Studies on opponent status and steroid mediation of aggression in female mice. *Behavioral Biology, 23,* 118–123.

Barraclough, C. A. (1967). Modifications in reproductive function after exposure to hormones during the prenatal and early postnatal period. In L. Martini and W. F. Ganong (eds.), *Neuroendocrinology* (Vol. 2, pp. 62–69). New York: Academic Press.

Baum, M. J. (1979). Differentiation of coital behavior in mammals: A comparative analysis. *Neuroscience and Biobehavioral Reveiws, 3,* 265–284.

Baum, M. J., Gallagher, C. A., Martin, J. T. Damassa, D. A. (1982). Effects of testosterone, dihydrotestosterone, or estradiol administered neonatally on sexual behavior of female ferrets. *Endocrinology, 111,* 773–780.

Baum, M. J., and Vreeburg, J. T. M. (1973). Copulation in castrated male rats following combined treatment with estradiol and dihydrotestosterone. *Science, 182,* 283–285.

Beach, F. A. (1942). Sexual behavior of prepuberal male and female rats treated with gonadal hormones. *Journal of Comparative Psychology, 34,* 285–292.

Beach, F. A. (1974). Behavioral endocrinology and the study of reproduction. *Biology of Reproduction, 10,* 2–18.

Beach, F. A., and Holz-Tucker, A. M. (1949). Effects of different concentrations of androgen upon sexual behavior in castrated male rats. *Journal of Comparative and Physiological Psychology, 42,* 433–441.

Beach, F. A., and Kuehn, R. E. (1970). Coital behavior in dogs X. Effects of androgenic stimulation during development on feminine mating responses in females and males. *Hormones and Behavior, 1,* 347–367.

Beach, G. A., and Westbrook, W. H. J. (1968). Dissociation of androgen effects on sexual morphology and behavior in male rats. *Endocrinology, 83,* 395–398.

Bean, N. J., and Connor, R. (1978). Central hormonal replacement and home-cage dominance in castrated rats, *Hormones and Behavior, 11,* 100–109.

Beatty, W. W. (1979). Gonadal hormones and sex differences in nonreproductive behaviors in rodents: Organizational and activational influences. *Hormones and Behavior, 12,* 112–163.

Beeman, E. A. (1947). The effect of male hormone on aggressive behavior in mice. *Physiological Zoology, 20,* 373–405.

Bell, R. (1978). Hormone influences on human aggression. *Irish Journal of Medical Science, 147* (Suppl. 1), 5–9.

Bernstein, I. S., Gordon, T. P., and Rose, R. M. (1983). The interaction of hormones, behavior, and social context in nonhuman primates. In B. Svare (ed.), *Hormones and aggressive behavior* (pp. 535–562). New York: Plenum Press.

Birch, H. G. and Clark, G. (1946). Hormonal modification of social behavior. II. The effects of sex-hormone administration on the social dominance status of the female-castrate chimpanzee. *Psychosomatic Medicine, 8,* 320–331.

Blaustein, J. D., and Feder, H. H. (1979). Cytoplasmic progestin receptors in guinea pig brain: Characteristics and relationship to the induction of sexual behavior. *Brain Research, 169,* 481–497.

Borgaonkar, D., and Shah, S. (1974). The XYY chromonsome male—or syndrome? In A. Steinberg and A. Bearn (eds.), *Progress in medical genetics* (Vol. 10). New York: Grune and Stratton.

Booth, J. E. (1977). Sexual behavior of neonatally castrated rats injected during infancy with oestrogen and dihydrotestosterone. *Journal of Endocrinology, 72,* 135–141.

Bowden, N. G., and Brain, P. F. (1978). Blockade of testosterone-maintained intermale fighting in albino laboratory mice by an aromatization inhibitor. *Physiology and Behavior, 20,* 543–546.

Breedlove, S. M., and Arnold, A. P. (1980). Hormone accumulation in a sexually dimorphic motor nucleus in the rat spinal cord. *Science, 210,* 564–566.

Bremer, J. (1959). *Asexualization: A follow-up study of 244 cases.* New York: Macmillan.

Bronson, F. H., and Desjardins, C. (1970). Neonatal androgen administration and adult aggressiveness in female mice. *General and Comparative Endocrinology, 15,* 320–325.

Brown, W. and Davis, G. (1975). Serum testosterone and irritability in man. *Psychosomatic Medicine, 37,* 87–97.

Carter, C. S., Clemens, L. G., and Hoekema, D. J. (1972). Neonatal androgen and adult sexual behavior in the golden hamster. *Physiology and Behavior, 9,* 89–95.

Ciaccio, L. A. Lisk, R. D., and Reuter, L. A. (1979). Prelordotic behavior in the hamster: A hormonally modulated transition from aggression to sexual receptivity. *Journal of Comparative and Physiological Psychology, 93,* 771–780.

Clark, C. R., and Nowell, N. W. (1980). The effect of the nonsteroidal antiandrogen flutamide on neural receptor binding of testosterone and intermale aggressive behavior in mice. *Psychoneuroendocrinology, 5,* 39–45.

Clemens, L. G., Gladue, B. A., and Coniglio, L. P. (1978). Prenatal endogenous androgenic influences on masculine sexual behavior and genital morphology in male and female rats. *Hormones and Behavior, 10,* 40–53.

Clemens, L. G., Popham, T. V., and Ruppert, P. H. (1979). Neonatal treatment of hamsters with barbiturate alters adult sexual behavior. *Developmental Psychobiology, 12,* 49–59.

Crowley, W. R., and Zemlan, F. P. (1981). The neurochemical control of mating behavior. In N. T. Adler (ed.), *Neuroendocrinology of Reproduction* (pp. 451–484). New York: Plenum.

Dalton, K. (1964). *The premenstrual syndrome.* Springfield, Ill.: Charles C. Thomas.

Dalton, K. (1982). Premenstrual tension: An overview. In R. C. Friedman (ed.), *Behavior and the menstrual cycle* (pp. 217–242). New York: Dekker.

Damassa, D. A., Smith, E. R., and Davidson, J. (1977). The relationship between circulating testosterone levels and sexual behavior. *Hormones and Behavior, 8,* 275–286.

D'Andrade, R. (1966). Sex differences and cultural institutions. In E. Maccoby (ed.), *The development of sex differences.* Stanford, Ca.: Stanford University Press.

Davidson, J. M. (1966). Activation of the male rat's sexual behavior by intracerebral implantation of androgen. *Endocrinology, 79,* 783–794.

Davidson, J. M., Kwan, M., and Greenleaf, W. J. (1982). Hormonal replacement and sexuality in men. In J. Bancroft (ed.), *Clinics in endocrinology and metabolism, diseases of sex and sexuality* (pp. 599–624). Philadelphia: Saunders.

Davidson, J. M., Rodgers, C. H., Smith, E. R., and Bloch, G. J. (1968). Stimulation of female sex behavior in adrenalectomized rats with estrogen alone. *Endocrinology, 82,* 193–195.

Davis, P. G., and Barfield, R. J. (1979). Activation of feminine sexual behavior in castrated male rats by intrahypothalamic implants of estradiol benzoate. *Neuroendocrinology, 28,* 228–233.

Davis, P. G., Chaptal, C. V., and McEwen, B. S. (1979). Independence of the differentiation of masculine and feminine sexual behavior in rats. *Hormones and Behavior, 12,* 12–19.

De Wied, D. (1971). Long-term effect of vasopressin in the maintenance of a conditioned avoidance response in rats. *Nature, 232,* 58–60.

Doering, C., Brodie, J., Kraemer, H., Moos, R., Becker, H., and Mechanic, D. (1975). Negative affect and plasma testosterone: A longitudinal human study. *Psychosomatic Medicine, 37,* 484–491.

Dorner, G. (1980). Sexual differentiation of the brain. *Vitamins and Hormones, 38,* 325–381.

Dorner, G., and Staudt, J. (1969). Structural changes in the hypothalamic ventromedial nucleus of the male rat, following neonatal castration and androgen treatment. *Neuroendocrinology, 4,* 278–281.

Edwards, D. A. (1969). Early androgen stimulation and aggressive behavior in male and female mice. *Physiology and Behavior, 4,* 333–338.

Edwards, D. A., and Burge, K. G. (1971). Early androgen treatment and male and female sexual behavior in mice. *Hormones and Behavior, 2,* 49–58.

Edwards, D. A., and Herndon, J. (1970). Neonatal estrogen stimulation and aggressive behavior in female mice. *Physiology and Behavior, 5,* 993–995.

Ehrenkranz, J., Bliss, E., and Sheard, M. (1974). Plasma testosterone: Correlation with aggressive behavior and social dominance in man. *Psychosomatic Medicine, 36,* 469–475.

Ehrhardt, A. A. (1979). Psychosexual adjustment in adolescence in patients with congenital abnormalities of their sex organs. In H. L. Vallet and I. H. Porter (Eds.), *Genetic mechanisms of sexual development* (Birth Defects Institute Symposia), pp. 473–484. Academic Press, New York.

Ehrhardt, A., and Baker, S. (1974). Fetal androgens, human central nervous system differentiation, and behavior sex differences. In R. Friedman, R. Richart, and R. Vande Wiele (eds.), *Sex differences in behavior.* New York: Wiley.

Erhardt, A. A., and Meyer-Bahlburg, H. F. L. (1981). Effects of prenatal sex hormones on gender-related behavior. *Science, 211,* 1312–1318.

Elias, M. (1981). Serum cortisol, testosterone and testosterone bindng globulin responses to competitive fighting in human males. *Aggressive Behavior, 7,* 215–224.

Ellis, D., and Austin, P. (1971). Menstruation and aggressive behavior in a correctional center for women. *The Journal of Criminal Law and Police Science, 62,* 388–395.

Erskine, M., Barfield, R. J., and Goldman, B. D. (1980). Postpartum aggression in rats. I. Effects of hypophysectomy. *Journal of Comparative and Physiological Psychology, 94,* 484–494.

Everitt, B. J., Herbert, J., and Hamer, J. D. (1971). Sexual receptivity of bilaterally adrenalectomized female rhesus monkeys. *Physiology and Behavior, 8,* 409–415.

Feder, H. H. (1984). Hormones and sexual behavior. *Annual Review of Psychology, 35,* 165–200.

Finney, H. C., and Erpino, M. J. (1976). Synergistic effect of estradiol benzoate and dihydrotestosterone on aggression in mice. *Hormones and Behavior, 7,* 391–400.

Floody, O. R. (1983). Hormones and aggression in female mammals. In B. Svare (ed.), *Hormones and aggressive behavior* (pp. 39–89). New York: Plenum.

Floody, O. R., and Pfaff, D. W. (1977). Aggressive behavior in female hamsters: The hormonal basis for fluctuations in female aggressiveness correlated with estrous state. *Journal of Comparative and Physiological Psychology, 91,* 443–464.

Gandelman, R. (1980). Gondal hormones and the induction of intraspecific fighting in mice. *Neuroscience and Biobehavioral Reviews, 4,* 133–140.

Gandelman, R. (1983). Gonadal hormones and sensory function. *Neuroscience and Biobehavioral Reviews, 7,* 1–17.

Gandelman, R., Howard, S. M., and Reinisch, J. M. (1981)., Perinatal esposure to 19-Nor-17 ethynyltestosterone (Norethindrone) influences morphology and aggressive behavior of female mice. *Hormones and Behavior, 15,* 404–415.

Gandelman, R., vom Saal, F. S., and Reinisch, J. M. (1977). Contiguity to male foetuses affects morphology and behavior of female mice. *Nature, 266,* 722–724.

Gerall, A. A., Dunlap, J. L., Hendricks, S. E. (1973). Effect of ovarian secretions on female behavioral potentiality in the rat. *Journal of Comparative and Physiological Psychology, 82,* 449–465.

Gerall, A. A., Hendricks, S. E., Johnson, L. L., and Bounds, T. W. (1967). Effects of early castration in male rats on adult sexual behavior. *Journal of Comparative and Physiological Psychology, 64,* 206–212.

Gessa, G. L., Paglietti, E., and Quarantotti, G. P. (1979). Induction of copulatory behavior in sexually inactive rats by naloxone. *Science, 204,* 203–205.

Gladue, B. A., Green, R., and Hellman, R. E. (1984). Neuroendocrine response to estrogen and sexual orientation. *Science, 225,* 1496–1499.

Goldfoot, D. A., Kravetz, M. A., Goy, R. W., and Freeman, S. K. (1976). Lack of effect of vaginal lavages and aliphatic acids on ejaculatory responses in rhesus monkeys: Behavioral and chemical analyses. *Hormones and Behavior, 7,* 1–28.

Goldfoot, D. A., and van der Werff ten Bosch, J. J. (1975). Mounting behavior of female guinea pigs after prenatal and adult administration of the propionates of testosterone, dihydrotestosterone, and androstanediol. *Hormones and Behavior, 6,* 139–148.

Gordon, H. W., and Galatzer, A. (1980). Cerebral organization in patients with gonadal dysgenesis. *Psychoneuroendocrinology, 5,* 235–244.

Gorski, R. A. (1979). Nature of hormone action in the brain. In T. H. Hamilton, J. H. Clark, and W. A. Sadler (eds.), *Ontogeny of receptors and reproductive hormone action* (pp. 371–392). New York: Raven.

Gorski, R. A., Gordon, J. H., Shryne, J. E., and Southam, A. M. (1978). Evidence for a morphological sex difference within the medial preoptic area of the rat brain. *Brain Research, 148,* 333–346.

Goy, R. (1970). Early hormonal influences on the development of sexual and sex-related behavior. In F. Schmitt, G. Quarton, T. Melnechuck, and G. Adelman (eds.), *The neurosciences: Second study program.* New York: Rockefeller University Press.

Goy, R. W., and McEwen, B. S. (1980). *Sexual differentiation of the brain.* Cambridge, Mass.: MIT Press.

Grady, K. L., Phoenix, C. H., and Young, W. C. (1965). Role of the developing rat testis in differentiation of the neural tissues mediating mating behavior. *Journal of Comparative and Physiological Psychology, 59,* 176–182.

Greenough, W. T., Carter, C. S., Steerman, C., and DeVoogd, T. J. (1977). Sex differences in dendritic patterns in hamster preoptic area. *Brain Research, 126,* 63–72.

Grunt, J. A., and Young, W. C. (1953). Consistency of sexual behavior patterns in individual male guinea pigs following castration and androgen therapy. *Journal of Comparative and Physiological Psychology, 46,* 138–144.

Hands, J., Herbert, V., and Tennent, G. (1974). Menstruation and behavior in a special hospital. *Medicine, Science, and the Law, 14,* 32–35.

Harding, C. (1983). Hormonal influences on avian aggressive behavior. In B. Svare (ed.), *Hormones and aggressive behavior* (pp. 435–468). New York: Plenum Press.

Harding, C., and Feder, H. H. (1976). Relation between individual differences in sexual behavior and plasma testosterone levels in the guinea pig. *Endocrinology, 98,* 1198–1205.

Harlan, R. E., Shivers, B. D., and Pfaff, D. W. (1983). Midbrain microinfusions of PRL increase the estrogen-dependent behavior, lordosis. *Science, 219,* 1451–1453.

Harris, G. W., and Jacobsohn, D. (1952). Functional grafts of the anterior pituitary gland. *Proceedings of the Royal Society, Series B, 139,* 263–276.

Harris, G. W., and Levine, S. (1965). Sexual differentiation of the brain and its experimental control. *Journal of Physiology, 181,* 379–400.

Hart, B. L. (1979). Sexual behavior and penile reflexes of neonatally castrated male rats treated in infancy with estrogen and dihydrotestosterone. *Hormones and Behavior, 13,* 256–268.

Heimer, L., and Larsson, K. (1966/1967). Impairment of mating behavior in male rats following lesions in the preoptic-anterior hypothalamic continuum. *Brain Research, 3,* 248–263.

Hines, M. (1981). Prenatal diethylstilbestrol esposure, human sexually dimorphic behavior and cerebral lateralization. *Dissertation Abstracts International, 42,* 423B.

Hyde, J. S., and Sawyer, T. F. (1977). Estrous cycle fluctuations in aggressiveness of house mice. *Hormones and Behavior, 9,* 290–295.

Imperato-McGinley, J., Guerrero, L., Gautier, T., and Peterson, R. E. (1974). Steroid 5-reductase deficiency in man: An inherited form of male pseudohermaphroditism. *Science, 186,* 1213–1215.

Imperato-McGinley, J., Peterson, R. E., and Gautier, T. (1976). Gender identity and hermaphroditism. *Science, 191,* 872.

Jacobson, C. D., and Gorski, R. A. (1981). Neurogenesis of the sexually dimorphic nucleus of the preoptic area in the rat. *Journal of Comparative Neurology, 196,* 519–529.

Katchadourian, H. A., and Lunde, D. T. (1980). *Fundamentals of Human Sexuality.* New York: Holt, Rinehart, and Winston.

Kislak, J. W., and Beach, F. A. (1955). Inhibition of aggressiveness by ovarian hormones. *Endocrinology, 56,* 684–692.

Klaiber, E. L., Broverman, D. M., Vogel, W., and Kobayashy, Y. (1976). The use of steroid hormones in depression. In T. M. Itil, G. Laudahn, and W. M. Herrmann (eds.), *Psychotropic action of hormones.* New York: Halsted Press.

Kobayashi, F. and Gorski, R. A. (1970). Effects of antibiotics on androgen-ization of the neonatal female rat. *Endocrinology, 86,* 285–289.

Kreuz, L., and Rose, R. (1972). Assessment of aggressive behavior and plasma testosterone in a young criminal population. *Psychosomatic Medicine, 34,* 321–332.

Kreuz, L., Rose, R., and Jennings, J. (1972). Suppression of plasma testosterone levels and psychological stress. *Archives of General Psychiatry, 26,* 479–482.

Larsson, K. (1966). Individual differences in reactivity to androgen in male rats. *Physiology and Behavior, 1,* 255–258.

Laschet, U. (1972). Antiandrogen in the treatment of sex offenders: Mode of action and therapeutic outcome. In J. Zubin and J. Money (eds), *Contemporary sexual behavior: Critical issues in the 1970s* (pp. 311–320). Baltimore: Johns Hopkins University Press.

LeMaire, E. (1956). Danish experiences regarding the castration of sexual offenders. *Journal of Criminal Law, Criminology, and Police Science, 47,* 294–310.

Leshner, A. I. (1978). *An introduction to behavioral endocrinology.* New York: Oxford.

Leshner, A. I., Walker, W. A., Johnson, A. E., Kelling, J. S., Kreisler, S. J., and Svare, B. (1973). Pituitary adrenocortical activity and intermale aggressiveness in isolated mice. *Physiology and Behavior, 11,* 705–711.

Levine, S. (1972). *Hormones and behavior.* New York: Academic.

Lieberburg, I., MacLusky, N. J., and McEwen, B. S. (1980). Androgen receptors in the perinatal rat brain. *Brain Research, 178,* 207–212.

Luttge, W. G. (1972). Activation and inhibition of isolation induced intermale fighting behavior in castrate male CD-1 mice treated with steroidal hormones. *Hormones and Behavior, 3,* 71–81.

Luttge, W. G., and Hall, N. R. (1973). Differential effectiveness of testosterone and its metabolites in the induction of male sexual behavior in two strains of albino mice. *Hormones and Behavior, 4,* 31–43.

Maccoby, E., and Jacklin, C. (1974). *The psychology of sex differences.* Stanford, Ca.: Stanford University Press.

Mallow, G. K. (1979). The relationship between aggression and cycle stage in adult female rhesus monkeys *(Macaca mulatta). Dissertation Abstracts International, 39,* 3194.

Mandell, A., and Mandell, M. (1967) Suicide and the menstrual cycle. *Journal of the American Medical Association, 200,* 792–793.

Mann, M. A., Konen, C., and Svare, B. (1984). The role of progesterone in pregnancy-induced aggression in mice. *Hormones and Behavior, 18,* 140–160.

Mann, M. A., and Svare, B. (1982). Factors influencing pregnancy-induced aggression in mice. *Behavioral and Neural Biology, 36,* 242–258.

Mann, M. A., and Svare, B. (1983). Prenatal testosterone exposure elevates maternal aggression in mice. *Physiology and Behavior, 30,* 503–507.

Masters, W. H., and Johnson, V. E. (1966). *Human sexual response.* Boston: Little, Brown.

Maxson, S. C., Shrenker, P., and Vigue, L. C. (1983). Genetics, hormones, and aggression. In B. Svare (ed.), *Hormones and aggressive behavior* (pp. 179–196). New York: Plenum.

Mazur, A., and Lamb, T. (1980). Testosterone, status, and mood in human males. *Hormones and Behavior, 14,* 236–246.

McCance, A. A., Luff, M. C., and Widdowson, E. C. (1952). Distribution of coitus during the menstrual cycle. *Journal of Hygiene, 37,* 571–611.

McDonald, P., Beyer, C., Newton, F., Brien, B., and Baker, R. (1970). Failure of 5-dihydrotestosterone to initiate sexual behavior in the castrated male rat. *Nature, 227,* 964–965.

McEwen, B. S., Lieberburg, I., Chaptal, C., and Krey, L. C. (1977). Aromatization: Important for sexual differentiation of the neonatal rat brain. *Hormones and Behavior, 9,* 249–263.

McGlone, J. (1980). Sex differences in human brain asymmetry: A critical survey. *Behavioral and Brain Sciences, 3,* 215–263.

McKinney, T. D., and Desjardins, C. (1973). Postnatal development of the testis, fighting behavior, and fertility in the house mouse. *Biology of Reproduction, 9,* 279–294.

Meyer-Bahlburg, H. F. L. (1977). Sex hormones and male homosexuality in comparative perspective. *Archives of Sexual Behavior, 6,* 297–325.

Meyer-Bahlburg, H. F. L., Boon, D., Sharma, M., and Edwards, J. (1973). Aggressiveness and testosterone measures in man. *Psychosomatic Medicine, 35,* 453.

Michael, R. P., and Zumpe, D. (1970). Aggression and gonadal hormones in captive rhesus monkeys *(Mucaca mulatta). Animal Behavior, 18,* 1–10.

Miczek, K., and Krsiak, M. (1981). Pharmacological analysis of attack and flight. In P. F. Brain and D. Benton (eds.), *A multidisciplinary approach to aggression research.* Amsterdam: Elsevier.

Mizejewski, B. J., Vonnegut, M., and Simon, R. (1980). Neonatal androgenization using antibodies to alpha-fetoprotein. *Brain Research, 188,* 273–277.

Money, J. (1975). Hormones, gender identity, and behavior. In B. E. Eleftheriou and R. L. Sprott (eds.), *Hormonal correlates of behavior* (pp. 325–340). New York: Plenum Press.

Money, J. (1976). Gender identity and hermaphroditism. *Science, 191,* 872.

Money, J. (1980). *Love and love sickness.* Baltimore: Johns Hopkins University Press.

Money, J., and Ehrhardt, A. A. (1968). Prenatal hormonal exposure: Possible effects on behavior in man. In R. P. Michael (ed.) *Endocrinology and human behavior* (pp. 32–48). London: Oxford University Press.

Money, J., and Ehrhardt, A. A. (1972). *Man and woman, boy and girl.* Baltimore: Johns Hopkins University Press.

Money, J., and Schwartz, M. (1976). Fetal androgens in the early treated adrenogenital syndrome of 46XX hermaphroditism: Influence on assertive and aggressive types of behavior. *Aggressive Behavior, 2,* 19–30.

Moos, R., and Lunde, D. T. (1969). Fluctuations in symptoms and moods during the menstrual cycle. *Journal of Psychosomatic Research, 13,* 37–44.

Morin, L. P., and Feder, H. H. (1974). Intracranial estradiol benzoate implants and lordosis behavior of overiectomized guinea pigs. *Brain Research, 70,* 95–102.

Morton, J., Additon, H., Addison, R., Hunt, C., and Sullivan, J. (1953). A clinical study of premenstrual tension. *American Journal of Obstetrics and Gynecology, 65,* 1182–1191.

Moss, R. L., and McCann, S. M. (1973). Induction of mating behavior in rats by LHRF. *Science, 181,* 177–179.

Nadler, R. D. (1968). Masculinization of female rats by intracranial implantation of androgen in infancy. *Journal of Comparative and Physiological Psychology, 66,* 157–167.

Netley, C. (1977). Dichotic listening of callosal agenesis and Turner's syndrome patients. In S. J. Segalowitz and F. A. Gruder (eds.), *Language development and neurological theory.* New York: Academic Press.

Noble, R. G., and Alsum, P. B. (1975). Hormone dependent sex dimorphisms in the golden hamster *(Mesocricetus auratus). Physiology and Behavior, 14,* 567–574.

Nock, B., and Feder, H. H. (1981). Neurotransmitter modulation of steroid action in target cells that mediate reproduction and reproductive behavior. *Neuroscienc and Biobehavioral Reviews, 5,* 437–447.

Nott, P., Franklin, M., Armitage, C., and Gelder, M. (1976). Hormonal changes and mood in the puerperium. *British Journal of Psychiatry, 128,* 379–383.

Owen, K., Peters, P. J., and Bronson, F. H. (1974). Effects of intracranial implants of testosterone propionate on intermale aggression in the castrated male mouse. *Hormones and Behavior, 5,* 83–92.

Palmer, R. K., Hauser, H., and Gandelman, R. (1984). Relationship between sexual activity and intraspecific fighting in male mice. *Aggressive Behavior, 10,* 317–324.

Payne, A. P., and Swanson, H. H. (1970). Agonistic behavior between pairs of hamsters of the same and opposite sex in a neutral observation area. *Behaviour, 36,* 259–267.

Payne, A. P., and Swanson, H. H. (1971). Hormonal control of aggressive dominance in the female hamster. *Physiology and Behavior, 6,* 366–357.

Persky, H., Charney, N., Lief, H. I., O'Brien, C. P., Miller, W. R., and Strauss, D. (1978). The relationship of plasma estradiol level to sexual behavior in young women. *Psychosomatic Medicine, 40,* 523–535.

Persky, H., Smith, K., and Basu, B. (1971). Relation of psychologic measures of aggression and hostility to testosterone production in man. *Psychosomatic Medicine, 33,* 265–277.

Peters, P. J., Bronson, F. H., and Whitsett, J. M. (1972). Noenatal castration and intermale aggression in mice. *Physiology and Behavior, 8,* 265–278.

Pfeiffer, C. A. (1936). Sexual differences in the hypophysis and their determination by the gonads. *American Journal of Anatomy, 58,* 195–226.

Phoenix, C. H. (1974). Effects of dihydrotestosterone propionate on sexual behavior of castrated male rhesus monkeys. *Physiology and Behavior, 12,* 1045–1055.

Phoenix, C. H., Goy, R. W., Gerall, A. A., and Young, W. C. (1959). Organizing action of prenatally administered testosterone propionate on the tissues mediating mating behavior in the female guinea pig. *Endocrinology, 65,* 369–382.

Plapinger, L., McEwen, B. S., Clemens, L. E. (1973). Ontogeny of estradiol-binding sites in rat brain. II. Characteristics of a neonatal binding macromolecule. *Endocrinology, 93,* 1129–1139.

Raisman, G., and Field, P. M. (1973). Sexual dimorphism in the neurophil of the preoptic area of the rat and its dependence on neonatal androgens. *Brain Research, 54,* 1–29.

Reinisch, J. M. (1977). Prenatal exposure of human foetuses to synthetic progestin and estrogen affects personality. *Nature, 266,* 561–562.

Reinisch, J. M. (1981). Prenatal exposure to synthetic progestins increases potential for aggression in humans. *Science, 211,* 1171–1173.

Roche, K. E., and Leshner, A. I. (1979). ACTH and vasopressin treatments immediately after a defeat increase future submissiveness in mice. *Science, 204,* 1343–1344.

Rose, R., Bernstein, I., and Gordon, T. (1975). Consequences of social conflict on plasma testosterone levels in rhesus monkeys. *Psychosomatic Medicine, 37,* 50–61.

Rose, R., Bourne, P., Poe, R., Mougey, E., Collins, D., and Mason, J. (1969). Androgen response to stress: II. Excretion of testosterone, epitestosterone, androsterone, and etiocholanolone during basic combat training and under threat of attack. *Psychosomatic Medicine, 31,* 418–436.

Rosenblatt, J. S., and Aronson, L. R. (1958). The decline in sexual behavior in male cats after castration with special reference to the role of prior sexual experience. *Behaviour, 12,* 285–338.

Rossi, A., and Rossi, P. (1980). Body time and social time: Mood patterns by menstrual cycle and day of week. In J. Parsons (ed.), *The psychobiology of sex differences and sex roles.* New York: McGraw-Hill.

Rowell, T. E. (1963). Behavior and female reproductive cycles of rhesus macaques. *Journal of Reproduction and Fertility, 6,* 193–203.

Rowell, T. E. (1967). Female reproductive cycles and the behavior of baboons and rhesus macaques. In S. A. Altmann (ed.), *Social communication among primates.* Chicago: University of Chicago Press.

Rubin, B. S., and Barfield, R. J. (1983). Progesterone in the ventromedial hypothalamus facilitates estrous behavior in ovariectomized estrogen-primed rats. *Endocrinology, 113,* 797–804.

Rubin, R. T., Reinisch, J. M., and Haskett, R. F. (1981). Postnatal gonadal steroid effects on human behavior. *Science, 211,* 1318–1324.

Schecter, D., and Gandelman, R. (1981). Intermale aggression in mice: Influence of gonadetomy and prior fighting experience. *Aggressive Behavior, 7,* 187–193.

Schecter, D., Howard, S. M., and Gandelman, R. (1981). Dihydrotestosterone promotes fighting behavior in female mice. *Hormones and Behavior, 15,* 233–237.

Schwartz, S. M., Blaustein, J. M., and Wade, G. N. (1979). Inhibition of estrous behavior by progesterone in rats: Role of neural estrogen and progestin receptors. *Endocrinology, 105,* 1078–1082.

Selmanoff, M. K., Goldman, B. D., and Ginsburg, B. E. (1977). Serum testosterone, agonistic behavior, and dominance in inbred strains of mice. *Hormones and Behavior, 8,* 107–119.

Shapiro, B. H., Levine, D. C., and Adler, N. T. (1980). The testicular feminized rat: A naturally occurring model of androgen independent brain masculinization. *Science, 209,* 418–420.

Sheridan, P. J., Sar, M., and Stumpf, W. E. (1974). Interaction of exogenous steroids in the developing rat brain. *Endocrinology, 95,* 1749–1753.

Short, R. V. (1974). Sexual differences of the brain of the sheep. In M. G. Forest and J. Bertrand (eds.), *Endocrinologie sexuele de la periode perinatale* (pp. 121–142). Paris: INSERM.

Simon, N. G. (1983). New strategies for aggression research. In E. C. Simmel, M. E. Hahn, and J. K. Walters (eds.), *Aggressive behavior: Genetic and neural approaches* (pp. 19–36). Hillsdale, NJ.: Lawrence Erlbaum.

Simon, N. G., and Gandelman, R. (1978). The estrogenic arousal of aggressive behavior in female mice. *Hormones and Behavior, 10,* 118–127.

Simon, N. G., Gandelman, R., and Howard, S. M. (1981). MER-25 does not inhibit the activation of aggression by testosterone in adult Rockland-Swiss mice. *Psychoneuroendocrinology, 6,* 131–137.

Simon, N. G., and Whalen, R. E. (In press). Hormonal regulation of aggression: Evidence for a relationship among genotype, receptor binding, and behavioral sensitivity to androgen and estrogen. *Aggressive Behavior.*

Singer, J. (1968). Hypothalamic control of male and female sexual behavior in female rats. *Journal of Comparative and Physiological Psychology, 66,* 738–742.

Slotnick, B. M., and Mullen, M. F. (1972). Intraspecific fighting in albino mice with septal forebrain lesions. *Physiology and Behavior, 8,* 333–338.

Stumpf, W. E., and Sar, M. (1979). Steroid hormone target cells in the extrahypothalamic brain stem and cervical spinal cord: neuroendocrine significance. *Journal of Steroid Biochemistry, 11,* 801–807.

Svare, B. (1977). Maternal aggression in mice: Influence of the young. *Biobehavioral Reviews, 1,* 151–164.

Svare, B. (1980). Testosterone propionate inhibits maternal aggression in mice. *Physiology and Behavior, 24,* 435–439.

Svare, B., ed. (1983). *Hormones and aggressive behavior.* New York: Plenum.

Svare, B., Davis, P. G., and Gandelman, R. (1974). Fighting behavior in female mice following chronic treatment during adulthood. *Physiology and Behavior, 12,* 399–403.

Svare, B., and Gandelman, R. (1975). Postpartum aggression in mice: Inhibitory effect of estrogen. *Physiology and Behavior, 14,* 31–36.

Svare, B., Mann, M. A., Broida, J., and Michael, S. D. (1982). Maternal aggression exhibited by hypophysectomized parturient mice. *Hormones and Behavior, 16,* 455–461.

Tiefer, L. (1970). Gonadal hormones and mating behavior in the adult golden hamster. *Hormones and Behavior, 1,* 189–202.

Toran-Allerand, C. D. (1980). Sex steroids and the development of the newborn mouse hypothalamus and preoptic area in vitro: II. Morphological correlates and hormonal specificity. *Brain Research, 189,* 413–427.

Turner, C. D., and Bagnara, J. T. (1976). *General endocrinology.* Philadelphia: Saunders.

Udry, J. R., and Morris, N. M. (1968). Distribution of coitus in the menstrual cycle. *Nature, 220,* 593–596.

Vermeulen, A., Rubens, R., and Verdonck, L. (1972). Testosterone secretion and metabolism in male senescence. *Journal of Clinical Endocrinology and Metabolism, 34,* 731–735.

Vito, C. C., and Fox, T. O. (1982). Androgen and estrogen receptors in embryonic and neonatal rat brain. *Developmental Brain Research, 2,* 97–110.

vom Saal, F. S. (1979). Prenatal exposure to androgen influences morphology and aggressive behavior of male and female mice. *Hormones and Behavior, 12,* 1–11.

vom Saal, F. S., and Bronson, F. H. (1978). In utero proximity of female mouse fetuses to males: Effect on reproductive performance in later life. *Biology of Reproduction, 19,* 842–853.

vom Saal, F. S., and Bronson, F. H. (1980). Sexual characteristics of adult female mice are correlated with their blood testosterone levels during prenatal development. *Science, 208,* 597–599.

vom Saal, F. S., Gandelman, R. and Svare, B. (1976). Aggression in male and female mice: Evidence for changed neural sensitivity in response to neonatal but not adult androgen exposure. *Physiology and Behavior, 17,* 53–57.

vom Saal, F. S., Grant, W. M., McMullen, C. W., and Laves, K. S. (1983). High fetal estrogen concentrations: Correlation with increased adult sexual activity and decreased aggression in male mice. *Science, 220,* 1306–1308.

Ward, I. L. (1972). Prenatal stress feminizes and demasculinizes the behavior of males. *Science, 175,* 82–84.

Ward, I. L., and Weisz, J. (1980). Maternal stress alters plasma testosterone in fetal males. *Science, 207,* 328–329.

Waxenberg, S. E., Drellick, M. G., and Sutherland, A. M. (1959). The role of hormones in human behavior: 1. Changes in female and sexuality after adrenalectomy. *Journal of Clinical Endocrinology and Metabolism, 19,* 193–202.

Weingartner, H. (1981). Effects of vasopressin on human memory functions. *Science, 211,* 601–603.

Weisz, J., and Ward, I. L. (1980). Plasma testosterone and progesterone titers of pregnant rats, their male and female fetuses, and neonatal offspring. *Endocrinology, 106,* 306–316.

Whalen, R. E., and Nadler, R. D. (1963). Suppression of the development of female mating behavior by estrogen administered in infancy. *Science, 141,* 273–274.

Wise, D. A. (1974). Aggression in the female golden hamster: Effects of reproductive state and social isolation. *Hormones and Behavior, 5,* 235–250.

Wise, D. A., and Pryor, T. L. (1977). Effects of ergocornine and prolactin on aggression in the postpartum golden hamster. *Hormones and Behavior, 8,* 30–39.

Witkin, H., Mednick, S., Schulsinger, G., Bakkestrom, E., Christiansen, K., Goodenough, D., Hirschhorn, K., Lundsteen, C., Owen, D., Philip, J., Rubin, D., and Stocking, M. (1976). Criminality in XYY and XXY men. *Science, 193,* 547–555.

Yalom, I. D., Lunde, D., Moos, R., and Hamburg, D. (1968). Postpartum "blues" syndrome: A description and related variables. *Archives of General Psychiatry, 18,* 16–27.

Yerkes, R. M. (1940). Social behavior of chimpanzees: Dominance between mates in relation to sexual status. *Journal of Comparative Psychology, 30,* 147–186.

Young, W. C. (1961). The hormones and mating behavior. In W. C. Young (ed.), *Sex and internal secretions* (pp. 1173–1239). Baltimore: Williams and Wilkins.

Zemlan, F. P., Ward, I. L., Crowley, W. R., and Margules, D. L. (1973). Activation of lordotic responding in female rats by suppression of serotonergic activity. *Science, 179,* 1010–1011.

Zucker, I. (1966). Facilitatory and inhibitory effects of progesterone on sexual responses of spayed guinea pigs. *Journal of Comparative and Physiological Psychology, 62,* 376–381.

Zumpe, D., and Michael, R. P. (1970). Redirected aggression and gonadal hormones in captive rhesus monkeys *(Macaca mulatta). Animal Behavior, 18,* 11–19.

CHAPTER 3

A Biosocial Theory of
Heterosexual Relationships*

DOUGLAS T. KENRICK AND MELANIE R. TROST

INTRODUCTION

In McDougall's classic text on social psychology, he discussed the "instinct of reproduction":

> It is unnecessary to say anything of the great emotional excitement that accompanies its exercise. One point of interest is its intimate connection with the parental instinct. . . . The biological utility of an innate connection of this kind is obvious. It would prepare the way for that cooperation between the male and female in which, even among the animals, a lifelong fidelity and mutual tenderness is often touchingly displayed. (1913:82)

When interest in the study of human sexual attraction and mating reemerged in social psychology during the second half of this century, researchers did not seek the causes of courtship progress in the evolution-based drives that McDougall was interested in. Cognitive theorists like Newcomb (1968) sought the causes of marital attraction in the same cerebral processes that presumably lead to any form of interpersonal preference. The important motivation for this approach was the search for aesthetic congruence between our beliefs and those of our partners. Reinforcement theorists like Byrne (1971) and Lott and Lott (1974) considered the role of affect as well as that of

* We wish to express our thanks to David Buss, Uriel Foa, Sara Gutierres, George Levinger, and D. W. Rajecki for their very helpful criticisms of an earlier draft of this chapter. We should note that not all of these colleagues agree with the view we have expressed here (which of course made their comments all the more useful).

cognition, but also regarded the process of attraction towards a potential mate as resulting from the same processes that lead to attraction towards a friend (or even towards a good restaurant). That is, the potential spouse was seen as an initially neutral stimulus that could take on rewarding value by association with primary reinforcers like food or sexual arousal. More recent "interactionist" theories of mate selection (e.g., Duck 1978; Levinger and Snoek 1972; Murstein 1933) have argued that mate choice is characterized by sequential changes in reinforcement patterns or in cognitions about the partner, but have continued to seek the causes of attraction and courtship progress mainly in cerebral processes (regarding perceived similarity, equity, and compatibility, for instance) (Morton and Douglas 1981).

Though McDougall's approach has not generally been followed by his social psychological descendents, the Darwinian significance of human mating has recently reemerged as a topic of interest among behavioral biologists. Encouraged by theoretical advances in explaining the interplay between social behaviors, ecological conditions, and organismic physiological states (Eibl-Eibesfeldt 1975; Lumsden and Wilson 1981; Wilson 1975), biological theorists have advanced a number of hypotheses about human courtship and sexual attraction (Barash 1977; Chagnon and Irons 1979; Daly and Wilson 1979; Mellen 1981; Symonds 1979).

These biologically based views, with occasional exceptions (e.g., Daly and Wilson 1979), have generally ignored the social psychological literature on "attraction" processes. For instance, most recent biological approaches to human attraction have not considered the sequential processes of human courtship with which social psychological "interactionist" theorists have been concerned. On the other hand, social psychologists interested in human courtship processes have not, for the most part, seriously considered the potentially analogous biological literature. Most of the offerings in Duck and Gilmour's (1981–1983) four volume series on human relationships, for instance, look to cognitively based, normative expectancies for their explanatory constructs of human courtship and divorce. There is, however, some recent budding awareness of the potential reciprocal relevance of the two literatures (e.g., Cunningham 1981; Kelley 1983), although we are not aware of any systematic attempts to integrate the two areas. The purpose of the present chapter is to outline a possible model of the development of human sexual relationships, based on the general assumptive framework of social biology but incorporating some of the insights of the social psychologically based, "interactionist" theories.

Although we will review evidence we believe is relevant, much of the framework we will advance is based upon tentative speculation.

We do not wish to claim that this model is "proved" by the current evidence. We do believe, however, that there is great promise in this direction. We feel a biosocial approach is potentially important because our current social psychological models may be "blind" to the causes of at least some of the variance in human relationships. At the very least, the framework has a good deal of heuristic potential, and disproofs can be as fascinating as proofs in this area. Note that in the study of altruism, some exciting developments have followed the puzzle posed by behaviors that are prima facie opposed to evolutionary principles (Campbell 1975, 1983).

There are some more general reservations about the application of evolutionary models to human behavior, and it may be useful to address several of them at the outset (borrowing partly from Blurton-Jones 1983):

1. One argument is that most complex adult human behavior is learned and not genetically "programmed." Current research in the learning area, however, indicates that learning does not occur outside the domain of biology, but that it is genetically *constrained* (e.g., Lumsden and Wilson 1981; Rozin and Kalat 1971; Seligman and Hager 1972; Shettleworth 1972). Not all associations are equally learnable—nausea conditions to novel tastes, for instance, but not to visual stimuli—and these findings apply to humans as well as to other species (Garb and Stunkard 1974). In a similar manner, recent reviews suggest there are biological constraints on human cognitive development (Keil 1981). This literature suggests that children learn certain constructs more readily than others. The extent of such constraints is not known, but we are fairly certain the slate is not totally blank at birth.

2. Another objection to evolutionary models is that people do not explain their behavior as being due to a desire to leave viable descendents. People's reasons for entering and maintaining heterosexual relationships, in particular, are multitudinous and, we suspect, only occasionally related to procreation. Our proximal "reasons" for our behavior, however, may be quite beside the point of their ultimate significance (Alcock 1979), and there is even some question about our accuracy in reporting the proximal reasons for our behaviour (Nisbett and Wilson 1977). As Blurton-Jones (1983) points out, other animals generally engage in genetically adaptive behaviors, and there is no need to assume they ever give any "thought" whatsoever to their descendents.

3. A related, but more crucial, problem comes from the obvious fact that modern day humans engage in a substantial amount of "recreational" (or nonprocreative) sex, and that, in fact, many of us

use birth control techniques to specifically avoid having offspring. For virtually all of the history of our species, however, recreational sex had the functional outcome of procreation, whatever the cognitive intentions of the participants. The fact that birth control technology has short-circuited a naturally functional program does not mean the program has gone away. Note that moderns still continue to copulate with vigorous frequency (Hunt 1974), just as we continue to consume sweet substances that have little nutritive value. Modern consumers of saccharine and aspartame (nutrasweet), like modern sexual rec-reators, are faithfully enacting proclivities that were highly adaptive for our pre-technological ancestors. It should also be pointed out that even primitive hunter-gatherers did not simply have as many offspring as their bodies could bear, but engaged in various techniques to optimize the number of *successful* offspring (Blurton-Jones 1983). The population-limiting tchniques of our ancesters ranged from sexual abstinence after childbirth to infanticide. Population limitation occurs in other animals as well, although it is important to note that the current evidence suggests that such behavior has tended, on the average, to maximize long-term success (see Alcock 1979, for a fuller discussion of these issues). Our present proclivities may well be adapted to an outmoded ecological niche, but their possible mala-daptiveness does not make those predispositions any less interesting. In fact, it may make understanding them all the more relevant.

4. Another objection to evolutionary based models is that they are not disprovable. As with all scientific theories (Laudan 1977), the central core of assumptions of Darwinian theory would be difficult to "disprove"; however, specific derivations from evolutionary models are eminently disprovable, and this is all one can ask of any general paradigm (Laudan 1977). Disproving one cognitive hypothesis does not lead the cognitive theorist to stop believing that people think. We feel there have been enough encouraging findings to assume that it is not absurd to attempt to derive hypotheses from a biosocial perspective (Lumsden and Wilson 1981). The ultimate fruitfulness of such an endeavor remains to be seen.

It is also important to note here that our approach is not intended to deny the importance of learning or cognition. For us, the fascinating questions are about how learning and cognition interact with bio-logical proclivities (see Kenrick, Montello and MacFarlane, 1985). Humans are not rigidly programmed by genes (or on a more proximate level, by hormones produced according to genetic instructions), but we are innately more sensitive to certain stimuli, innately predisposed to express certain responses more readily, and innately predisposed to certain arousal states under certain conditions (Lumsden and

Wilson 1981). We do presume that our absorption of culture is neither totally random nor totally rational.

5. One final objection to evolutionary based approaches is that humans are unique as a species. This is no doubt true, as it is true that every individual, every relationship, and every family are unique among humans. But just as most psychologists believe that nomothetic generalizations can be made about groups of people, social biologists believe generalizations can be made about groups of animals. Primates, social carnivores, and pair-bonded birds all share common ecological pressures and/or morphological features with humans, and certain generalizations separate those groupings from other groupings of species. We are already accustomed to assuming that some cross-species generalizations can be made—that is, from conditioning experiments done with dogs, rats, and pigeons as well as with humans—and social biologists have generally focused more upon the *differences* between species than we psychologists have. Much of the literature in this area has been concerned with the particular ecological characteristics of human evolution, for instance (e.g., Mellen 1981). So our approach will in no way deny the uniqueness of the human species, although it does presume that comparison with other species can sometimes yield a helpful perspective.

In the remainder of the introduction, we will briefly review (1) some general assumptions regarding mating strategies (across different species and within the human species in particular); (2) some general assumptions in social psychological interactionist models; and (3) some "interactionist" courtship models from ethology. We intend to give here only the "bottom line" of these three areas and not to present either the evidence or the fine details of any of these approaches. We refer the interested reader to Daly and Wilson (1979), Duck and Gilmour (1981–1983), and Lehrman (1966) for more detailed treatments of the respective areas. We follow this general review with a discussion of our own proposed model.

General Sociobiological Assumptions

There are three generalizations from ethology-based studies of courtship strategies that are important to note at the outset:

Variable Strategies.   Referring to mating strategies across different species, sociobiologists have accumulated much evidence suggesting that different categories of species-typical mating strategies are related to certain ecological factors, such as density and resource scarcity (see Barash 1977; Daly and Wilson 1979). Reproductive strategies can be considered along a dimension characterized at one end by high investment in a small number of offspring (referred to as the K-selected strategy) and, at the other end, by high fecundity with little investment in any particular offspring (r strategy). The K strategy is associated with resource scarcity and high density and is characterized by monogamy and territoriality. Conversely, the r strategy is associated with more abundant resources (which are not spatially fixed), low density, and promiscuity. In r-selected species, females are more likely to mate with highly selected, dominant males who are larger and more ostentatious than the females. This selectivity occurs because males in such species contribute only their genes to the offspring. Females in r-selected species can therefore be highly selective, and, consequently, there are large differences between males in their reproductive success. In K-selected species, the male contributes more, there is less sexual differentiation, and there is likely to be a lengthy period of courtship that allows both the male and female to estimate the fitness and reliability of a potential mate. It is generally assumed that r and K strategies have differential thresholds within species, and that individuals can sometimes shift to the alternative strategy when ecological conditions favor it. Nevertheless, there are presumed to be differential genetic tendencies favoring r and K strategies between species as well as within species.

Human Pair Bonds. Social biologists presume that humans vary their reproductive strategies, but that they are strongly disposed towards pair-bonding (unlike most mammals, who are extremely promiscuous). Our bias toward pair-bonding has supposedly been selected because of the long period of dependency of human offspring and the advantages of the human male directly contributing resources to those offspring (Mellen 1981). Daly and Wilson (1979) have reviewed cross-cultural research suggesting that every human cultural group has some form of marriage. We are, therefore, generally considered a K strategy species.

Human "pair bonds" are not always monogamous. Where bonding is not monogamous, there is a strong tendency for polygyny to be more prevalent than polyandry. Surveying marital customs in 849 human societies studied by anthropologists, polygyny is found to be usual or occasional in 708, while polyandry is permitted in only 4; the remaining 137 are strictly monogamous (Murdock 1967).

Sex Differences and Parental Investment. Generalizing across species, ethologists have gathered evidence suggesting that there are sex differences in the optimal mating strategy (Trivers 1972). Particularly for mammals, females have a lower ceiling on the number of potential offspring they can have than males do. Males therefore compete amongst themselves for reproductive opportunities and are presumed less selective than females about taking advantage of any particular mating opportunity (having less to lose). Females presumably select a male either because of evidence that he has genes that will contribute to successful survival, or (in bonding species) because of evidence that the male is willing to invest time and energy towards the care of any offspring resultant from mating. Males in species that adopt bonding strategies have much to lose from being cuckolded—that is, they thereby invest their own energies in offspring not their own—therefore males are presumed to be selected for jealously guarding against such a possibility. Females may lose the energy that an unfaithful partner invests in another mating opportunity, but they are never in doubt as to which offspring are theirs. Lengthy courtship occurs in bonding species, and is presumed to allow for careful assessment of the characteristics of the partner as well as ensuring against the existence of other mates.

With specific regard to the human species, then, social biological theorists presume that females will be relatively selective in their choice of a mate and will look for evidence of a willingness to contribute time and resources to potential offspring. Human males, like males in other species generally, are seen to be more willing to take advantage of a promiscuous mating opportunity, but to be selective in their choice of pair-bonded mates. Within pairbonds, males are thought by sociobiologists to be more jealous than females because of the differential uncertainty of paternity (as opposed to maternity, which is unambiguous). Again, we will not here attempt to review the evidence for these assumptive generalizations, instead the reader is referred to Daly and Wilson (1979) and Barash (1977), who have conducted such reviews.

General Assumptions in Social Psychological Interactionist Models

Interactionist models of attraction arose in reaction to questions about the possible artificiality of earlier, laboratory-based research on interpersonal attraction. Although generally in agreement with the importance of factors such as attitudinal similarity and physical attractiveness, interactionist theorists argued that laboratory studies had not fully addressed some important issues, such as the following.

Temporal Changes in Relationships. Murstein (1971), for instance, argued that rewards important early in a relationship (such as physical attractiveness) are less crucial at later phases. Following the reasoning of Winch (1958), Murstein presumed a series of "filters" within relationships that serve to screen potential partners in successively more selective ways. Many potential partners satisfy one another's "stimulus" requirements for initial dates (e.g., looks and clothing). Upon closer examination, however, potential partners might find that their "values," regarding religion, politics, and so on, do not coincide sufficiently. Finally, according to Murstein (1971), many partners who satisfy the requirements of the "stimulus" and "value" screenings do not pass the "role" requirements, that is, the couple is not compatible in mutual interaction (both may desire to dominate decision making in the relationship, for example).

Levinger and Snoek (1972) developed another well-known interactionist model that viewed couples as progressing from zero contact, to unilateral awareness through surface contact, and on to greater and greater levels of mutually shared interaction. In recent years, interactionist theorists have become increasingly interested in later "stages," and they consider the maintenance of established relationships as well as their termination (e.g., Levinger 1983; Kelley et al. 1983; Duck and Gilmour 1981–1983). There has also been some question about whether the "stages" are rigidly sequenced, and researchers in this area now tend to view these "stages" as more flexible and overlapping "phases" (Levinger 1983).

Reciprocal Exhange of Rewards within a Relationship. Interactionist theorists point out that when we are looking for an ideally rewarding mate, we consider not only his/her objective characteristics but also our own. Most interactionist theorists hold to some variation of equity theory (Walster, Walster, and Berscheid 1978) and believe that partners consider their own assets and liabilities against a potential partner's before entering a relationship. It is also presumed that partners reevaluate each other's inputs before proceeding to more committed phases in the courtship sequence (Murstein 1971).

Progressive Access to More Intimate Information Several interactionist theorists have viewed the progressive escalation of the exchange of intimate information as central to relationship progress (Altman 1974; Duck 1978; Morton and Douglas 1981). For instance, Altman (1974) conceived of relationship formation as a process of "social penetration," in which partners self-disclose more and more intimate information as time goes on. Altman suggests an interesting metaphor to help visualize his viewpoint. He envisions relationship formation as a peeling back of the layers of an onion, revealing ever more deeply enclosed and protected areas. In a sense, this progressive change in the intimacy of information exchanged represents a combination of the two points above, and the focus on "information" illustrates the cognitive emphasis of most interactionist models (Morton and Douglas 1981).

Interactionist Courtship Models in Ethology

Although recent sociobiological approaches to human sexual attraction (e.g., Daly and Wilson 1979; Mellen 1981; Symonds 1979) have not been centrally concerned with sequential changes in relationships, there are several classical studies of animal courtship that are, in this respect, similar to the human interactionist models we have just discussed. Several animal researchers have considered "response chaining" between mates (Lehrman 1966; Morris 1958). For instance, Tinbergen (1951) observed that mating in stickleback fish involved a relatively fixed sequence, in which behaviors of one sex elicited reciprocal behaviors from the opposite sex that, in turn, led to a new set of behaviors, and so on in an escalatory fashion until spawning and fertilization. Morris (1958) found that the probability of any mating behavior in the stickleback was strongly tied to the stage the partners had reached in mutual interaction. "Zig zag dancing" by the male occurred only upon confronting a novel female and was terminated by the female's courting movements to be replaced by "leading" movements, and so on.

Lehrman and his colleagues have shown that such courtship interactions are accompanied by physiological changes that, in turn, alter behavioral probabilities. These researchers have intensively studied the mating behaviors of the ring dove *(Streptopelia risoria)* and have found a systematic, reciprocal interplay, linked in a more or less lock-step fashion, between the behaviors and physiological states of one member of a mating pair and the behaviors and physiological states of the partner. For instance, the initial courtship behaviors of the male (strutting, bowing, and cooing) elicit estrogen secretion in the female, which is associated with increased nest-building behaviors. After several days of nest-building have passed, other hormonal changes have occurred in the pair that increase the likelihood of egg-sitting behaviors. Later, the cries of the young enhance production of prolactin and thereby increase production of the "crop-milk" that the young are fed.

In sum, ethologists and comparative psychologists have observed that animal mating behaviors are (1) sequential or stagelike; (2) reciprocally interactive; and (3) accompanied by and facilitated by certain physiological changes.

Overview of a Biosocial Model

As we just mentioned, the sequential models from the ethological literature deal with some issues similar to those being addressed by social psychological interactionists. Both groups focus on sequencing and reciprocal interaction in courtship, for instance. The biological models, however, are different from the psychological models in several crucial ways, and these differences will be emphasized in our discussion of courtship progress. Three assumptions from the biological models form the foundation of our approach.

1. Reproduction is the central organizing theme of courtship. This emphasis contrasts with the social psychologist's focus on more proximal cognitive and/or normative motivations. In the model we will advance, cognitive satisfactions are not seen as ends in themselves. To a large extent, we will view cognition as serving the larger goal of enhancing reproductive success and as somewhat constrained by biology. There are two corollaries of this assumption. It is presumed that information about a potential partner will be particularly salient to the extent that it relates to (1) the partner's possession of adaptive characteristics (that may be inherited by the offspring); and (2) the partner's potential direct contribution to the offspring (i.e., in terms of resources he or she will provide).

2. Courtship progress interacts with physiologically based states of readiness. These physiological states are, in turn, keyed to environmental events, particularly to the traits and behaviors of the partner and to the ecological conditions related to the success of the different reproductive strategies (such as population density and resource scarcity).

3. There are differential strategies for the two sexes (the "parental investment" argument [Trivers 1972] discussed above). In particular, females are more selective than males, that is they have a higher threshold at which they will take advantage of an opportunity to mate, and, once pair-bonding has occurred, males are presumably more jealous than females.

Purely biological models, however, ignore the very important effects of the social environment. In keeping with the learning models, we believe that individual differences in socialization experiences will influence preferences and courtship behaviors. In keeping with the cognitive models, we believe that ongoing interpretation of social events can influence our satisfactions and our choice of behavioral strategies. But learning and cognition do not occur in a vacuum. We presume, instead, that learning and cognitive expectancies operate within biological constraints. Although humans are capable of a multiplicity of *topographical* variations on the human mating theme (Levinger 1983), we believe there are certain underlying regularities that more or less fit the sociobiological generalizations we reviewed above.

RELATIONSHIP FORMATION

In this paper, relationship formation will be conceptualized as involving five more or less sequential tasks, each of which can be roughly defined in terms of a certain goal or end state. These tasks are (1) *stimulus search*—engaging in a general search for persons possessing reproductively desirable stimulus characteristics: (2) *establishing contact;* (3) *trait assessment*—searching for cues about fitness that are not immediately obvious; (4) *establishing physical intimacy*—copulation; and (5) *bond maintenance/termination.*

Tasks 1, 2, and 4 must obviously occur in this sequence for any species, that is copulation must be preceded by contact, which must be preceded by some choice regarding which organism to interact with. In species with any degree of courtship, assessment of the partner's nonobvious traits seems most likely to occur after establishing contact and before copulation. In humans, the process of assessment can begin before contact is made (via reputation and/or observation), and this assessment likely continues after first intercourse. It nevertheless makes some sense to presume that the most significant increments in information about traits are obtained after contact is made but before copulation occurs. The process of bond maintenance is discussed after copulation because, from the biological perspective on pair-bonding, the latter issue is presumed to be more crucial after mating has occurred. Relationship termination is probably also more problematic for established couples. Like trait assessment, however, the bond maintenance process no doubt overlaps a bit with other tasks, and it seems reasonable to presume that bond formation is initiated in some degree very soon after initiating contact. From our theoretical perspective, though, the process is not nearly as crucial or as powerfully motivated until courtship has progressed to (or nearly to) the point where potential offspring are involved.

In the discussion that follows, we will not attempt to review all the vast social psychological literature on sexual attraction and relationship formation. For each phase of the courtship process, however, we will first select what we consider to be the most relevant general findings from the literature, following with a discussion of theory and research that relates to a biosocial perspective (including other sociological or psychological findings that seem relevant). Three questions were most salient in developing our discussion of these issues:

1. On the most proximate level, are there any physiological mechanisms that relate to the phase in question?

2. On a more distal or "ultimate" level of analysis, how might the social psychological findings be relevant to adaptive reproduction strategies?

3. Are there sex differences in human mating strategies that fit the notion of differential parental investment?

STIMULUS SEARCH

Social Psychological Findings

Social psychologists have directed a good deal of research to the question of which factors influence attraction before interaction begins. Several generalizations can be made.

1. People are in reasonable agreement about who is morphologically attractive (Berscheid and Walster 1974), and such "physical attractiveness" apparently carries a great deal of weight when choosing dating partners (Berscheid and Walster 1974; Kenrick and Gutierres 1980; Walster, Aronson, Abrahams, and Rottman 1966). Although the question of what subjects are agreeing about when they call someone "physically attractive" has not been definitively answered, evidence suggests that symmetrical features are attractive, while facial asymmetry, irregular scarring, or evidence of disease are unattractive (Berscheid and Walster 1974; Symonds 1979). Cross-cultural research suggests that a clear, healthy complexion is universally attractive (Ford and Beach 1951). Illsley (1955) found that taller and healthier women were more likely to marry upward. With regard to physique, Lavrakas (1975) found that a V-shaped physique in males (broad, well-developed chest and shoulders with a narrow waist) is considered attractive.

2. Familiar faces are rated as more attractive than unfamiliar ones (Moreland and Zajonc 1982). It has been suggested that this attraction may partially explain the tendency for mates to be chosen from among those living in very close proximity (Bossard 1932; Katz and Hill 1958).

3. Similarity with regard to any number of overt characteristics is attractive. We are here discussing similarity on overt variables such as race (Kerchoff 1974) and height (Pearson and Lee 1903). Obviously, much of the information regarding "similarity" is not overtly available, but emerges only with a more probing assessment. This issue will therefore be returned to later. However, information about religion, ethnicity, or ideology can be revealed in behavior or adornments (such as crucifixes or stars worn around the neck).

The Biosocial Perspective

From a biological perspective, concern with physical attractiveness, familiarity, and similarity are quite relevant to successful mating. Judgments of physical attractiveness involve, at least in part, a search for any signs of ill health or genetic abnormality. Facial asymmetry is associated with minor genetic defects, and poor complexion and facial scar tissue may be associated with previous diseases (Symonds 1979). Lott (1979) has speculated that, since humans have been selected for their upright stature and bipedal gait, morphological features of the walking apparatus such as buttocks and legs should be importantly related to attractiveness, and such features have been found to be important for both females (Wiggins, Wiggins, and Conger 1977) and males (Beck, Ward-Hull, and McLear 1976).

Regarding similarity of mate choice, geneticists have noted a general tendency toward assortive mating among animals. Phenotypical characteristics within a pair are generally more similar than would be expected at random (McClearn and DeFries 1973; Wallace 1979). Geneticists regard the optimal genetic strategy to be mating with an organism whose genetic makeup is neither highly different from one's own (which might result in the loss of characteristics adapted to a particular habitat and/or infertility of the offspring) nor so identical as to increase the probability of pairing harmful recessive genes (Wilson 1978). Throughout most of the history of the species, humans apparently lived in groups of twenty-five to fifty closely related individuals (Lee and DeVore 1968; Tiger and Fox 1971). These groups were connected to larger, neighboring dialectic tribes composed of ten to twenty such groups who were related to one another (Wilson 1978) and who spoke and dressed similarly and had similar customs. Mates were generally chosen either from one's own group or from the slightly larger dialectic tribe. Thus, the tendency to be attracted to familiar and similar-appearing others who live nearby would have accomplished the task of assortive mating for our ancestors.

We mentioned above that there is a disadvantage in mating with individuals that are too closely related. Sibling matings result in an increase in genetic defects (Wilson 1978). Van den Berghe (1983) reviews evidence suggesting that humans are innately predisposed to avoid strong sexual attraction toward siblings. Shepher (1971) has noted that Israeli children raised like siblings in small, mixed sex groups do not show sexual attraction towards one another as adults. Of nearly three thousand marriages involving individuals raised in such groups, none occurred between two persons raised together from birth, despite the existence of no normative pressure to the contrary and the general tendency toward a preference for neighbors.

One might argue here that the recent exposés of incest among Americans disprove the existence of an innate bias against incest (see van den Berghe 1983). Note, however, that (1) much of the reported "incest" does not qualify by biological criteria—that is, it involves nonbiological step-relatives, occurs before puberty, and/or does not involve intercourse; (2) participants seem to become less rather than more attracted to one another; and (3) a biological predisposition does not imply 100 percent certainty of the expression of that behavior under all environmental conditions, only a lower than otherwise expected frequency (see van den Berghe [1983] for a more extensive discussion of these issues).

The argument that males and females differ in parental investment would lead us to expect certain sex differences in judgments about sexual attractiveness. One such difference relates to the relatively greater importance of dominance as a characteristic of males. Given that females are limited in the number of offspring they can produce, it is presumed that males will compete with each other for opportunities to reproduce. By choosing males that have successfully competed with other males, a female gains a potential genetic advantage for her offspring, as well as access to any resources controlled by the male. Among animals in general and primates in particular (e.g., DeVore 1965; Saayman 1971), there is a tendency for females to mate preferentially with dominant males. Females have an a priori higher parental investment among mammals—they carry and nurse the young, for instance. Since females are making an initially higher direct contribution to the offspring, they are presumed to be in a position to "demand" more evidence of adaptive characteristics from the male than vice-versa. The male is presumed to demonstrate his adaptiveness by successful competition with other males.

With regard to human mating choice, there is evidence that females are, in fact, more influenced than males by signs of high social status (Daly and Wilson 1979). Sadalla, Kenrick, and Vershure (1981) found evidence that nonverbal expressions of social dominance significantly enhanced the sexual attractiveness of a male stimulus person, but had no effect on the ratings of a female. The attractiveness of the V-shaped physique (Lavrakas 1975) may be related to its association with the socially dominant, mesomorphic body build.

In nonhuman species, there are unlearned social stimuli that can elicit attraction. For instance, specific olfactory stimuli have been found to exert an influence on sexual arousal in several different species (Michael and Keverne 1968; Parkes and Bruce 1961; Vandenberg 1969). With regard to humans, a number of biological writers have speculated on the existence of specific visual and olfactory stimuli that "automatically" trigger sexual arousal. These stimuli include female breasts (Eibl-Eibesfeldt 1975; Morris 1972), broad shoulders in males (Eibl-Eibesfeldt 1975; Wallace 1979), and sexual pheromones (see Rogel 1978, for a review on the pheromone research).

Using the research of Lehrman and his colleagues as a model, we would speculate that perceptions regarding the attractiveness of the opposite sex, as well as the inclination to pay attention to sexual features of potential mates, can be influenced by hormonal states. Consistent with this speculation, there is evidence that sexual arousal (produced by reading an erotic passage) enhances the perceived attractiveness of a potential date (Stephan, Berscheid, and Walster 1971).

Summary

The biosocial perspective sees the differential attraction toward healthy, symmetrical, familiar, and similar others (excepting our siblings) as having served to promote optimal assortive mating. Females' differential preference for dominance and muscularity in males is consistent with findings from other species, and is also consistent with the argument that females' greater parental investment in offspring will result in their greater selectiveness from intrasexually competing males. At the proximate level, some writers have speculated on the existence of specifically predisposed "trigger" stimuli for human sexual attraction, and, finally, sexual arousal seems to enhance the perceived attractiveness of a potential date's stimulus characteristics.

ESTABLISHING CONTACT

Although many pairs may meet each other's stimulus requirements, they may, nevertheless, "pass in the night." What determines which pairs will make contact, and how does this contact proceed?

Social Psychological Findings

Social psychologists have devoted a good deal of research to how potential partners are perceived, but less to the conditions associated with moving from a perception of attractiveness to actual contact (Huston and Levinger 1978). Some research has suggested a relationship between the actor's self-evaluations and his/her likelihood of approaching a potential date. Kiesler and Baral (1970) found that males whose self-esteem had been raised were more likely to make romantic advances toward an attractive female. Conversely, males whose self-esteem had been lowered expressed less interest in an attractive female, but made relatively more approach responses toward an unattractive female. In a related vein, Walster (1965) looked at the effect of self-esteem on responses to romantic overtures and found that female subjects whose self-esteem had been raised were relatively less attracted to a good-looking male who asked them for a date. Finally, individuals who are independently judged as physically attractive have been found to have a more stringent set of criteria for an acceptable date (Walster, Aronson, Abrahams, and Rottmann 1966).

Social psychological studies have found evidence of sex differences in initiating interactions. Males have been found to push conversations with strange females toward higher levels of intimacy (Davis 1978). Males' cognitions also appear to bias them toward escalating an encounter with a woman. Abbey (1982) found that when females act friendly in a first encounter, males are prone to interpret this behavior as flirtatious and seductive.

Some attention has been directed towards the nonverbal behaviors associated with initial interactions. Subjects who have been instructed to elicit attraction in another sit closer to that person, lean towards them, and make more direct eye contact (Mehrabian 1969). Subjects who have been led to believe another is similar to them, or who have been introduced to a physically attractive person, likewise sit closer to that person and make more direct eye contact (Byrne, Ervin, and Lamberth 1970). Patterson (1976) reviews evidence suggesting that intimate, nonverbal signals such as eye contact and proximity seem to increase arousal and facilitate the dominant response occurring in an interpersonal encounter. Such cues thus serve to enhance aggressiveness in an interaction as well as pleasantness, depending on the context. In a situation involving two mutually attracted persons of the opposite sex, such nonverbal intimacies will facilitate attraction. Consistent with the findings just discussed (Davis 1978), males in mixed sex dyads have been found to initiate touching more frequently (Henly 1977).

The physical and social setting has also been found to have implications for establishing contact. Rosenblatt and Cozby (1972) note that in societies that allow freedom in mate selection, dances are frequently used as a meeting place. Additionally, Roebuck and Spray (1967) described a middle-class lounge that younger women frequented in order to meet wealthier men. Although the women knowingly placed themselves in the situation, it was left to the men to make the advances toward them. It has already been mentioned that residential proximity is related to attraction, and that this relationship is probably due, in part, to the convenience and low-response cost of making contact with neighbors (Myers 1983).

The Biosocial Perspective

As we just mentioned, Roebuck and Spray (1967) found that, in the cocktail lounge they studied, contact initiation was made by the male. This finding is relevant to the sociobiological assumption of differential strategies for male and female courtship. Again, the parental investment argument is that males are selected for active "salesmanship" in courtship, and females (with more to lose from an ill-chosen mating) are presumed to be selected for "sales resistance" (Barash 1977). The fact that active initiation of courtship is made by the male, not just in middle-class cocktail lounges but generally across cultures, is in line with this argument (Daly and Wilson 1979; Ford and Beach 1951). Findings that males escalate intimacy in coversation and nonverbal contact (discussed above) also support the parental investment prediction.

Studies of animal courtship have revealed fixed behavioral displays that are made in response to attractive members of the opposite sex (Barash 1977). Eibl-Eibesfeldt (1975) has discovered that females in divergent cultures respond to a flirtatious greeting with a common sequence of motor actions. This response involves a short-duration smile and "eyebrow flash" (wide opening of the eyes accompanied by raising the eyebrows), followed by dropping and turning the head, and then by a sidelong glance. This finding emerged from careful analysis of subtle movements captured on slow motion film. G. D. Jensen (1973) has noted that male dominance displays in chimpanzees (including piloerection and "swaggering") are incorporated in courtship displays, and he suggests that humans engage in analogous displays. This suggestion is in line with Rubin's (1973) finding of increased eye contact between lovers, and it has been pointed out that such behavior also occurs in agonistic exchanges (Patterson 1976).

At the outset of this section, we mentioned the relationship between self-evaluation and approaches to (or receptivity to) the opposite sex. It is a general primate characteristic to be attentive to one's relative hierarchical position in comparison with the rest of one's social group (Lancaster 1975). There is evidence that sexual hormone levels interact with hierarchical position in other primates. A series of studies done by Rose and his colleagues suggest that increases in testosterone level accompany elevations in a monkey's position in a dominance hierarchy (Rose, Holaday, and Bernstein 1971). Mazur and Lamb (1980) have predicted a similar relationship for humans. Consistent with that prediction they found that graduation from medical school was accompanied by increases in testosterone level. Likewise, a clear victory in a tennis match was followed by increased testosterone levels (Mazur and Lamb 1980).

Summary

In this section, we have argued that males' tendency to initiate and nonverbally escalate first contacts fit with the parental investment argument. The relationship between self-perceived status and approaches to the opposite sex aligns with findings from primate studies. On a proximate level, there is some evidence of nonverbal flirtation gestures that may be innate, and alterations in testosterone level are related to changes in human dominance. As we will discuss in more detail below, testosterone level is strongly related to experienced sexual desire. The findings that females prefer to mate with dominant males, therefore, lends some sense to the fact that increased dominance leads to increased testosterone production.

TRAIT ASSESSMENT

Social Psychological Findings

The process of information exchange within developing relationships has occupied a central place in social psychological models. The social penetration model developed by Altman sees the self-disclosure of progressively more intimate and hidden information as the key to relationship progress (Altman 1974; Morton and Douglas 1981). Several researchers have, in fact, found that the more attractive or desirable another is, the more a subject will self-disclose to him/her (Brundage, Derlega, and Cash 1977; Kleinke and Kahn 1980). In a similar vein, Duck's (1978) theory assumes that the central theme of relationship formation is the search for "depth" information about the partner's personality. Newcomb (1961), one of the pioneering researchers in this area, believed that individuals were motivated by a desire for informational congruence (i.e., agreement about important issues).

Huston and Levinger (1978) have reviewed evidence suggesting that the association between attraction within a dyad and disclosure of information about oneself is not perfectly symmetrical. Initial attraction does apparently lead to a reciprocal self-disclosure process, but the effects of that self-disclosure upon increased attraction are contingent (1) on the extent to which the content revealed is socially desirable; and (2) on the timing of the disclosure, which suggests knowledge of appropriate social skills. So, although initial attraction does lead to the exchange of "depth" information, the informational content and style of delivery may act as filters to further escalations in the relationship.

Regarding the content of the information exchanged, a substantial literature has accumulated supporting the importance of agreement on attitudes about religion and politics (Byrne 1971; Kerchoff and Davis 1962; Newcomb 1961). Evidence also exists suggesting that similarity on a wide range of personality characteristics increases attraction (e.g., Buss 1985; Byrne, Griffitt, and Stefaniak 1967; Meyer and Pepper 1977; Pursell and Banikiotes 1978).

There are some exceptions to this preference for similar personality traits, particularly when one end of a trait dimension is more socially valued. For instance, Hendrick and Brown (1971) found that both introverts and extroverts regarded extroversion to be an attractive characteristic. Seyfried and Hendrick (1973) found that females preferred males with traditionally masculine (vs. feminine) sex role attitudes. Consistent with this finding, there is evidence that assessments of physical attractiveness are elevated by the perception of high intelligence (Solomon and Saxe 1977) and friendliness (Gross and Crofton 1977).

Some research has found a sex difference between males' and females' trait preferences, with females expressing more interest in a male's social status and scholastic ability (e.g., Coombs and Kenkel 1966).

The Biosocial Perspective

From our perspective, information about the potential partner's traits is also crucially relevant, but not as an end in itself. As noted by Kenrick (1979), a purely cognitive analysis can fall prey to a view of man as a "disembodied cortex," seeking information for its own sake. We hold that the actor seeks "depth" information about the partner as a means of estimating the partner's likely direct and indirect contributions to potential offspring.

Hogan (1982) has proposed a very useful framework regarding the adaptiveness of certain personality characteristics, and we will adopt this model for our discussion. There are three main tenets to Hogan's argument: (1) much of the variance in personality research can be explained by only a few personality dimensions through which humans evaluate each other—we consider the other's adjustment, intelligence, likeability, level of ambition (dominance), or degree of prudence (conscientiousness); (2) such characteristics are important to the survival of the individual and his/her social group; and (3) the tendency to attend to these characteristics is innate.

There are clear genetic selection advantages to the individual who scores highly on these personality characteristics. Some of the advantages are more direct, as in the intelligence and prudence dimensions. For instance, high intelligence allows one to maximize problem-solving strategies involved in the attainment of resources. A tendency to work hard, attend to odds, avoid unnecessary risks, and consider long-term consequences (indicators of prudence or conscientiousness) should also directly affect survival. Since humans are a social species and each individual is interdependent with the rest of his/her social group (Campbell 1975; Lancaster 1975), a number of indirect advantages will also accrue to those scoring high on the likeability and ambitiousness dimensions. For instance, other members of a group are likely to reward an individual for being unhostile, uncomplaining, and predictable (components of likeability) in conjunction with the other traits. Likewise, for males, "ambitious," consisting of assertiveness, competitiveness, success orientation, and so on, is related to the attainment of status, with all the concomitant selection advantages accruing therefrom (Wilson 1975).

The most important indirect reward for possessing these characteristics, from the perspective of this paper, is greater access to more desirable members of the opposite sex. Both males and females should gain selection advantages for their own offspring by mating with an individual possessing traits such as intelligence and conscientiousness in at least two ways: (1) since for humans both parents are likely to share some of the responsibilities of caring for the offspring, the resources accruing (directly and indirectly) from those traits will be invested in any offspring of the match; and (2) the offspring themselves are likely to inherit those useful traits.

Other research suggests there are differences between the sexes' mating strategies when it comes to personality preference. For instance, Symonds (1979) reviewed evidence suggesting that males look for characteristics that indicate the female will be a compatible sexual companion, mate, and mother (i.e., cleanliness, industry, and temperament). Females, on the other hand, expressed a preference for personality dimensions that indicate the male will be a good provider and have an acceptable level of social status (i.e. industry, ability, wealth, and the social prominence of his father). Although this sort of a sexual division of labor may be outmoded in contemporary technological society, it apparently reflects a universal sexual division of labor among our hunter-gatherer ancestors (Mellen 1981).

Regarding the importance of similar attitudes and beliefs, we have already mentioned the genetic advantages to "assortive mating" that could predispose an individual toward marrying others within his/her own tribe or social group. As indicated above, research from several divergent theoretical perspectives has generally supported the importance of similar attitudes in attraction. Also supporting the "same tribe" hypothesis is evidence that individuals prefer partners whose attitudes are similar to those of their parents (Murstein 1971; Strauss 1946).

Rosenbaum (1984) has reanalyzed several studies on the similarity/ attraction phenomenon and produced some of his own data that argues it is not so much that similarity is rewarding as that dissimilarity is aversive. This argument is perhaps even more compatible with our viewpoint, since it posits an easy "rule of thumb"—rather than weighting all possible dimensions of similarity, the actor simply looks for any evidence that the other is from a different "tribe" and is disposed to move away if any such evidence is uncovered.

Summary

The biosocial perspective views the well-documented concern with depth information about a partner's personality as relevant to genetic fitness. Searching for an intelligent, sociable, and conscientious mate has the ultimate result of increasing direct resources to, and ensuring desirable genes for, one's offspring. Sex differences in preferences have been interpreted to reflect the division of labor in our hunter-gatherer ancestors (Mellen 1981; Symonds 1979), and the preference for trait similarity is in line with the assortive mating argument advanced earlier. We are aware of no evidence relating perceptions of the partner's personality to physiological states. Based upon our earlier discussion of the relationship between hormonal states and environmental stimuli, however, we would expect that information indicating the potential partner is well adjusted, intelligent, dependable, friendly, and similar to the actor would lead to increases in sexual arousability and facilitate advancement to the stage of intimate physical contact.

INTIMATE PHYSICAL CONTACT

Social Psychological Findings

Although they have placed much more emphasis upon the cognitive and/or normative levels of analysis (Morton and Douglas 1981), social psychologists have not been blind to the importance of physical intimacy. Rubin (1970), for instance, noted that close physical proximity and touching occurred more frequently in dating couples that described themselves as relatively more in love. Survey data has continued to indicate that premarital sexual intercourse is most likely to occur among couples who are either engaged to be married or dating steadily (Hunt 1974).

Peplau, Rubin, and Hill (1977) found their dating couples could be divided into "traditionals," for whom intercourse occurred only after professed love and commitment, and "liberals," for whom sexual intercourse was seen as an acceptable dating goal in itself and was considered to be one possible route to developing intimacy.

One group of social psychologists studied the "hard to get female" phenomenon. Walster, Walster, Piliavin, and Schmidt (1973) found that males preferred to date females who were "selectively hard to get"—that is, easy for the subject to get, but difficult for other males to get. The female who was uniformly interested in dating many males ("easy" to get) was perceived as less attractive and potentially sexually unfaithful by subjects.

The Biosocial Perspective

Obviously, from our perspective, the establishment of a physically intimate relationship is a central task. After all, mating provides the primary motivation for the formation of heterosexual relationships of the sort we are discussing, and the desire to mate (and successfully rear offspring) is central in the other tasks we have discussed. Barash (1977) notes that behavioral and hormonal intercoordination is essential in all animal courtship, and that there is no reason to presume an exception for *Homo sapiens*.

Writing from a biological perspective, Morris (1972) has observed that human couples engage in intercourse only after a series of progressively more intimate nonverbal behaviors. The sequence, Morris argues, proceeds through eye contact, vocal contact, hand contact, shoulder to waist contact, kissing, intimate fondling and mutual masturbation, to intercourse. The steps are generally escalated only gradually so that mutual appraisal and bond formation will precede the possibility of offspring. "Foreplay" for most other primates is much less prolonged and ritualized, partners often copulating only minutes after "introduction." This behavior contrasts with the prolonged mating rituals in pair-bonded birds, like those studied by Lehrman (1966). Unlike other primates, who are less formalized and gradual in their mating, Morris (1972) argues that humans have been selected for pair-bonding due to the long period of gestation and offspring dependency.

Given the parental investment argument we have discussed, it is to be expected that males and females will differ in their threshold for sexual contact. Males should be more inclined to initiate first intercourse, and they should also be relatively less selective in their choice of sexual partners. Daly and Wilson (1979) review a good deal of evidence supporting these assumptions. Females should generally be more hesitant to become sexually involved, and cross-cultural evidence suggests it is the male who makes the initial invitation to sexual intercourse. Survey data have generally indicated that the average male has more sexual experience with more partners and in more diverse forms (with some females being very active) (Hunt 1974; Kinsey, Pomeroy, Martin, and Gebhard 1953). Males are also much more likely to engage in extramarital sexual liaisons (Hunt 1974; Kinsey et al. 1953). These trends continue even into the most recent survey data. Among the most liberal and egalitarian youthful samples, sex without love is considered much more acceptable for males than for females (Daly and Wilson 1979). Foa, Anderson, Urbansky, Mulhausen, and Tornblom (1984) used an evolutionary model to predict male/female differences in cognitions about the relationship between sex and love. Consistent with the general thrust of findings reviewed above, Foa et al. (1984) found that males are less likely than females to categorize sex and love as belonging together.

Research relating hormones to sexual desire has found strong evidence that testosterone is necessary for male sexual arousal (Bancroft 1978). Bancroft (1978) also reviews evidence that females show substantial decreases in sexual activity if they are no longer producing testosterone. Conversely, the administration of exogenous testosterone to females apparently increases sexual desire and frequency (Bancroft 1978). Both male and female humans produce testosterone in their adrenal glands, but males produce a much greater quantity in their testes. These hormonal findings appear to be directly related to the differential male/female thresholds in the desire for sexual intimacy.

As indicated earlier, sociobiologists assume that mating patterns will vary between and within species. Human beings have generally been thought to be predisposed towards K strategies, like pair-bonding, but to have the potential for a more "promiscuous" r strategy (Daly and Wilson 1979). This reasoning leads us to speculate that there might be individual differences related to these thresholds for pair-bonding as opposed to promiscuous strategies.[1] Perhaps Peplau et al.'s distinction between "traditional" and "liberal" daters is relevant here. If so, one would expect such tendencies to be heritable, and to be associated with territoriality (vs. mobility) and number of offspring.

There are several findings that are potentially relevant to this hypothesis. First, Eysenck (1976) and his colleagues have, in fact, found a heritable component in strength of sex drive, as well as in age at first sexual intercourse (Martin, Eaves, and Eysenck 1977), thereby supporting the possible existence of heritable differences in sexual strategies. Second, Jessor, Costa, Jessor, and Donovan (1983) found that early intercourse was associated with higher independence and less attachment to parents. Third, Rosen, Herskovitz, and Stack (1982) found that early intercourse among females was associated with a tendency to view love and sex as unrelated. Fourth, individuals who have several premarital partners are more likely to later divorce (Newcomb and Bentler 1981). Finally, Kelley, Pilchowicz, and Byrne (1981) found that, when females took the initiative in beginning a sexual relationship, it tended to be short-lived. Taken in combination, these findings suggest that a tendency toward promiscuity might be (1) heritable, (2) associated with the earlier onset of intercourse, (3) associated with a tendency to view love and sex as unrelated, and (4) associated with a lower commitment to family.

Summary

In this section, we presented findings of a male/female difference in thresholds for initiating sexual intercourse that seem to fit the parental investment argument. We have also suggested the possibility that there are individual differences in sexual intercourse thresholds that are in line with the r vs. K distinction made by ethologists. On a physiological level, the fact that males produce markedly higher levels of testosterone, and that this hormone is related to sexual desire in both sexes, is in line with the parental investment argument.

BOND MAINTENANCE AND TERMINATION

Social Psychological Findings

Until recent years, relationship researchers were more concerned with the processes of dating and courtship than with relationship maintenance, apparently presuming that couples "lived happily ever after." In recent years, more attention has been directed to the factors associated with relationship continuity and termination.

A number of social psychological studies have found that the romantic or passionate love associated with the early phases of a relationship generally fails to withstand the test of time. As Paul Geraldy notes, "the history of a love affair is the drama of its fight against time" (Berscheid and Walster 1974:359). Consistent with this observation, empirical studies have found that passionate love decreases over the course of a relationship (Cimbalo, Faling, and Mousaw 1976; Driscoll, Davis, and Lipetz 1972).

Hunt (1974) found a strong association between sexual pleasure and marital happiness. A large majority of his sample of males and females who described marital coitus as very pleasurable for the preceding year also rated their marriages as emotionally close. Furthermore, 60 percent of the women and 40 percent of the men who rated their marriage as distant or not close found marital sex lacking or even unpleasant.

Mills and Clark (1982) have noted that, in established couples, there is a shift from a concern with equity of inputs to a more communal spirit, in which rewards are exchanged without "record-keeping." Such a communal arrangement probably stems from, and in turn increases, the level of trust between partners, as well as making for more hassle-free interactions. There is also evidence to support the argument that attention to attitudinal disagreement is attenuated once the partners have become committed to one another (Byrne and Blaylock 1963).

Several factors have been associated with marital longevity. For instance, Hill, Rubin, and Peplau (1979) found that similarity of age, highest educational degree planned, IQ, and physical attractiveness were important. Several different researchers have noted that the husband's income is positively related to marital stability (Ross and Sawhill 1975; Scanzoni 1979). Wives' independent income, on the other hand, is inversely related to marital stability (Levinger 1979). Interracial marriages tend to be quite unstable (Norton and Glick 1979). Gross psychopathology is associated with divorce, as is the number of premarital partners (Newcomb and Bentler 1981). Extramarital sex is associated with divorce, particularly when it involves the female (Glass and Wright 1977).

The Biosocial Perspective

The processes by which relationships are maintained and the factors associated with termination are of particular relevance to our model, which presumes humans are predisposed to bond together to care for their offspring. Regarding sex differences, Daly and Wilson (1979) have noted that divorced men are twice as likely to report their spouses' infidelity as having been important in divorce, even though females are only about half as likely to be unfaithful. These authors interpret these findings in sociobiological terms—the male is more uncertain about paternity and must guard his parental investment against cuckoldry.

There is one finding that runs contrary to the argument regarding differential parental investment: women are more likely to petition for divorce than are men (Newcomb and Bentler 1981). This behavior may simply be due to the fact that women are more anxious to legally formalize a separation (in order to facilitate finding a new mate or to receive child support) and not to the fact that women desire a breakup in the first place. Certainly, males are more content to engage in extramarital affairs while formally married (Hunt 1974). From the present perspective, however, this sex difference requires further investigation. We would expect that female termination of a marriage would not occur during the early years of offspring dependency, and/or that females are only interested in legally terminating an already broken relationship. Evidence to the contrary could not be explained within the present framework.

It is, however, consistent with this model that the husband's income serves as a bond-facilitator, while the reverse is true regarding the wife's independent income. When the wife's relative resources are high, the need for a "providing" male investment decreases. When the male is not "providing," the need for the bond is reduced.

In 1891, Willcox found that the divorce rate was 3–4 times higher among childless couples; such a relationship continues into the present (Rasmussen 1981). Interestingly, this relationship holds despite the fact that children decrease perceived satisfaction with one's partner (Houseknecht 1979). Rasmussen (1981) has discussed the sociobiological significance of divorce following infertility, and he notes that a similar pattern has been observed in pair-bonding birds by Lack (1966). Pairs that were unsuccessful in raising young during one season were more likely to seek new partners for the following season. In this case, poor success followed production of either too few eggs or too many in a clutch. Rasmussen (1981) notes that, among humans, divorce not only follows from childlessness, but tends to be more frequent among couples with very large numbers of offspring as well. In line wtih Rasmussen's line of reasoning, Hoffman and Manis (1978) found that, although children decreased the quality and quantity of interactions between spouses, they nevertheless *increased* marital commitment.

We noted above that passionate love is strongest at the beginning of a relationship, but fades with time. Rather than view this decline as the lamentable plight of the human race, however, such a tendency can easily be incorporated within the present functionalist viewpoint. Simply, it would seem highly inefficient if, once a pair bond were formed, the initial high levels or arousal and continual courtship behaviors were maintained continuously. In fact, such a state of affairs would likely interfere with the task of providing for any offspring resulting from that bond.

On the other hand, studies such as those mentioned above (Cimbalo et al. 1976; Driscoll et al. 1972), although reporting decreases in passionate arousal over the course of a relationship, nevertheless find increases in other indices of attraction (e.g., "liking" for spouse) and in interrelatedness between spouses over time. Our position is that intense arousal is again instigated, however, with any threat to the relationship. Along these lines, it is interesting to note that the well-known Holmes and Rahe (1967) assessment of life stressors assigns the most weight to "death of a spouse" and "divorce." Such events are associated with high levels of anxiety, depression, and psycho-physiological distress. Much to the dismay of friends and relatives whose "cold" cognitive analysis (Zajonc 1980) of the "worthlessness" of a given marriage leads them to applaud its dissolution, after a brief separation the partners themselves frequently terminate their unpleasant autonomic arousal by reestablishing the bond.

The basic mechanism by which love relationships transform themselves from passionately arousing states into addiction-like patterns maintained by negative arousal upon termination is documented in Solomon's (1980) paper on "opponent-process" theory. Solomon notes that any affectively arousing stimulus becomes neutral over time, as a function of the development of a physiologically opposite reaction. This opponent process neutralizes the affective response to the original stimulus but is slow to dissipate after the stimulus is removed. This delay results in an unpleasant "hangover" when a positive stimulus is removed. Addiction results as a means to avoid these unpleasant aftereffects, but is associated with less of a "rush" in the presence of the pleasant stimulus (due to the strongly developed opponent process). Solomon (1980) notes that such a process is associated with bond formation during imprinting, and he suggests its applicability to human love.

Given our earlier discussion of *r* versus *K* strategies and their relationship with ecological factors, we would predict that divorce rates would go down with economic threat and with increasing population density, and that promiscuity would be associated with economic well-being and low density conditions. We are not aware of the existence of an appropriate analysis, but it is of interest that the divorce rate declined during the recent economic recession and that there has been much talk of the reversal of the "sexual revolution" since that time. We would expect that the present perception of economic recovery will be associated with a recovery of the sexual revolution.

We would also expect individual differences in the strength of bonding associated with *r* versus *K* strategists. It is consistent that there is an association between earlier promiscuity and later proneness to divorce, and also that a proneness to divorce seems to "run" in families (Pope and Mueller 1979). These findings have been explained with reference to more proximate factors, but those explanations are neither proved nor necessarily incompatible with a biosocial perspective.

From our discussion of Lehrman's research on mating sequences, we would expect internal arousal to be important in maintaining the couples' bond. Generalized autonomic arousal seemingly plays an important role in conditioning processes (Hull 1943; Killeen, Hanson, and Osborne 1978) and should play a role in conditioning attraction for cues associated with one's partner. Interestingly, sociopaths seem to have chronically low levels of generalized autonomic arousal (Lykken 1957; Schachter and Latane 1964), and one of the diagnostic indicators of sociopathy is "incapacity for love and attachment" (Davison and Neale 1978:227). In a somewhat related vein, Morris (1972) has speculated that alcohol's role in inhibiting arousal levels may explain the relative ease with which "one night stands" can be terminated.

Summary

Males' greater concern about their spouses' fidelity and the greater importance of male income in maintaining a marriage fit with the parental investment argument, but the finding that females are more likely to file for divorce does not. The finding that divorce is higher among couples without children—even though those couples are happier with one another—supports the importance of reproduction in courtship maintenance. The fact that passionate arousal seems to decrease over the course of a relationship, but is aroused again at the threat of termination, was also interpreted as having a possible adaptive significance. Interestingly, the stress of marital separation appears unrelated to the reported happiness of the couple (Weiss 1975). Solomon (1980) has suggested a physiologically based explanation of these changes in passionate arousal over the course of relationship formation and termination. Finally, there is some evidence of a connection between chronic autonomic arousability and the capacity for long-term relationships.

CONCLUSION

We have presented a model of relationship formation that combines several aspects of existing social psychological models with assumptions emerging from research on animal courtship. Traditional social psychological models have focused on cognitive and/or normative levels of analysis in discussing the motivations for courtship and relationship maintenance. The biosocial perspective assumes that successful reproduction is the ultimate organizing theme of courtship. "Information" about the partner is, in fact, viewed as relevant, but it is seen as ultimately related to the partner's adaptive characteristics and potential contribution to any potential offspring (although individuals' "explanations" may focus on more proximate motivations). The present model further presumes an interplay between courtship progress and physiological states and, finally, that courtship strategies are somewhat different for males and females.

We have presented some suggestive findings regarding our model, but at this point much additional research is called for to address questions such as the following:

1. What exactly is the interplay between hormonal states and courtship progress at the various stages? Which hormones are involved, and what is the effect of their absence?

2. How exactly do ecological conditions such as density and resource scarcity affect progress through the stages of courtship and the strategies of courtship used?

3. Are there heritable factors associated with varying strategies of courtship? How do such predispositions operate at a proximate level?

4. How do learning experiences, cognition, and biological factors interact to determine adult courtship patterns?

Some Problematic Issues for the Model

At this point, it is useful to consider the possible limitations of the model.

There are gaps in the evidence. In discussing the need for additional research, it strikes us that there are at least as many pieces of the puzzle missing as there are on the table. Again, we wish to stress that we offer this model in a tentative fashion and not as "proven fact." For this very reason, however, we think the model has a good deal of heuristic promise. Theories drive our search for new data, and this model provides a map that suggests a search in places where current social psychological models would not lead us to look.

Is the notion of stages or phases really necessary? For reasons we discussed at the outset, it seems necessary to presume that intimate sexual contact generally follows acquaintance, which follows stimulus assessment. It also seems reasonable to assume that at least some degree of depth assessment precedes intimate sexual contact, but that depth assessment and maintenance processes overlap with the other tasks. Our theory makes a stronger commitment to a sequential model, since we predict that different physiological processes will be associated with different relationship phases. We would expect, for instance, that information about the brilliant intellectual capacities of an opposite-sexed other would *quite literally* "turn on" testosterone production. This information would not be as important, however, if the individual was dealing with a noneligible acquaintance who had expressed no interest in the perceiver. Neither would we expect such information to have much effect on a spouse of five years as opposed to a new flame.

Alteration of the sequence is certainly not impossible—prostitutes and "swingers" in southern California alter the sequence all the time—but, in line with Morris' (1972) reasoning, such alterations would be associated with decreased bonding. On the other hand, biological differences in the production of various hormones should influence the flow of the sequence outlined here.

There are many difficulties in "proving" that behavior has been naturally selected for. It is not enough to simply demonstrate that a given behavior is "functional" to prove that it is a product of biological evolution. Colwell and King (1983) argue that, in addition to making an experimental or rhetorical case that individuals who demonstrate a certain behavioral trait have a reproductive or survival advantage, it is necessary to show that the characteristic in question is genetically transmitted from one generation to the next. This task becomes particularly difficult when one notes that parents pass on cultural patterns as well as genes to their offspring, so a trait may follow a lineage without really being genetically passed on (Colwell and King 1983; Rajecki 1984).

We do not claim that the necessary genetic evidence (e.g., from twin and adoptee studies) exists for most of the behaviors we have discussed. Nevertheless, although "indisputable" proof of the natural selection argument for adult human behaviors awaits more powerful genetic data, we feel it worthwhile to consider these possibilities with the present data. As we already mentioned, it seems unlikely we would ever *begin* looking for biosocial evidence given only the present theories. In addition, we feel that a biologically based explanation is simply *more plausible* than a normatively based explanation *for at least some* of the findings we have discussed, for example, (1) Shepher's data on "incest" avoidance for those raised on the kibbutz; (2) Eibl-Eibesfeldt's data on the existence of cross-culturally universal flirtation gestures; and (3) the data showing a strong association between testosterone production, gender, and sexual interest. All these findings stand out as being difficult for normatively based theories to explain parsimoniously.

Even for those uninterested in doing research on a genetic level, there may be advantages to considering comparative data. For instance, Rajecki and Flanery (1981) point out that there are three ways to make parallels across different species. A *homology* exists when the behavior or morphological feature is the result of common ancestry. For instance, penis erection in humans and chimpanzees can be presumed *not* to have evolved separately, but to have its genesis in a common, genetically coded trait. An *analogy* exists when a parallel trait is the result of common ecological pressures, but has evolved separately. The human penis and the anal fin on a male guppy *(Lebistus reticulatus)* are both used to inseminate females, but they can be presumed to have evolved from somewhat different morphological structures. Finally, a *model* is the term Rajecki and Flanery use to describe parallels based neither in common genes nor in convergent evolution to similar ecological demands, but that may nevertheless yield fruitful insights. As Rajecki and Flanery put it, ". . . organisms on this planet can function in only so many ways, and . . . for whatever reason, certain functions in different animals will happen to be alike" (1981:97). When we use the term evolution to refer both to culturally transmitted and to genetically transmitted traits, we are, in some sense, using a "model" as opposed to a homology or an analogy (although this use may be more general than Rajecki and Flanery intended). In this paper, our comparison of the testosterone/dominance link in monkeys and humans is a *homology*—that is, it is a mechanism based partly on common ancestry and acting in a similar fashion across different species. Our comparison of humans and ring doves is probably better regarded as an *analogy*—a parallel based upon common ecological pressures rather than on shared genes. We think, however, that the biosocial theory is fruitful even if one only considers courtship in similar species as occasionally instructive *models* of human courtship. As such, they suggest a number of hypotheses that are eminently testable, with data that may be more readily accessible than the genetic evidence needed to test a *homology*-based theory.

Sex is only a small part of human courtship relationships. One might object that the reasons for human mating bonds are not limited solely to copulation but include such things as a desire for companionship or financial stability. It might also be noted that relationships continue beyond the years of fertility, when no more offspring can be expected. In response to this objection, we agree that adult human behavior is no doubt multiply determined, but we continue to argue that the potential for procreation explains much of the variance in the differential strength of and effort surrounding marital bonds, as generally compared with other relationships. This statement does not deny that friendship, social standing, and financial considerations are in themselves important, we are simply saying that procreation is, ultimately, even more important. Note that successful procreation was not just related to acts of intercourse for our ancestors, but it involved providing a stable and resourceful environment for the offspring. Returning to the parallel with pair-bonded birds, copulation for them is often extremely brief and confined to a short period in the whole process, but the "name of the game" of nest-building, care of offspring, and so on, is reproduction.

Regarding our tendency to maintain bonds after the reproductive years, this objection is in itself not a "problem" for the idea that their *initial* formation was linked to reproduction. For one thing, what an organism does after fertility is quite irrelevant to natural selection. Moreover, human grandparents frequently continue to accumulate resources that they share with or pass on, not to posterity in general, but to their own descendents.

The Relationship Between Culture and Genes

This is a good time to reiterate that we do not presume that genetic influences operate oblivious to cultural inputs. There are several ways for a genetically based tendency to interact with postnatal experience:

1. The biologically based trait may be expressed under virtually all environmental conditions. Except in relatively rare circumstances, females develop vaginas and males do not, for instance.

2. The genetic trait may emerge only with appropriate experience or be facilitated by experiential factors. Menstruation in human females occurs only when the amount of body fat is adequate to support a fetus, for instance (Frisch and McArthur 1974). On an even more proximate level, testosterone and estrogen secretions are markedly increased by intimate physical contact (Bancroft 1973).

3. Environmental factors may regularly act in opposition to the trait. Campbell (1975, 1983) brings up this issue in his discussion of human selfishness versus cultural pressures for altruism, and we may presume that the religious preachings that harshly oppose premarital sexuality (e.g., Messenger 1972; Masters and Johnson 1970) fall into this category, as do practices prevalent in some cultures of segregating opposite-sexed adolescents (Symonds 1979).

4. Environmental factors may operate largely independently of genetic factors when genetic constraints on certain types of learning are either weak or nonexistent. The varying stylistic preferences for attractiveness across generations probably fall into this category. A

long-haired, bearded, and beaded male wearing bell-bottoms and a paisley, Nehru shirt was once provocative, but is now passé.

The prevailing viewpoint in American social science in general, and in the study of sexuality in particular, has exclusively favored the last alternative. That is, the tendency has been to view humans as either *tabulae rasae* or to view social inputs as regularly overriding a weakly written genetic code (Bandura 1977; Simon and Gagnon 1977). This position is becoming more untenable, however, in light of recent evidence (Lumsden and Wilson 1981, 1983).

The Interaction of Learning, Cognition, and Biology. We have argued elsewhere that there are three possible outcomes to the argument about the relationship between social learning, social cognition, and social biological explanations of behavior (Kenrick, Montello, and MacFarlane, 1985): (1) one of these approaches (learning, cognitive, or biological) will win the day and negate the applicability of the others; (2) it will become acceptable to operate solely at one level of analysis without considering the others; (3) biological factors, learning experiences, and cognition will be found to interact in nonadditive ways, and complete models of human behavior will neither ignore nor negate any of these levels of analysis. Kenrick et al. (1985) favor the third alternative, and we argue that such an approach will be the most fruitful for studying sexual relationships in particular.

In the domain of courtship formation, our perceptions of and cognitions about potential partners are likely to be influenced by cultural learning as well as by hormonal states (e.g., Dermer and Pyszcynski 1978; Stephan, Berscheid, and Walster 1971). These hormonal states are no doubt also strongly influenced by attentional and cognitive processes, many of which are learned (e.g., Byrne and Lamberth 1971; Masters and Johnson 1966; Stock and Geer 1982). The process of learning, by which we develop cognitive expectancies and preferences, is also likely to be influenced by biological factors (e.g., van den Berghe 1983). There is much exciting work for psychologists to do in examining exactly how genes, mind, and culture interact.

In addition to its advantages as an heuristic tool, we believe a biosocial perspective helps organize our thinking about a number of disparate influences on courtship. Rather than generating a "laundry list" of potentially relevant variables, a biosocial perspective considers the interplay of variables such as ecology, physiology, family background, social interaction, and individual differences as parts of a sensible and functional whole.

We opened this paper with a reference to McDougall's classical text on social psychology. If the benefits of a Darwinian perspective are anywhere obvious, it is in the area of sexual behavior. If our own ancestors had not operated within the laws of natural selection in this of all domains, we would not be around to theorize about it.

REFERENCES

Abbey, A. (1982). Sex differences for friendly behavior: Do males misperceive females' friendliness? *Journal of Personality and Social Psychology, 42,* 830–838.

Alcock, J. (1979). *Animal behavior: An evolutionary approach.* Sunderland, MA: Sinauer.

Altman, I. (1974). The communication of interpersonal attitudes: An ecological approach. In T. L. Huston (ed.), *Foundations of interpersonal attraction.* New York: Academic Press.

Argyle, M., and Dean, J. (1965). Eye-contact, distance and affiliation. *Sociometry, 28,* 289–304.

Bancroft, J. (1978). The relationship between hormones and sexual behavior in humans. In J. B. Hutchison (ed.), *Biological determinants of sexual behavior.* Chichester, England: John Wiley & Sons.

Bandura, A. (1977). *Social learning theory.* Englewood Cliffs, NJ: Prentice-Hall.

Barash, D. P. (1977). *Sociobiology and behavior.* New York: Elsevier.

Barash, D. P. (1982). From genes to mind to culture: Biting the bullet at last. *Behavioral and Brain Sciences, 5,* 7.

Beck, S. B., Ward-Hull, C. I., and McLear, P. M. (1976). Variables related to women's somatic preferences of the male and female body. *Journal of Personality and Social Psychology, 34,* 1200–1210.

Berscheid, E., and Walster, E. (1974). Physical attractiveness. In L. Berkowitz (ed.), *Advances in experimental social psychology* (Vol. 7). New York: Academic Press.

Blurton-Jones, N. G. (1983). Two investigations of human behavior guided by evolutionary theory. In G. C. L. Davey (ed.), *Animal models of human behavior* (pp. 179–204). New York: Wiley & Sons.

Bossard, J. H. S. (1932). Residential propinquity as a factor in mate selection. *American Journal of Sociology, 38,* 219–224.

Brundage, L. E., Derlega, V. J., and Cash, T. F. (1977). The effects of physical attractiveness and need for approval on self-disclosure. *Personality and Social Psychology Bulletin, 3,* 63–66.

Buss, D. M. (1985). Human mate selection. *American Scientist, 73,* 47–51.

Byrne, D. (1971). *The attraction paradigm.* New York: Academic Press.

Byrne, D., and Blaylock, B. (1963). Similarity and assumed similarity of attitudes between husbands and wives. *Journal of Abnormal and Social Psychology, 67,* 636–640.

Byrne, D., Ervin, C. R., and Lamberth, J. (1970). Continuity between the experimental study of attraction and real-life computer dating. *Journal of Personality and Social Psychology, 16,* 157–165.

Byrne, D., Griffitt, W., and Stefaniak, D. (1967). Attraction and similarity of personality characteristics. *Journal of Personality and Social Psychology, 5,* 82–90.

Byrne, D., and Lamberth, J. (1971). Cognitive and reinforcement theories as complementary approaches to the study of attraction. In B. I. Murstein (ed.), *Theories of attraction and love.* New York: Springer.

Campbell, D. T. (1975). On the conflicts between biological and social evolution and between psychology and moral tradition. *American Psychologist, 30,* 1103–1126.

Campbell, D. T. (1983). The two distinct routes beyond kin selection to ultrasociality: Implications for the humanities and social sciences. In D. Bridgeman (ed.), *The nature of prosocial development: Interdisciplinary theories and strategies.* New York: Academic Press.

Chagnon, N. A., and Irons, W. (1979). *Evolutionary biology and human social behavior.* North Scituate, MA: Duxbury.

Cimbalo, R. S., Faling, V., and Mousaw, P. (1976). The course of love: A cross-sectional design. *Psychological Reports, 38,* 1292–1294.

Colwell, R. K., and King, M. C. (1983). Disentangling genetic and cultural influences on human behavior: Problems and prospects. In D. W. Rajecki (ed.), *Comparing behavior: Study man studying animals.* Hillsdale, NJ: Lawrence Erlbaum Associates.

Coombs, R. H., and Kenkel, W. F. (1966). Sex differences in dating aspirations and satisfaction with computer-selected partners. *Journal of Marriage and the Family, 23,* 62–66.

Cunningham, M. R. (1981). Sociobiology as a supplementary paradigm for social psychological research. In L. Wheeler (ed.) *Review of personality and social psychology.* Beverly Hills, CA: Sage.

Daly, M., and Wilson, M. (1979). *Sex, evolution, and behavior.* N. Scituate, MA: Duxbury.

Davis, J. D. (1978). When boy meets girl: Sex roles and the negotiation of intimacy in an acquaintance exercise. *Journal of Personality and Social Psychology, 36,* 684–692.

Davison, G. C. and Neale, J. M. (1978). *Abnormal psychology: An experimental clinical approach* (2nd ed.). New York: John Wiley & Sons.

Dermer, M. and Pyszcynski, T. A. (1978). Effects of erotica upon men's loving and liking responses for women they love. *Journal of Personality and Social Psychology, 36,* 1302–1309.

DeVore, B. I. (1965). *Primate behavior: Field studies of monkeys and apes.* New York: Holt, Rinehart & Winston.

Driscoll, R., Davis, K., and Lipetz, M. (1972). Parental interference and romantic love: The Romeo and Juliet effect. *Journal of Personality and Social Psychology, 24,* 1–10.

Duck, S. (1978). *The study of acquaintance.* Westmead, England: Saxon House.

Duck, S., and Gilmour, R. (1981–1983). *Personal relationships.* London: Academic Press.

Eibl-Eibesfeldt, I. (1975). *Ethology: The biology of behavior.*New York: Holt, Rinehart & Winston.

Eysenck, H. J. (1976). *Sex and personality.* London: Open Books.

Foa, U. G., Anderson, B., Urbansky, W. A., Mulhausen, S. M., and Tornblom, K. Y. (1984). *Gender differences in sexual preferences: Some cross-cultural evidence of evolutionary selection.* Paper presented at the meeting of the Society for Experimental Social Psychology, Snowbird, Utah.

Ford, C. S., and Beach, F. A. (1951). *Patterns of sexual behavior.* New York: Harper & Row.

Frisch, R. E., and McArthur, J. W. (1974). Menstrual cycles: Fatness as a determinant of minimum weight for height necessary for their maintenance or onset. *Science, 185,* 949–951.

Garb, J. L., and Stunkard, A. (1974). Taste aversions in man. *American Journal of Psychiatry, 131,* 1204–1207.

Glass, S. P., and Wright, T. L. (1977). The relationship of extramarital sex, length of marriage, and sex differences on marital satisfaction and romanticism: Athanaslou's data reanalyzed. *Journal of Marriage and Family, 39,* 691–703.

Gross, A.E., and Crofton, C. (1977). What is good is beautiful. *Sociometry, 40,* 85–90.

Hendrick, C., and Brown, S. R. (1971). Introversion, extroversion and interpersonal attraction. *Journal of Personality and Social Psychology, 20,* 31–36.

Henly, N. M. (1977). *Body politics: Power, sex, and nonverbal communication.* Englewood Cliffs, NJ: Prentice Hall.

Hill, C. T., Rubin, Z., and Peplau, L. A. (1979). Breakups before marriage: The end of 103 affairs. In G. Levinger and O. Moles (eds.), *Divorce and separation* (pp. 64–82). New York: Basic Books.

Hoffman, L. W., and Manis, J.D. (1978). Influences of children on marital interaction and parental satisfactions and dissatisfactions. In R. M. Lerner and G. B. Spanier (eds.), *Child influences on marital and family interaction.* New York: Academic Press.

Hogan, R. (1982). A socioanalytic theory of personality. In M. Page and R. Dienstbier (eds.), *Nebraska symposium on motivation, 1981.* Lincoln: University of Nebraska Press.

Holmes, T. H., and Rahe, R. H. (1967). The social readjustment scale. *Journal of Psychosomatic Research, 11,* 213–218.

Houseknecht, S. K. (1979). Childlessness and marital adjustment. *Journal of Marriage and the Family, 41,* 259–265.

Hull, C. L. (1943). *Principles of behavior.* New York: Appleton-Century-Crofts.

Hunt, M. (1974). *Sexual behavior in the 1970s.* Chicago: Playboy Press.

Huston, T. L., and Levinger, G. (1978). Interpersonal attraction and relationships. *Annual Review of Psychology, 29,* 115–156.

Illsley, R. (1955). Social class selection and class differences in relation to stillbirths and infant deaths. *British Medical Journal, 24,* 1520–1524.

Jensen, G. D. (1973). Human sexual behavior in primate perspective. In J. Zubin and J. Money (eds.), *Contemporary sexual behavior: Critical issues in the 1970s.* Baltimore: Johns Hopkins University Press.

Jessor, R., Costa, F., Jessor, L., and Donovan, J. E. (1983). Time of first intercourse: A prospective study. *Journal of Personality and Social Psychology, 44,* 608–626.

Katz, A. M., and Hill, R. (1958). Residential propinquity and marital selection: A review of theory, method, and fact. *Marriage and Family Living, 20,* 327–335.

Keil, F. C. (1981). Constraints on knowledge and cognitive development. *Psychological Review, 83,* 197–227.

Kelley, H. H. (1983). Love and commitment. In H. H. Kelley, E. Berscheid, A. Christensen, J. H. Harvey, T. L. Huston, G. Levinger,E. McClintock, L. A. Peplau, and D. R. Peterson (eds.), *Close relationships* (pp. 256–314). New York: W. H. Freeman & Co.

Kelley, H. H., Berscheid, E., Christensen, A., Harvey, J. H., Huston, T. L., Levinger, G., McClintock, E., Peplau, L. A., and Peterson, D. R., (eds.) (1983). *Close relationships.* New York: W. H. Freeman & Co.

Kelley, K., Pilchowicz, E., and Byrne, D. (1981). Response of males to female-initiated dates. *Bulletin of the Psychonomic Society, 17,* 195–196.

Kenrick, D. T. (1979). The science of friendship: A model of friends as scientists. *Contemporary Psychology, 24,* 505.

Kenrick, D. T., and Gutierres, S. E. (1980). Contrast effects and judgments of physical attractiveness: When beauty becomes a social problem. *Journal of Personality and Social Psychology, 38,* 131–140.

Kenrick, D. T., Montello, D., and MacFarlane, S. (1985). Personality: Social learning, social cognition, or sociobiology? In R. Hogan and W. Jones (eds.), *Perspectives in personality* (Vol. 1 pp. 201–234). Greenwich, CT: JAI Press.

Kerchoff, A. C. (1974). The social context of interpersonal attraction. In T. L. Houston (ed.), *Foundations of interpersonal attraction.* New York: Academic Press.

Kerchoff, A. C., and Davis, K. E. (1962). Value consensus and need complementarity in mate selection. *American Sociological Review, 27,* 295–303.

Kiesler, S., and Baral, R. (1970). The search for a romantic partner: The effects of self-esteem and physical attractiveness on romantic behavior. In K. Gergen and D. Marlowe (eds.), *Personality and social behavior.* Reading, MA: Addison-Wesley.

Killeen, P. R., Hanson, S. J., and Osborne, S. R. (1978). Arousal: Its genesis and manifestation as response rate. *Psychological Review, 85,* 571–581.

Kinsey, A. C., Pomeroy, W. B., Martin, C. E., and Gebhard, P. H. (1953). *Sexual behavior in the human female.* Philadelphia, PA: Saunders.

Kleinke, C. L., and Kahn, M. L. (1980). Perceptions of self-disclosers: Effects of sex and physical attractiveness. *Journal of Personality, 48,* 190–205.

Lack, D. (1966). *Population studies of birds.* Oxford, England: Clarendon Press.

Lancaster, J. B. (1975). *Primate behavior and the emergence of human culture.* New York: Holt, Rinehart, Winston.

Laudan, L. (1977). *Progress and its problems: Toward a theory of scientific growth.* Berkeley: University of California Press.

Lavrakas, P. J. (1975). Female preferences for male physiques. *Journal of Research in Personality, 9,* 324–334.

Lee, R. B., and DeVore, I., eds. (1968). *Man the hunter*. Chicago: Aldine.

Lehrman, D. S. (1966). The reproductive behavior of ring doves. In S. Coopersmith (ed.), *Frontiers of psychological research*. San Francisco: W. H. Freeman & Co.

Levinger, G. (1974). A three-level approach to attraction: Toward an understanding of pair relatedness. In T. Huston, (ed.), *Foundations of interpersonal attraction*. New York: Academic Press.

Levinger, G. (1979a). Marital cohesiveness at the brink: The fate of applications for divorce. In G. Levinger and O. Moles (eds.), *Divorce and separation* (pp. 137–150). New York: Basic Books.

Levinger,G. (1979b). A social psychological perspective on marital dissolution. In G. Levinger and O. Moles (eds.),*Divorce and separation* (pp. 37–60). New York: Basic Books.

Levinger, G. (1983). Development and change. In H. H. Kelley, E.Berscheid, A. Christensen, J. H. Harvey, T. L. Huston, G. Levinger, E. McClintock, L. A. Peplau, and D. R. Peterson (eds.), *Close relationships* (315–359). New York: W. H. Freeman & Co.

Levinger, G., and Moles, O., eds. (1979). *Divorce and separation*. New York: Basic Books.

Levinger, G., and Snoek, J. E. (1972). *Attracting in relationship: A new look at interpersonal attraction*. Morristown, NJ: General Learning.

Lott, A., and Lott, B. (1974). The role of reward in the formation of positive interpersonal attitudes. In T. Huston (ed.), *Foundations of interpersonal attraction*. New York: Academic Press.

Lott,D.F. (1979). A possible role for generally adaptive features in mate selection and sexual stimulation. *Psychological Reports, 45*, 539–546.

Lumsden, C. J., and Wilson, E. O. (1981). *Genes, mind, and culture: The coevolutionary process*. Cambridge, MA: Harvard University Press.

Lumsden, C. J., and Wilson, E. O. (1983). *Promethean fire*. Cambridge, MA: Harvard University Press.

Lykken, D. T. (1957). A study of anxiety in the sociopathic personality. *Journal of Abnormal and Social Psychology, 55*, 6–10.

Martin, N. G., Eaves, L. J., and Eysenck, H. J. (1977). Genetical, environmental, and personality factors influencing the age of first sexual intercourse in twins. *Journal of Biosocial Science, 9*, 91–97.

Masters,W. H., and Johnson, V. E. (1966). *Human sexual response*. Boston, MA: Little, Brown, & Co.

Masters, W. H., and Johnson, V. E. (1970). *Human sexual inadequacy*. Boston, MA: Little, Brown, & Co.

Mazur, A., and Lamb, T. (1980). Testosterone, status, and mood in human males. *Hormones and Behavior, 14*, 236–246.

McClearn, G. E., and DeFries, J. C. (1973). *Introduction to behavioral genetics*. San Francisco: W. H. Freeman.

McDougall,W. (1913). *Social psychology: An introduction*. London: Methuen.

Mehrabian, A. (1969). Significance of posture and position in the communication of attitudes and status relationships. *Psychological Bulletin, 71*, 359–372.

Mellen, S. L. W. (1981). *The evolution of love*. San Francisco: Freeman.

Messenger, J. C. (1972). Sex and repression in an Irish folk community. In D. S. Marshall and R. C. Suggs (eds.), *Human sexual behavior: Variations in the ethnographic spectrum.* Englewood Cliffs, NJ: Prentice-Hall.

Meyer, J. P., and Pepper, S. (1977). Need compatibility and marital adjustment in young married couples. *Journal of Personality and Social Psychology, 35,* 331–342.

Michael, R. P., and Keverne, E. B. (1968). Pheromones in the communication of sexual status in primates. Nature, 218, 746–749.

Mills, J., and Clark, M. S. (1982). Exchange and communal relationships. In L. Wheeler (ed.), *Review of personality and social psychology* (Vol. 3). Beverly Hills, CA: Sage.

Moreland, R. L., and Zajonc, R. B. (1982). Exposure effects in person perception: Familiarity, similarity, and attraction. *Journal of Experimental Social Psychology, 18,* 395–415.

Morris, D. (1958). The reproductive behavior of the ten spined stickleback (Pygosteus pungitius L.). *Behaviour, 6.*

Morris, D. (1972). *Intimate behaviour.* New York: Random House.

Morton, T. L., and Douglas, M. (1981). Growth of relationships. In S.W. Duck and R. Gilmour (eds.), *Personal relationships 2: Developing personal relationships.* London: Academic Press.

Murdock, G. P. (1967). *Ethnographic atlas.* Pittsburgh: University of Pittsburgh Press.

Murstein, B. (1971). A theory of marital choice. In B. Murstein (ed.), *Theories of attraction and love.* New York: Springer.

Murstein, B. I. (1983). Process, filter, and stage theories of attraction. In M. Cook (ed.), *The bases of human sexual attraction.* London: Academic Press.

Myers, D. G. (1983). *Social psychology.* New York: McGraw-Hill.

Newcomb, M. D., and Bentler, P. M. (1981). Marital breakdown. In S. Duck and R. Gilmour (eds.), *Personal relationships, volume 3: Personal relationships in disorder* (pp. 57–94). London: Academic Press.

Newcomb, T. M. (1961). *The acquaintance process.* New York: Holt, Rinehart & Winston.

Newcomb, T. M. (1968). Interpersonal balance. In R. P. Abelson (ed.), *Theories of cognitive consistency: A source book.* Chicago: Rand-McNally.

Nisbett, R. E., and Wilson, T. D. (1977). Telling more than we can know: Verbal reports on mental process. *Psychological Review, 84,* 231–259.

Norton, A. J., and Glick, P.C. (1979). Marital instability in America: Past, present and future. In G. Levinger and O. Moles (eds.), *Divorce and separation* (pp. 6–19). New York: Basic Books.

Parkes, A. S., and Bruce, H. M. (1961). Olfactory stimuli in mammalian reproduction. *Science, 134,* 1049–1054.

Patterson, M. L. (1976). An arousal model of interpersonal intimacy. *Psychological Review, 83,* 235–245.

Pearson, K., and Lee, A. (1903). On the laws of inheritance in man: I. Inheritance of physical characters. *Biometrike, 2,* 372–377.

Peplau, L. A., Rubin, Z., and Hill,C. T. (1977). Sexual intimacy in dating relationships. *Journal of Social Issues, 33,* 86–109.

Pope, H., and Mueller, C. W. (1979). The intergenerational transmission of marital instability: Comparisons by race and sex. In G. Levinger and O. Moles (eds.), *Divorce and separation* (pp. 99–113). New York: Basic Books.

Pursell, S. A., and Banikiotes, P. G. (1978). Androgyny and initial interpersonal attraction. *Personality and Social Psychology Bulletin, 4,* 235–243.

Rajecki, D. W. (1984). On inferring evolutionary adaptation. *The Behavioral and Brain Sciences, 1*(1), 161–162.

Rajecki, D. W., and Flanery,R. C. (1981). Social conflict and dominance in children: A case study for a primate homology. In M. E. Lamb and A. L. Brown (eds.), *Advances in developmental psychology* (Vol. 9). Hillsdale, NJ: Erlbaum.

Rasmussen, D. R. (1981). Pair bond strength and stability and reproductive success. *Psychological Review, 88,* 274–290.

Roebuck, J. B. and Spray, S. L. (1967). The cocktail lounge: A study of heterosexual relations in a public organization. *American Journal of Sociology, 72,* 386–396.

Rogel, M. J. (1978). A critical evaluation of the possibility of higher primate reproductive and sexual pheromones. *Psychological Bulletin, 85,* 810–830.

Rose, R. M., Holaday, J. W., and Bernstein, I. (1971). Plasma testosterone, dominance rank, and aggressive behavior in male rhesus monkeys. *Nature, 231,* 366–368.

Rosen, R. H., Herskovitz, L., and Stack, J. M. (1982). Timing of the transition to nonvirginity among unmarried adolescent women. *Population Research and Policy Review, 1,* 153–170.

Rosenbaum, M. (1984). *The repulsion hypothesis: On the nondevelopment of relationships.* Paper presented at a meeting of the Society of Experimental Social Psychology, October, Snowbird, Utah.

Rosenblatt, P. C., and Cozby, P. C. (1972). Courtship patterns associated with freedom of choice of spouse. *Journal of Marriage and the Family, 34,* 689–695.

Ross, H. L., and Sawhill, I. V. (1975). *Time of transition: The growth of families headed by women.* Washington, DC: The Urban Institute.

Rozin, P., and Kalat, J. W. (1971). Specific hungers and poison avoidance as adaptive specializations of learning. *Psychological Review, 19,* 259–276.

Rubin, Z. (1970). Measurement of romantic love. *Journal of Personality and Social Psychology, 16,* 265–273.

Rubin,Z. (1973). *Liking and loving: An invitation to social psychology.* New York: Holt, Rinehart, & Winston.

Saayman, G. S. (1971). Behavior of the adult males in a troop of free-ranging chaema baboons *(Papio ursinus). Folia Primatologica, 15,* 36–57.

Sadalla, E. K., Kenrick, D. T., and Vershure, B. (1981). *Dominance and heterosexual attraction: Sociocultural and sociobiological models.* Paper presented at the annual meeting of the American Psychological Association, New York.

Scanzoni, J. (1979). A historical perspective on husband-wife bargaining power and marital dissolution. In G. Levinger and O. Moles (eds.), *Divorce and separation* (pp. 20–36). New York: Basic Books.

Schachter, S., and Latane, B. (1964). Crime, cognition, and the autonomic nervous system. In D. Levine (ed.), *Nebraska symposium on motivation* (Vol. 12). Lincoln: University of Nebraska Press.

Seligman, M. E. P., and Hager, M., eds. (1972). *Biological boundaries of learning.* New York: Appleton-Century-Crofts.

Seyfried, B., and Hendrick, C. (1973). When do opposites attract? When they are opposite in sex and sex-role attitudes. *Journal of Personality and Social Psychology, 25,* 15–20.

Shepher, J. (1971). Mate selection among second generation kibbutz adolescents and adults: Incest avoidance and negative imprinting. *Archives of Sexual Behavior, 1,* 293–307.

Shettleworth, S. J. (1972). Constraints on learning. In D. S. Lehrman, R. A. Hinde, and E. Shaw (eds.), *Advances in the study of behavior.* New York: Academic Press.

Simon, W., and Gagnon, J. (1977). Psychosexual development. In D. Byrne and L. A. Byrne, (eds.), *Exploring human sexuality.* New York: Thomas Y. Crowell.

Solomon, R. L. (1980). The opponent-process theory of acquired motivation: The costs of pleasure and the benefits of pain. *American Psychologist, 35,* 691–712.

Solomon, S., and Saxe, L. (1977). What is intelligent, as well as attractive, is good. *Personality and Social Psychology Bulletin, 3,* 670–673.

Stephan, W., Berscheid, E., and Walster, E. (1971). Sexual arousal and heterosexual perception. *Journal of Personality and Social Psychology, 20,* 93–101.

Stock, W. E., and Geer, J. H. (1982). A study of fantasy-based sexual arousal in women. *Archives of Sexual Behavior, 11,* 33–47.

Strauss, A. (1946). The influence of parent-images upon marital choice. *American Sociological Review, 11,* 554–559.

Symonds, D. (1979). *The evolution of human sexuality.* New York: Oxford University Press.

Tiger, L., and Fox, R. (1971). *The imperial animal.* New York: Holt, Rinehart & Winston.

Tinbergen, N. (1951). *The study of instinct.* Oxford: Oxford University Press.

Touhey, J. C. (1972). Comparison of two dimensions of attitude similarity on heterosexual attraction. *Journal of Personality and Social Psychology, 23,* 8–10.

Trivers, R. L. (1972). Parental investment and sexual selection. In B. Campbell (ed.), *Sexual selection and the descent ofman.* Chicago: Aldine.

Vandenberg, J. G. (1969). Endocrine coordination in monkeys: Male sexual responses to the females. *Physiology and Behavior, 4,* 261–264.

van den Berghe, P. L. (1983). Human inbreeding avoidance: Culture in nature. *Behavioral and Brain Sciences, 6,* 91–123.

Wallace, R. A. (1979). *The ecology and evolution of animal behavior.* Santa Monica, CA: Goodyear Publishing.

Walster, E. (1965). The effect of self-esteem on romantic liking. *Journal of Experimental Social Psychology, 1,* 184–197.

100   DOUGLAS T. KENRICK AND MELANIE R. TROST

Walster, E., Aronson, V., Abrahams, D., and Rottman, L. (1966). Importance of physical attractiveness in dating behavior. *Journal of Personality and Social Psychology, 4,* 506–516.

Walster, E. H., Walster, G. W., and Berscheid, E. (1978). *Equity: Theory and research.* Boston: Allyn & Bacon.

Walster, E., Walster, G. E., Piliavin, J., and Schmidt, L. (1973). Playing hard-to-get: Understanding an elusive phenomenon. *Journal of Personality and Social Psychology, 26,* 113–121.

Weiss, R. S. (1975). *Marital separation.* New York: Basic Books.

Wiggins, J. S., Wiggins, N. and Conger, J. C. (1977). Social Correlates of heterosexual somatic preference. *Journal of Experimental Social Psychology, 13,* 253–268.

Wilson, E. O. (1975). *Sociobiology: The new synthesis.* Cambridge, MA: Harvard University Press.

Wilson, E. O. (1978). *On human nature.* Cambridge, MA: Harvard University Press.

Winch, R. F. (1958). *Mate selection: A study of complementary needs.* New York: Harper & Row.

Zajonc, R. B. (1980). Feeling and thinking: Preferences need no inferences. *American Psychologist, 35,* 151–175.

NOTE

[1] Our thanks to Richard C. Keefe for suggesting this possibility.

CHAPTER 4

The Premenstrual Syndrome

BEVERLY ROLKER-DOLINSKY

Interestingly, although premenstrual syndrome was first described in 1931, only in the past few years has it gained widespread attention from the general public, the mass media, and over-the-counter pharmaceutical companies. Polls have shown that up to 95 percent of women *report* that they suffer from premenstrual syndrome. When specifically asked what they experience just prior to menstruation, some women report physical changes such as an increase in weight or headaches. Other women report psychological changes such as irritability and depression. Still others report various combinations of both physical and psychological changes. The severity of premenstrual symptoms also varies from woman to woman. Some women report that these symptoms are very mild and hardly noticeable, while others report symptoms so severe that they are unable to perform their normal daily responsibilities. As an example of how our culture is now recognizing the potential severity of premenstrual syndrome, note that a court of law in Great Britain recently accepted a plea of diminished capacity due to premenstrual syndrome as an adequate explanation for murder (Laws 1983).

What is this syndrome from which such a large number of women in the United States reportedly suffer but for which the type and severity of symptoms vary so widely? Can it really predispose a woman to murder? Does it really even exist? If so, what are the causes behind premenstrual syndrome?

DOES PREMENSTRUAL SYNDROME EXIST?

Prior to answering the question regarding premenstrual syndrome's existence, it would first be helpful to define the syndrome itself. In

The author wishes to thank Kathryn Kelley and Gary Dolinsky for their critical reading of early drafts of this manuscript.

general, premenstrual syndrome can be thought of as physical/psychological symptoms that begin just prior to the onset of menstruation and that decrease significantly at least during the week following menstruation.

When one notes that up to 95 percent of women report experiencing premenstrual symptoms and that several drug companies are marketing products specifically geared towards the premenstrual sufferer, questions regarding the existence of premenstrual syndrome appear moot. However, as will become apparent, if one were to review the inconsistent and contradictory findings reflective of premenstrual syndrome research, a conclusion of *nonexistence* would not be surprising or unusual. It would, nonetheless, be premature. Though the lack of clear, concise results may be due to the nonexistence of any premenstrual syndrome, it may also be due to the fact that premenstrual syndrome research has been characterized by diverse, poorly designed, and ill-controlled methodologies. Furthermore, despite the contradictions and inconsistencies in premenstrual syndrome research, one cannot ignore that the majority of women do report physical/psychological symptoms just prior to and during menstruation. Regardless of whether these reports are based on an actual physiological abnormality, personality trait, or simply one's expectations, premenstrual syndrome does exist.

In the general public, premenstrual syndrome seems to be too easily accepted at face value. On the other hand, the scientific community seems too eager to dismiss the syndrome. By providing a historical perspective on the definition of premenstrual syndrome, and by detailing the research surrounding its etiological bases, it is hoped that those too eager to accept the concept will begin to see that this area is plagued by controversy and that there are many questions in need of answers. On the other hand, for those inclined to discard the concept, it is hoped that this chapter will demonstrate that there is empirical support for both the existence of a premenstrual syndrome and its hypothetical etiological bases, although it is recognized that further research is certainly necessary.

A HISTORICAL PERSPECTIVE OF THE DEFINITION OF PREMENSTRUAL SYNDROME

Unlike other medical "illnesses," premenstrual syndrome has not been an easily defined phenomenon, primarily due to a lack of concensus among researchers. Not only have researchers disagreed on the definition of premenstrual syndrome, they have also disagreed on what it should be called. A review of the literature on the topic reveals that it is most often referred to as premenstrual syndrome.

It has also, however, been referred to as (1) premenstrual tension (Frank 1931); (2) premenstrual tension syndrome; (3) menstrual distress (Moos 1969); (4) premenstrual affective syndrome (Kashiwagi, McClure, and Wetzel 1976); (5) premenstrual changes (Harrison, Endicott, Rabkin, and Nee 1984); and even (6) cyclical syndrome (Sutherland and Stewart 1965). The varying names reflect valid, differing opinions about the type, timing, severity, and course of premenstrual symptoms.

Frank (1931) first described premenstrual tension as an increase in fatigue and irritability, a lack of concentration, and an attack of pain seven to ten days prior to the onset of menstruation. He believed these changes were due to an excess amount of estrogens. In 1959, Dalton defined premenstrual syndrome as "symptoms which recur regularly in the same phase of each menstrual cycle followed by a symptom free phase in each cycle" (Dalton 1980:61). She differentiated premenstrual syndrome from menstrual distress by defining the latter as an increase in reported symptoms during the premenstrual phase, although the same symptoms are present throughout the entire menstrual cycle. Generally, in most research performed in the area of premenstrual syndrome, investigators have operationally defined the syndrome in a manner more closely resembling Dalton's definition of menstrual distress rather than her definition of premenstrual syndrome. A proposed explanation for this definition is that it is extremely difficult to identify a *true* premenstrual sufferer as defined by Dalton, who experiences symptoms regularly during the same phase of each cycle but has no such symptoms during the rest of the cycle. For example, it is very difficult to find women who *only* experience negative mood states such as depression, irritability, and anxiety, some of the major symptoms used to define premenstrual syndrome, just prior to menses (Clare 1980). Apparently, most researchers have found it more reasonable to define the syndrome in terms of cyclic symptoms, which increase significantly during the premenstrual phase.

In an attempt to define premenstrual syndrome by its reported symptomology, Moos (1969) identified over 150 symptoms associated with the syndrome. Using factor analysis, it was found that these symptoms could be categorized into eight separate but empirically intercorrelated clusters of symptoms. These eight categories were labeled (1) pain (headaches, cramps, etc.); (2) concentration (forgetfulness, confusion, etc.); (3) behavioral change (lowered work/school performance, etc.); (4) autonomic reactions (dizziness, nausea, etc.); (5) water retention (weight gain, swollen breast, etc.); (6) negative affect (crying, loneliness, anxiety, etc.); (7) arousal (affectionate, excited, etc.); and (8) control (feelings of suffocation, chest pain, ringing in ears, etc.). Moos has suggested that the contradictory findings concerning the etiology of premenstrual syndrome may be due in part to the fact that premenstrual syndrome should really be referred to as premenstrual syndromes. Researchers have also suggested that certain subtypes of premenstrual syndrome are related to hormonal factors while others are more related to psychosocial factors, and that the lack of verification among studies may be due to a lack of differentiation between these subtypes (Moos and Leiderman 1978).

The idea that premenstrual syndrome may be more than one entity has recently been expounded upon by Halbreich, Endicott, Schacht, and Nee (1982). Agreeing with Moos and Leiderman (1978) that the great variability in premenstrual symptoms implies the existence of more than one syndrome, Halbreich et al. have developed a new assessment form (the Premenstrual Assessment Form), which takes this possibility into account. The Premenstrual Assessment Form differs from the assessment form used by Moos (the Menstrual Distress Questionnaire), since it includes an even broader variety of possible syndromes (eighteen possible subtypes) and more specific descriptions of positive as well as negative behavior, mood, and physical changes. Using the Premenstrual Assessment Form, Halbreich et al. have found that premenstrual sufferers most commonly fall into one or more of the following premenstrual subtypes: (1) major depressive syndrome (depression, appetite change, decreased energy, etc.); (2) water retention syndrome (breast pain, weight gain, abdominal discomfort, etc.); (3) general discomfort syndrome (headaches, backaches, abdominal discomfort, etc.); (4) Implusive syndrome (violent, lack of self-control, irritability); and (5) impaired social functioning syndrome (decreased judgment, lowered performance, avoidance of social activities, etc.) (Endicott, Halbriech, Schacht, and Nee 1981).

It is commonly believed that a reduction in task performance and/ or cognitive abilities constitutes defining symptoms of premenstrual syndrome. This assumption is reflected in Frank's definition of premenstrual tension, Endicott et al.'s definition of impaired social functioning syndrome, and the self-reports of many premenstrual sufferers. Due to this definition, a great deal of research has been performed to determine whether there are cyclic variations in cognitive abilities and perceptual-motor skills. Unfortunately, a majority of this research has been characterized by contradictory and/or nonreplicable results. Despite these methodological weaknesses, reviews of the literature have led to the firm conclusion that perceptual-motor skills and cognitive abilities do *not* vary with the menstrual cycle (Asso 1983; Sommer 1983). Specifically, the research indicates that the menstrual cycle does not influence a woman's ability to think, solve problems, learn, recall learned material, or make decisions. On an individual level, Asso has tentatively suggested that a reduction in cognitive skills or task performance may be more reflective of the negative beliefs a woman has towards the physical/emotional changes that occur during the menstrual cycle rather than of an actual cyclic impairment. The influence of negative expectations towards the menstrual cycle and its relationship to premenstrual syndrome will be discussed later in this chapter.

Because of the various definitions and assessment techniques used to operationalize those definitions, researchers have found an incredible variety of explanations regarding the timing, severity, and course of premenstrual symptoms. For example, based on the varying definitions, estimates of the incidence of premenstrual syndrome among women in the United States vary from 15 to 95 percent (Paige 1973).

Given these definitional problems, it is not surprising that research on the etiological basis of premenstrual syndrome has also been characterized by a variety of explanations and contradictory findings. The remainder of this chapter will review this latter research. The physiological determinants of premenstrual syndrome will first be discussed, followed by a discussion of the psychological factors that have been suggested as playing a role in the etiology of premenstrual syndrome.

THE PHYSIOLOGICAL BASIS OF PREMENSTRUAL SYNDROME

Before detailing the major hypotheses that have been developed to explain the physiological basis of premenstrual syndrome, it would be helpful first to describe a normal menstrual cycle with its hormonal/physiological fluctuations. During a twenty-eight-day menstrual cycle, the anterior pituitary gland secretes follicle stimulating hormone (FSH) a few days before menses. FSH stimulates the development of an ovarian follicle with its egg and also stimulates the ovary to secrete estrogens. Estrogens are principally involved in the buildup of the uterine lining. Estrogen secretion peaks around day twelve. This peak stimulates the production of luteinizing hormone, which is followed by ovulation. This part of the menstrual cycle is known as the follicular phase. Following ovulation, the ovarian follicle becomes a corpus luteum that triggers the release of the hormone progesterone. Progesterone causes further development of the uterine lining. If fertilization does not occur, progesterone begins to decline around day twenty four. This decrease leads to a sloughing off of the uterine lining and to menstruation. The part of the cycle following ovulation is known as the luteal phase (Abraham, Elsner, and Lucas 1978).

Numerous physiological factors have been identified as playing a role in the etiology of premenstrual syndrome (Reid and Yen 1981); however, the majority of research has generally focused on three factors: (1) the cyclic fluctuations of estrogens and progesterone; (2) the cyclic fluctuation of prolactin; and (3) the renin-angiotensin-aldosterone system.

Estrogens and Progesterone

Because negative mood states frequently occur premenstrually, postpartum, and at menopause in women, hormonal influences in premenstrual symptomology have frequently been hypothesized. As previously mentioned, it was initially believed that an excess of estrogens during the premenstrual phase was the cause of premenstrual symptoms. This theory has not been substantiated, however, since there is apparently no symptomology reflective of premenstrual syndrome during the follicular phase of the menstrual cycle, in which estrogen levels are known to peak. In fact, there appears to be a sense of well-being during the preovulatory estrogen peak (Backstrom, Sanders, Leask, Davidsen, Warner, and Bancroft 1983).

Consequently, the suggestion has been made that premenstrual symptoms are caused by a deficiency in progesterone during the luteal phase (Dalton 1959). Supporting this hypothesis, a few studies have found that progesterone levels are significantly lower two to five days prior to the onset of menstruation in women who complain of premenstrual symptoms when compared to women reporting no premenstrual symptomology (Backstrom and Carstensen 1974; Backstrom, Wide, Sodergard, and Carstensen 1976; Munday, Brush, and Taylor 1981). These findings, however, have been challenged by O'Brien, Selby, and Symonds (1980), who found progesterone levels of premenstrual sufferers to be significantly higher just prior to menses. To make matters more confusing, there have been other studies that have shown no significant differences in progesterone levels between premenstrual sufferers and non-sufferers (Sampson 1980; Taylor 1979).

Assuming that a deficiency in progesterone was the causal factor of premenstrual syndrome, many physicians have used human and synthetic progesterone to treat the syndrome. Dalton claims an 83 percent success rate in alleviating premenstrual symptoms with progesterone treatment. Not surprisingly, this claim has been disputed (Clare 1980; Sampson 1979; Smith 1975). In a carefully controlled study, Sampson (1979) alternately gave subjects progesterone and then a placebo for a two-month period. Premenstrual symptoms were rated both retrospectively and through the use of daily self-reports.

The results indicated that progesterone did not significantly reduce reported symptomology as compared to the placebo. In fact, in the majority of cases, the placebo was rated as being more effective, although not significantly so.

Rather than an excess of estrogens or an insufficient amount of progesterone, it has been suggested that premenstrual syndrome is due to the lack of balance between these hormones, with the imbalance caused by a relative excess of estrogens and a deficiency in progesterone (Morton 1950). In women with normal menstrual cycles, Abplanalp, Rose, Donnelly, and Livingston-Vaughan (1979) found no relationship between mood states and absolute levels of estrogen and progesterone; however, an association between relatively high levels of estrogens to relatively low levels of progesterone in premenstrual sufferers has been found in several studies (Backstrom et al. 1974; Munday et al. 1981; Persky, O'Brien, and Kahn 1976; Taylor 1979). Because of these findings, oral contraceptives containing both estrogen and progesterone are often used as a treatment for premenstrual syndrome. Importantly, however, although many studies have reported the effectiveness of oral contrtaceptives in reducing premenstrual depression, very few of these studies have used well-controlled designs (Clare 1979). Properly designed studies that have used double-blind, placebo procedures have not found the use of oral contraceptives to be effective in reducing premenstrual symptoms (Cullberg 1972; Morris and Udry 1972; Smith 1975).

A relatively new treatment based on the estrogen/progesterone imbalance hypothesis is the administration of pyridoxine (Vitamin B_6). Double-blind, placebo designs have found that pyridoxine decreases estrogens, increases progesterone, and decreases the symptoms of premenstrual nervousness, tension, mood swings, and irritability (Abraham 1983; Abraham and Hargrove 1980; Kerr 1977). A major problem associated with pyridoxine treatment has been the association of a very high dose of pyridoxine with sensory neuropathy (Schaumberg, Kaplan, and Windebank 1983). Sensory neuropathy is characterized by gradually progressive deficits in sensation, especially in the distal limb sensation of position and vibration. This finding suggests that the treatment of pyridoxine for premenstrual syndrome should be used with caution.

Prolactin

Elevated levels of the hormone prolactin have been associated with increases in water, sodium, and potassium retention, with a reduction in glucose tolerance, and with the stimulation of progesterone synthesis (Andersen, Larsen, Steenstrup, Svendstrup, and Nielsen 1977;

Horrobin, Karmali, Mtabaji, Manko, and Nassar 1976). During a normal menstrual cycle, serum prolactin levels are slightly higher in the luteal phase as compared to the follicular phase (Horrobin et al. 1976; Vekemans, Delvoye, L'Hermite, and Robyn 1977). Because water retention-related symptoms such as bloatedness, swollen breasts, and weight gain are often associated with premenstrual experiences, prolactin has often been suggested as playing a crucial role in premenstrual symptomology (Carroll and Steiner 1978). Specifically, the hypothesis is that premenstrual symptoms are caused by an increase in the concentration of prolactin during the premenstrual phase. Characteristic of premenstrual syndrome research in general, both support (Halbreich, Ben-David, Assael, and Bornstein 1976; Horrobin et al. 1976) and a lack of support (Epstein, McNeilly, Murray, and Hockaday 1975; McNeilly and Chard 1974; O'Brien and Symonds 1982) have been found for this hypothesis.

Under the assumption that excess prolactin does play a role in premenstrual symptomology, many premenstrual sufferers have been treated with bromocriptine, known to suppress prolactin production. Treatment with bromocriptine has been associated with improvement in bloatedness, depression, anxiety, irritability, and breast swelling (Andersch, Hahn, Wendestam, Ohman, and Abrahamsson 1978; Benedek-Jasmann and Hearn-Sturtevant 1976; Graham, Harding, Wise, and Berriman 1978; Ylostalo, Kauppila, Puulakka, Ronnberg, and Janne 1982). The possibility that the beneficial effects of bromocriptine are simply representative of a placebo effect still needs to be addressed (Andersen et al. 1977; Elsner, Buster, Schindler, Nessim, and Abraham 1980; Ghose and Coppen 1977; Kullander and Svanberg 1979).

The Renin-Angiotensin-Aldosterone System

The secretion of aldosterone has been implicated as a cause of premenstrual symptoms, primarily because it is the most potent, naturally occurring sodium-retaining hormone known. As with prolactin, the hypothesis is that there is a significantly higher amount of aldosterone secretion in women who complain of premenstrual symptoms than in women without any premenstrual symptomology.

Simultaneously measuring emotional changes, weight increase, and sodium retention, Janowsky, Berens, and Davis (1973) found that negative affect, weight, and the sodium-potassium ratio all increased approximately eleven days before menstruation, peaked a day before menstruation, and began to decrease dramatically with the onset of menstruation. Noting that there is no evidence showing that aldosterone directly influences behavior, Janowsky et al. hypothesized that angiotensin, as activated by renin, is the substance that produces cyclic behavioral changes. Angiotensin secretion is known to fluctuate in parallel with aldosterone secretion and has been found to influence animal behavior. Janowsky et al. therefore hypothesized that premenstrual syndrome is due to a complex interaction within the renin-angiotensin-aldosterone system. In support of their hypothesis, Janowsky et al. found a significantly higher amount of aldosterone during the premenstrual phase in women suffering from premenstrual symptoms. More recently, though, the relationship between excess aldosterone and premenstrual symptoms has not been found to be significantly different between premenstrual sufferers and nonsufferers (Munday 1977; Munday et al. 1981; O'Brien, Craven, Selby, and Symonds 1979). Despite these contradictory findings, O'Brien et al. have found that the administration of spirolactone, an aldosterone antagonist, does significantly reduce the number of reported symptoms in women who suffer from premenstrual syndrome. Furthermore, Abraham (1983) has found that the suppression of aldosterone through the use of pyridoxine significantly reduces the premenstrual symptoms of breast tenderness, abdominal bloating, and the sensation of weight gain.

The hypotheses that prolactin and/or the renin-angiotensin-aldosterone system are involved in the etiology of premenstrual syndrome are both highly dependent upon the assumption that premenstrual sufferers do experience water retention and weight gain. Unfortunately, even this basic assumption can not be consistently supported. As previously mentioned, Janowsky et al. did find a significant increase in sodium retention and weight gain in premenstrual sufferers. Reeves, Garvin, and McElin (1971) have produced similar results. There are several studies, however, that have found no consistent relationship between premenstrual weight gain and symptomology (Andersch, Andersson, and Isaksson 1978; Bruce and Russell 1962; Golub, Menduke, and Conly 1965; Herzberg 1971).

Summary

As can be seen in Table 1, no one, physiologically based etiological cause has been firmly supported by data. In reviewing the data from a methodological perspective, Rubinow and Roy-Byrne (1984) have concluded that the inconsistencies among findings on premenstrual syndrome etiology are due to (1) the lack of a clear, consistently used definition of premenstrual syndrome; (2) improper sampling methods and the use of heterogeneous samples; (3) differences in methodology and statistical analysis; and (4) the probability that there is more than one factor involved in the etiology of premenstrual syndrome.

Table 1. *Summary of Hormonally Based Theories of Premenstrual Syndrome Etiology*

Theory	Source
Excess of Estrogen:	
Supported	Frank (1931)
Not Supported	Backstrom et al. (1983)
Deficiency of Progesterone:	Backstrom and Carstensen (1974);
Supported	Backstrom et al. (1976); Dalton (1959);
	Munday et al. (1981)
Not Supported	O'Brien et al. (1980); Sampson (1980);
	Taylor (1979)
Imbalance of Estrogen/	Backstrom and Carstensen (1974);
Progesterone Levels:	Munday et al. (1981); Persky et al.
Supported	(1976); Taylor (1979)
Not Supported	Cullberg (1972); Morris and Udry
	(1972); Smith (1975)
Excess of Prolactin:	Carroll and Steiner (1978); Halbreich
Supported	et al. (1976); Horrobin et al. (1976)
Not Supported	Epstein et al. (1975); McNeilly and
	Chard (1974); O'Brien and Symonds
	(1982)
Excess of Aldosterone:	
Supported	Janowsky et al. (1973)
Not Supported	Munday (1977); Munday et al. (1981);
	O'Brien et al. (1979)

Despite the lack of consistency in the research findings, there is enough evidence to conclude that there is a hormonal influence in premenstrual symptomology. To become more specific and conclude that premenstrual syndrome is due to an excess of estrogens, a deficiency in progesterone, or an excess of prolactin or aldosterone, is currently impossible. More than likely, future research will show that the physiological basis of premenstrual syndrome is a complex interaction among these hormones. Until the aforementioned methodological weaknesses are addressed, however, it will be impossible to make any specific conclusions regarding the physiological etiology of premenstrual syndrome.

THE PSYCHOLOGICAL BASIS OF PREMENSTRUAL SYNDROME

Just as there have been several physiological factors implicated in the etiology of premenstrual syndrome, so have there been several proposed psychological factors. Specifically, premenstrual syndrome has been related to, or hypothesized as a function of, psychiatric disorders, neurotic disorders, affective disorders, attitudes towards femininity and sexuality, and attitudes and expectations regarding the menstrual cycle itself.

Psychiatric Tendencies and Premenstrual Syndrome

Repeatedly, a consistent relationship has been found between admissions of women to psychiatric hospitals and the phase of the menstrual cycle the women are in. In general, the highest frequency of psychiatric admissions occurs among women who are menstruating. The premenstrual phase is the second highest with respect to the frequency of psychiatric admissions. The lowest frequency of psychiatric admissions is associated with the midcycle (Abramowitz, Baker, and Fleischer 1982; Endo, Daiguji, Asano, Yamashita, and Takahashi 1978; Glass, Heninger, Lansky, and Tulan 1971; Janowsky, Gorney, Castelnuovo-Tedesco, and Stone 1969; Luggin, Bernsted, and Petersson 1984). Furthermore, women diagnosed as having a psychiatric disorder are found to score significantly higher on measures assessing premenstrual syndrome than are women with no history of a mental disorder (Clare 1983; Zola, Meyerson, Reznikoff, Thornton, and Concool 1979). Given the relationship between premenstrual syndrome, psychiatric admissions, and psychiatric patient reports of premenstrual symptoms, it has been suggested that psychiatric tendencies may play a role in the etiology of premenstrual syndrome. The research however, has not supported this hypothesis. In a well-designed study, Wetzel, Reich, McClure, and Wald (1975) prospectively studied the relationship between psychiatric disorders and premenstrual syndrome. Eight hundred and seventy-four women beginning their first year at Washington University in St. Louis, Michigan, filled out questionnaires assessing their experiences during the menstrual cycle. Each woman was then diagnosed for premenstrual affective syndrome, characterized by the experience of premenstrual depression. Over the next few years, the names of each of the subjects were checked against student health files from the student health center's psychiatric services. The results indicated that 135 of the 874 women were seen in psychiatric services. Of these 135 women, women diagnosed as experiencing premenstrual affective syndrome were significantly more likely to attend the clinic and be diagnosed as suffering from an *affective* disorder rather than from a psychiatric disorder. Kashiwagi et al. (1976) lent support to the findings of Wetzel et al. by discovering that the reported rate of premenstrual affective syndrome was not significantly different in subjects diagnosed with a psychiatric disorder other than depression, as compared to those subjects with no history of a psychiatric disorder.

In general, the research appears to indicate that psychiatric disorders do not play a major role in the etiology of premenstrual syndrome. Although women diagnosed as having a psychiatric disorder tend to report more severe premenstrual symptoms, the actual rate of incidence of premenstrual syndrome in psychiatric patients is no higher than in a normal population of women.

Is Premenstrual Syndrome a Type of Neurosis?

Neuroticism, as defined by the Maudsley Personality Inventory, is characterized by a general emotional lability of the personality, emotional overresponsiveness, and increased likelihood of a neurotic breakdown under stress. Coppen and Kessel (1963) correlated the Maudsley Personality Inventory with dysmenorrhea and premenstrual syndrome. They found no significant relationship between dysmenorrhea and neuroticism, however, they did find that the psychological symptoms of irritability, depression, and tension were positively correlated with neuroticism and that these symptoms were significantly worse just prior to menstruation. Several other studies have also found significant positive correlations between neuroticism and the premenstrual symptoms of tension, irritability, and depression (Gruba and Ruhrbaugh 1975; Levitt and Lubin 1967).

Given this correlation between neuroticism and premenstrual symptoms, one would expect a significantly higher incidence of premenstrual syndrome in women diagnosed as neurotic. Coppen (1965) examined the incidence of premenstrual syndrome in neurotic patients, schizophrenic patients, and patients suffering from affective disorders. The results indicated that neurotic patients complained significantly more of menstrual pain, premenstrual irritability, tension, depression, anxiety, and headaches than did the schizophrenic group, the affective disorder group, or a control group of women with no history of mental disorder. Discussing the results, Coppen concluded that the incidence of premenstrual syndrome in neurotic patients is significantly higher than expected by chance. When correlating the incidence of premenstrual syndrome with psychiatric admission, Kramp (1968) found that 42 percent of the women admitted during a one-year period were admitted during the premenstrual phase. The data also showed that 60 percent of the women diagnosed as suffering from premenstrual syndrome were also diagnosed as having a non-psychotic disorder (e.g., neurosis, character neurosis, or psychopathic personality). Of additional interest, Kramp found that the incidence of neurotic symptoms during childhood and early youth was of significant importance in predicting subsequent premenstrual syndrome.

Kashiwagi, McClure, and Wetzel (1976) differentiated between different types of neuroticism and found that, when those neurotic patients who had a life history of depression were excluded, no significant correlation was found between neuroticism and premenstrual syndrome. Kashiwagi et al. concluded that the occurrence of premenstrual syndrome depends more on a history of depression than on a neurotic disorder in general.

The correlation between neuroticism and premenstrual syndrome implies that women suffering from premenstrual syndrome should have a higher level of trait anxiety than would nonsufferers. The results are mixed with respect to this hypothesis. Golub (1976) did not find a significant correlation between trait anxiety and the premenstrual symptoms of anxiety and depression. In fact, the results indicated that premenstrual sufferers were as well adjusted as nonsufferers and were well within the normal levels of trait anxiety. Halbreich and Kas (1977), however, have found trait anxiety to be significantly higher in premenstrual sufferers than in nonsufferers and have concluded that women with trait anxiety are predisposed to premenstrual syndrome.

It is important to point out that there is little evidence that indicates premenstrual syndrome is a neurotic disorder in and of itself. Although Rees (1953) did find a positive correlation between the intensity of premenstrual symptoms and the severity of neurosis, he also found that severe premenstrual symptoms occur in women with little evidence of a neurotic predisposition. In support of this result, Walker (1974) found no differences with respect to neurotic tendencies or personal functioning between women who suffer from severe premenstrual symptoms and women who do not experience premenstrual symptoms.

In general, a neurotic predisposition apparently increases the probability that a women will experience premenstrual symptoms. However, the data clearly show that to be diagnosed neurotic does not guarantee a diagnosis of premenstrual syndrome and that experiencing premenstrual symptoms does not mean a woman has neurotic tendencies.

Premenstrual Syndrome and Its Relationship to Affective Disorders

Several studies have consistently shown a relationship between the menstrual cycle and mood changes. During the premenstrual and menstrual phases, many women report increases in negative mood states such as depression, anxiety, tension, and irritability. The midcycle and follicular phases are generally characterized by more positive feelings of well-being and pleasantness (Campos and Thurow 1978; Dennerstein and Burrows 1979; Ivey and Bardwick 1968; Silbergeld, Brast, and Noble 1971; Sanders, Warner, Backstrom, and Bancroft 1983; Smith 1976).

Because of this relationship between cyclic mood changes and the premenstrual phase, it has been suggested that premenstrual syndrome may be etiologically related to or influenced by affective disorders (McClure, Reich, and Wetzel 1971; Schuckit, Daly, Herrman, and Hineman 1975). As previously mentioned, Wetzel et al. (1975) and Kashiwagi et al. (1976) both found a significant relationship between premenstrual affective syndrome and affective disorders in general. Diamond, Rubinstein, Dunner, and Fieve (1976) have lent further support to these findings by demonstrating that the frequency of premenstrual and menstrual *affective* complaints are significantly higher in patients with affective disorders than in women with no history of affective disorders. Importantly, Diamond et al. also found that there were no significant differences in the frequency, severity, or type of *somatic* premenstrual complaints between affective disorder patients and control subjects. Endicott, Halbreich, Schacht, and Nee (1981) found that significantly more women diagnosed as suffering from an affective disorder were likely to experience certain premenstrual subtypes—major depressive syndrome, water retention syndrome, general discomfort syndrome, and impaired social functioning syndrome—than were women diagnosed with a nonaffective mental disorder or women who had no history of any mental disorder.

The results of the Diamond et al. and Endicott et al. studies indicate that there is a relationship between premenstrual syndrome and affective disorders, *but* that this relationship is highly dependent upon the type of symptoms included when defining premenstrual syndrome. To be an affective disorder, premenstrual syndrome should be characterized by the symptoms of recurrent depression, anxiety, and/or hostility. Haskett, Steiner, Osmon and Carroll (1980) have found, however, that none of these affective states *alone* can be considered as the major symptom of premenstrual syndrome. Haskett et al. finally concluded that premenstrual syndrome should not be thought of as some type of recurrent affective disorder.

If premenstrual syndrome is an affective disorder, one could hypothesize that treatment with an antidepressive medication would reduce reports of premenstrual symptomology. This hypothesis has not, however, been borne out. Using a single-blind, placebo design, Harrison, Endicott, Rabkin, and Nee (1984) found that antidepressive medication is no better than a placebo in reducing premenstrual symptoms. Reviews of the research relating premenstrual syndrome to affective disorders have concluded that the relationship between the two is very weak (Gitlin and Pasnau 1983; Lahmeyer 1984).

The Influence of Attitudes toward Femininity and Sexuality on Premenstrual Syndrome

Since 1939, several psychodynamic personality theorists have suggested that premenstrual syndrome represents a rejection of the feminine and sexual roles, aggression toward the mother and males in general, and a form of self-punishment (Bernsted, Luggin, and Petersson 1984; Foresti, Ferraro, Reithaar, Berlanda, Volpi, Drago, and Cerutti 1981; Fortin, Wittkower, and Kalz 1958; May 1976; Menninger 1939; Paulson 1961; Shader and Ohly 1970; Shainess 1961). When looking at the relationship between premenstrual symptoms and rejection of the feminine role, Berry and McGuire (1972) found that role acceptance, as defined by Paulson (1961), was significantly and negatively correlated with the Moos Menstrual Distress Questionnaire (MMDQ) subscales of pain, concentration, autonomic reaction, and control. Although Berry and McGuire concluded that rejection of the female role is related to menstrual distress symptoms, they emphasized that there was no empirical evidence to support a psychological etiological basis for premenstrual syndrome.

Rejection of the female sexual role has also been hypothesized as being related to premenstrual symptom experiences (Delaney, Lupton, and Toth (1976). In support of this hypothesis, a few studies have demonstrated that premenstrual sufferers hold significantly more negative attitudes towards their bodies, genitals, and sex than do nonsufferers (Osofsky and Fisher 1967; Paige 1973; Watts, Dennerstein, and Horne 1980). In corroboration with these findings, Wood, Larsen, and Williams (1979) have found that premenstrual tension sufferers are significantly more likely to report "problems" with their sex lives than are nonsufferers. Not surprisingly, the relationship between negative sexual attitudes and premenstrual syndrome severity is not perfect. For example, May (1976) found that premenstrual sufferers hold significantly more *positive* attitudes towards sex than do nonsufferers.

The adherence to more traditional feminine sex role attitudes has also been suggested as an etiological factor in premenstrual syndrome (Brattesani and Silverthorne 1978; Gough 1975; Schneider and Scheider-Duker 1974). Beck (1970) supported this hypothesis by finding that more traditional attitudes towards marriage were associated with reports of psychological premenstrual symptoms. Kehoe (1978) also found a positive correlation between traditional sex role attitudes and premenstrual symptoms. Furthermore, the results did not support the previously mentioned hypothesis in which premenstrual sufferers are thought to reject traditional feminine values. Finding similar results, Waggener (1981) has found that women who report the highest number of premenstrual symptoms also hold more traditional values with respect to sex roles. Interestingly, severe premenstrual syndrome sufferers were also found to be under the highest amounts of marital and life stress.

The correlation between traditional feminine values and premenstrual syndrome is not universal. Watts, Dennerstein, and Horne (1980) have found no difference between premenstrual sufferers and nonsufferers with respect to feminine values. In a later study, Spencer-Gardner, Dennerstein, and Burrows (1983) again found no support for the hypotheses that premenstrual sufferers hold more traditional feminine beliefs or that they reject the traditional female role. Instead, Spencer-Gardner et al. found that women suffering from premenstrual syndrome have lower self-esteem, negative attitudes towards menstruation, and feel they have little control over the events in their lives.

Although based solely on correlational data, attitudes towards femininity and sexuality do appear to influence the severity of premenstrual symptoms. Based on the data for the relationship between premenstrual syndrome and traditional female values, Waggener has proposed a hierarchical model with respect to the etiology of premenstrual syndrome. This model is based on the hypothesis that some minimum level of physiological sensitivity is required for a woman to experience premenstrual syndrome. Additional factors such as beliefs and stress levels are thought to contribute to the actual severity of the syndrome.

The Powerful Influence of Expectations

It has been hypothesized that premenstrual syndrome is the result of our expectations and attitudes toward menstruation, and that the reports of premenstrual symptoms are simply reflective of stereotypic beliefs concerning menstruation rather than of symptoms actually experienced. The suggestion has also been made that using the retrospective questionnaire as the primary assessment method for premenstrual syndrome is actually assessing stereotypic beliefs concerning menstruation. While assessing whether the Moos Menstrual Distress Questionnaire (MMDQ) is actually a measure of stereotypic beliefs, Parlee (1974) found that male and female subjects make very similar responses to questions about what women experience during the menstrual cycle. Parlee concluded that the MMDQ was a measure of stereotypic beliefs rather than a measure of the actual experiences occurring premenstrually. To support this conclusion, several other researchers have compared womens' reports of premenstrual experiences using retrospective questionnaires with daily self-reports of physical/psychological changes. Most studies have found *no* relationship between retrospectively reported premenstrual symptom experiences and actual premenstrual experiences as measured by daily self-reports. Therefore, although most women report physical/psychological changes just prior to menstruation, daily self-reports indicate there is minimal change in the majority of women (Abplanalp, Donnelly, and Rose 1979; Englander-Golden, Whitmore, and Dienstbier 1978; May 1976). In further support of these findings, Brooks, Ruble, and Clark (1977) have found that women report significantly more negative premenstrual experiences when asked to respond to the MMDQ as if they were in the premenstrual phase as compared to when they are asked to respond to the questionnaire as if they were in the midcycle phase.

Using an ingenious design, Ruble (1977) led subjects to believe it was possible to detect exactly when a subject was going to menstruate. The results indicated that subjects who were led to believe they were premenstrual but, in reality, were in the midcycle phase, reported significantly more premenstrual symptoms than did those who were correctly told that they were in the midcycle of the menstrual phase. Ruble concluded that the experience of premenstrual symptoms may be highly related to a woman's awareness of the menstrual phase she is in and not due only to hormonal fluctuations.

While assessing whether retrospective measures assess beliefs towards menstruation rather than actual experiences, Slade (1984) found that daily self-reports indicated that the physical symptoms of pain and water retention did significantly increase during the premenstrual and menstrual phases; however, reports of cyclic variations of psychological symptoms were not found. Slade concluded that the effects of the menstrual cycle are less significant on women than previously believed.

As can be surmised, the above findings caused an ensuing debate regarding whether premenstrual syndrome is an actual syndrome caused by abnormal hormonal flunctuation or simply a psychological manifestation. An excellent way to answer this question was to examine women who had undergone simple hysterectomies. The hormones that are the possible causes of premenstrual syndrome are still operating in such women, however the negative expectations concerning menstruation should no longer play a part since they no longer experience menstruation (Osborn 1981). This design, unfortunately, has not yielded consistent findings. Beumont, Richards, and Gelder (1975) found that hysterectomized patients showed no significant cyclic changes with respect to mental or physical symptoms, thus supporting the hypothesis that premenstrual syndrome is more a belief than an actuality. More recently, however, Backstrom, Boyle, and Baird (1981) did find cyclical changes in premenstrual symptoms, with feelings of tension, irritability, depression, and breast tenderness all significantly increasing during the late luteal phase of hysterectomized patients.

What can be made of these contradictory findings? Does premenstrual syndrome have a physiological basis, or is it simply a psychological manifestation experienced by a very large group of women? Given the large amount of evidence correlating hormonal fluctuations and premenstrual symptoms, and the finding that at least some hysterectomized patients still experience premenstrual symptoms, it seems unlikely that premenstrual syndrome is reflective only of women's expectations towards menstruation.

Summary

Although most studies concerned with the role psychological factors play in the etiology of premenstrual syndrome have been poorly designed, the high rate of placebo effectiveness and the high retrospective reports of symptom experience reflect the important role psychological factors play in the reporting and experience of premenstrual symptoms. As can be seen from Table 2, it is not yet possible to make any firm conclusions regarding the influence of psychological factors on premenstrual syndrome. Tentatively, the research does seem to indicate that, given a hormonal predisposition to premenstrual syndrome, various psychological factors such as psychotic, neurotic, or affective disorder predispositions, or attitudes towards femininity, sexuality, and menstruation can influence the perceived occurrence and severity of premenstrual symptoms.

Given the relationship between various psychological factors and premenstrual symptoms, it has been suggested that psychotherapy would be a useful treatment for premenstrual syndrome. Short-term therapy emphasizing the development of coping skills, the improvement of attitudes towards femininity and menstruation, an increase in self-esteem, and the development of relaxation skills should all theoretically help women deal more effectively with the experience of premenstrual syndrome. At this point in time, no adequately controlled studies have been able to demonstrate the effectiveness or noneffectiveness of psychotherapy in the treatment of premenstrual syndrome (Green 1982).

CONCLUSION

The topic of study known as premenstrual syndrome is plagued by controversy and contradiction. Currently, any conclusions made

Table 2. *Summary of Psychologically Based Theories of Premenstrual Syndrome Etiology*

Related to	Source
Neurotic Disorders: Supported	Coppen and Kessel (1963); Gruba and Ruhrbaugh (1975); Levitt and Lubin (1967)
Not Supported	Kashiwagi et al. (1976); Rees (1953)
Psychiatric Disorders: Supported	Clare (1983); Zola et al. (1979);
Not Supported	Kashiwagi et al. (1976); Wetzel et al. (1975)
Affective Disorders: Supported	Diamond et al. (1976); Endicott et al. (1981); Kashiwagi et al. (1976); Wetzel et al. (1975)
Not Supported	Gitlin and Pasnau (1983); Harrison et al. (1984); Haskett et al. (1980); Lahmeyer (1984)
Rejection of the Female Role: Supported	Berry and McGuire (1972)
Not Supported	Kehoe (1978); Spencer-Gardner et al. (1983); Watts et al. (1980)
More Traditional Female Sex Role Attitudes: Supported	Beck (1970); Kehoe (1978); Waggener (1981)
Not Supported	Spencer-Gardner et al. (1983); Watts et al. (1980)
Negative Attitudes and Expectations towards Menstruation: Supported	Beumont et al. (1975); Brooks et al. (1977); Ruble (1977)
Not Supported	Backstrom et al. (1981)

with respect to the symptomology, physiological etiology, psychosocial etiology, or even the name premenstrual syndrome itself is highly dependent upon the particular research article being reviewed. Although many women report that they suffer from premenstrual symptoms, it has been sufficiently demonstrated that a majority of these reports are reflective more of the beliefs women hold towards menstrual experiences rather than of actual experiences as measured by daily self-reports. There is a sufficient amount of evidence to conclude that there are both physiological and psychological factors influencing the occurrence and severity of premenstrual symptoms. Unfortunately, more definite and specific conclusions are not possible since the research on premenstrual syndrome has been characterized by poorly designed and controlled studies.

For more definite conclusions to be made, several methodological improvements will have to be made. These methodologies should include the use of (1) a clear, consistently used definition of premenstrual syndrome; (2) prospective methods of data collection; (3) better sampling methods; (4) controls for experimenter bias and demand characteristics; and (5) notations on at what point in the cycle data is collected (Abplanalp 1983). Due to the lack of consistency surrounding the definition and etiology of premenstrual syndrome, it is not surprising that no single treatment has been demonstrably effective in reducing premenstrual symptoms.

REFERENCES

Abplanalp, J. M. (1983). Psychologic components of the premenstrual syndrome: Evaluating the research and choosing the treatment. *The Journal of Reproductive Medicine, 28,* 517–524.

Abplanalp, J. M., Donnelly, A. F., and Rose, R. M. (1979). Psychoendocrinology of the menstrual cycle: I. Enjoyment of daily activities and moods. *Psychosomatic Medicine, 41,* 587–604.

Abplanalp, J. M., Rose, R. M., Donnelly, A. F., and Livingston-Vaughan, L. (1979). Psychoendocrinology of the menstrual cycle: II. The relationship between the enjoyment of activities, moods and reproductive hormones. *Psychosomatic Medicine, 41,* 605–615.

Abraham, G. E. (1983). Nutritional factors in the etiology of the premenstrual tension syndromes. *Journal of Reproductive Medicine, 28,* 446–464.

Abraham, G. E., Elsner, C., and Lucas, L. A. (1978). Hormonal and behavioral changes during the menstrual cycle. *Senologia, 3,* 33–38.

Abraham, G. E., and Hargrove, J. (1980). Effect of B_6 on premenstrual symptomology in women with premenstrual tension syndrome: A double-blind crossover study. *Infertility, 3,* 155–159.

Abramowitz, E. S., Baker, A. H., and Fleischer, S. F. (1982). Onset of depressive psychiatric crisis and the menstrual cycle. *American Journal of Psychiatry, 139,* 475–478.

Andersch, B., Andersson, M., and Isaksson, B. (1978). Body water and weight in patients with premenstrual tension. *British Journal of Obstetrics and Gynecology, 85,* 546–550.

Andersch, B., Hahn, L., Wendestam, C., Ohman, R., and Abrahamsson, L. (1978). Treatment of premenstrual tension syndrome with bromocriptine. *Acta Endocrinologica, Supplement 216, 88,* 165–174.

Andersen, A. N., Larsen, J.F., Steenstrup, O. R., Svendstrup, B., and Nielsen, J. (1977). Effect of bromocriptine on the premenstrual syndrome: A double-blind clinical trial. *British Journal of Obstetrics and Gynaecology, 84,* 370–374.

Asso, D. (1983). *The real menstrual cycle.* Chichester: John Wiley and Sons.

Backstrom, C. T., Boyle, H., and Baird, D. T. (1981). Persistance of symptoms of premenstrual tension in hysterectomized women. *British Journal of Obstetrics and Gynaecology, 88,* 530–536.

Backstrom, T., and Carstensen, H. (1974). Estrogen and progesterone in plasma in relation to premenstrual tension. *Journal of Steroid Biochemistry, 5,* 257–260.

Backstrom, T., Sanders, D., Leask, R., Davidsen, D., Warner, P., and Bancroft, J. (1983). Mood, sexuality, hormones and the menstrual cycle II:

Hormone levels and their relationship to the premenstrual sundrome. *Psychosomatic Medicine, 45,* 503–507.

Backstrom, T., Wide, L., Sodergard, R., and Carstensen, H. (1976). FSH, LH TeBG–capacity, estrogen and progesterone in women with premenstrual tension during the luteal phase. *Journal of Steroid Biochemistry, 7,* 473–476.

Beck, A. C. (1970). Chronological fluctuations of six premenstrual tension variables and their relation to traditional-modern sex-role stereotypes. *Dissertation Abstracts International, 31(4),* 4980B.

Benedek-Jaszmann, L.T., and Hearn-Sturtevant, M.D. (1976). Premenstrual tension and functional infertility: Aetiology and treatment. *Lancet, 1,* 1095–1098.

Bernsted, L., Luggin, R., and Petersson, B. (1984). Psychosocial considerations of the premenstrual syndrome. *Acta Psychiatrica Scandinavica, 69,* 455–460.

Berry, C., and McGuire, F. L. (1972). Menstrual distress and acceptance of sexual role. *American Journal of Obstetrics and Gynecology, 114,* 83–87.

Beumont, P. J. V., Richards, D. H., and Gelder, M. O. (1975). A study of minor psychiatric and physical symptoms during the menstrual cycle. *British Journal of Psychiatry, 126,* 431–434.

Brattesani, K., and Silverthorne, C. P. (1978). Social psychological factors of menstrual distress. *The Journal of Social Psychology, 106,* 139–140.

Brooks, J., Ruble, D., and Clark, A. (1977). College women's attitudes and expectations concerning menstrual related changes. *Psychosomatic Medicine, 39,* 288–298.

Bruce, J., and Russell, G. F. (1962). Premenstrual tension: A study of weight changes and balances of water, sodium and potassium. *Lancet, 2,* 267–271.

Campos, F., and Thurow, C. (1978). Attributions of moods and symptoms to the menstrual cycle. *Personality and Social Psychology Bulletin, 4,* 272–276.

Carroll, B. J., and Steiner, M. (1978). The psychobiology of premenstrual dysphoria: The role of prolactin. *Psychoneuroendocrinology, 3,* 171–180.

Clare, A. W. (1979). The treatment of premenstrual symptoms. *British Journal of Psychiatry, 135,* 576–579.

Clare, A. W. (1980). Progesterone, fluid, and electrolytes in premenstrual syndrome. *British Medical Journal, 281* 810–811.

Clare, A. W. (1983). Psychiatric and social aspects of premenstrual complaint. *Psychological Medicine, 4,* 1–58.

Coppen, A. (1965). The prevalence of menstrual disorders in psychiatric patients. *British Journal of Psychiatry, 111,* 155–167.

Coppen, A., and Kessel, N. (1963). Menstruation and personality. *British Journal of Psychiatry, 109,* 711–721.

Cullberg, J. (1972). Mood changes and menstrual symptoms with different gestagen/estrogen combinations. *Acta Psychiatrica Scandinavica, Supplement 236,* 1–86.

Dalton, K. (1959). Menstruation and acute psychiatric illness. *British Medical Journal, 1,* 148–149.

Dalton, K. (1980). Progesterone, fluid, and electrolytes in premenstrual syndrome. *British Medical Journal, 281,* 61.

Delaney, J., Lupton, M. J., and Toth, E. (1976). *The curse: A cultural history of menstruation.* Toronto: Clarke, Irwin and Company Limited.

Dennerstein, L., and Burrows, G. D. (1979). Affect and the menstrual cycle. *Journal of Affective Disorders, 1,* 77–92.

Diamond, S. B., Rubinstein, A. A., Dunner, D. L., and Fieve, R. R. (1976). Menstrual problems in women with primary affective illness. *Comprehensive Psychiatry, 17,* 541–548.

Elsner, C. W., Buster, J. E., Schindler, R. A., Nessim, S. A., and Abraham, G. E. (1980). Bromocriptine in the treatment of premenstrual tension syndrome. *Obstetrics and Gynecology, 56,* 723–726.

Endicott, J., Halbreich, U., Schacht, S., and Nee, J. (1981). Premenstrual changes and affective disorders. *Psychosomatic Medicine, 43,* 519–529.

Endo, M., Daiguji, M., Asano, Y., Yamashita, I., and Takahashi, S. (1978). Periodic psychosis recurring in association with the menstrual cycle. *Journal of Clinical Psychiatry, 39,* 456–466.

Englander-Golden, P., Whitmore, M. R., and Dienstbier, R. A. (1978). Menstrual cycle as focus of study and self reports of moods and behavior. *Motivation and Emotion, 2,* 75–86.

Epstein, M. T., McNeilly, A. S., Murray, M. A., and Hockaday, T. D. (1975). Plasma testosterone and prolactin in the menstrual cycle. *Clinical Endocrinology, 4,* 531–535.

Foresti, G., Ferraro, M., Reithaar, P., Berlanda, C., Volpi, M., Drago, D., and Cerutti, R. (1981). Premenstrual syndrome and personality traits: A study of 110 pregnant patients. *Psychotherapy and Psychosomatics, 36,* 37–42.

Fortin, J. N., Wittkower, E. D., and Kalz, F. (1958). A psychosomatic approach to the premenstrual tension syndrome: A preliminary report. *Canadian Medical Association Journal, 79,* 978–981.

Frank, R. T. (1931). The hormonal causes of premenstrual tension. *Archives of Neurology and Psychiatry, 26,* 1053–1057.

Ghose, K., and Coppen, A. (1977). Bromocriptine and premenstrual syndrome: Controlled study. *British Medical Journal, 1,* 147–148.

Gitlin, M. J., and Pasnau, R. O. (1983). Depression in obstetric and gynecology patients. *Journal of Psychiatric Treatment and Evaluation, 5,* 421–428.

Glass, G. S., Heninger,G. R., Lansky, M., and Tulan, K. (1971). Psychiatric emergency related to the menstrual cycle. *American Journal of Psychiatry, 128,* 705–711.

Golub, L. J., Menduke, H., and Conly, S. S. (1965). Weight changes in college women during the menstrual cycle. *American Journal of Obstetrics and Gynecology, 91,* 89–94.

Golub, S. (1976). The magnitude of premenstrual anxiety and depression. *Psychosomatic Medicine, 38,* 4–12.

Gough, H. G. (1975). Personality factors related to reported severity of menstrual distress. *Journal of Abnormal Psychology, 84,* 59–65.

Graham, J. J., Harding, P. E., Wise, P. H., and Berriman, H. (1978). Prolactin suppression in the treatment of premenstrual syndrome. *The Medical Journal of Australia, Special Supplement, 2,* 18–20.

Green, J. (1982). Recent trends in the treatment of premenstrual syndrome; A critical review. In R. C. Friedman (ed.), *Behavior and the menstrual cycle* (pp. 367–395). New York: Marcel-Dekker, Inc.

Gruba, G. H., and Ruhrbaugh, M. (1975). MMPI correlates of menstrual distress. *Psychosomatic Medicine, 37,* 265–273.

Halbreich, U., Ben-David, M., Assael, M., and Bornstein, R. (1976). Serum-prolactin in women with premenstrual syndrome. *Lancet, 2,* 654–656.

Halbreich, U., Endicott, J., Schacht, S., and Nee, J. (1982). The diversity of premenstrual changes as reflected in the premenstrual assessment form. *Acta Psychiatrica Scandinavica, 65,* 46–65.

Halbreich, U., and Kas, D. (1977). Variations in the Taylor Manifest Anxiety Scale of women with premenstrual syndrome. *Journal of Psychosomatic Research, 21,* 391–393.

Harrison, W. M., Endicott, J., Rabkin, J. G., and Nee, J. (1984). Treatment of premenstrual dysphoric changes: Clinical outcome and method-ological implications. *Psychopharmacology Bulletin, 20,* 118–122.

Haskett, R. F., Steiner, M., Osmun, J. N., and Carroll, B. J. (1980). Severe premenstrual tension: Delineation of the syndrome. *Biological Psychiatry, 15,* 121–139.

Herzberg, B. N. (1971). Body composition and premenstrual tension. *Journal of Psychosomatic Research, 15,* 251–257.

Horrobin, D. F., Karmali, R. A., Mtabaji, J. P., Manko, M.S., and Nassar, B. A. (1976). Prolactin and mental illness. *Postgraduate Medical Journal, 52,* 79–85.

Ivey, M. E., and Bardwick, J. M. (1968). Patterns of affective fluctuations in the menstrual cycle. *Psychosomatic Medicine, 30,* 336–345.

Janowsky, D. S., Berens, S. C., and Davis, J. M. (1973). Correlations between mood, weight, and electrolytes during the menstrual cycle: A renin-angiotensin-aldosterone hypothesis of premenstrual tension. *Psychosomatic Medicine, 35,* 143–154.

Janowsky, D. S., Gorney, R., Castelnuovo-Tedesco, P., and Stone, C. B. (1969). Premenstrual-menstrual cycle increases in psychiatric hospital admission rates. *American Journal of Obstetrics and Gynecology, 103,* 189–191.

Kashiwagi, T., McClure, J. N., and Wetzel, R. D. (1976). Premenstrual affective syndrome and psychiatric disorders. *Diseases of the Nervous System, 37,* 116–119.

Kehoe, P. (1978). Psychological factors in the experience of premenstrual and menstrual symptomology. *Dissertation Abstracts International, 38,* 6161B.

Kerr, G. D. (1977). The management of the premenstrual syndrome. *Current Medical Research and Opinion, 4,* 29–34.

Kramp, J. L. (1968). Studies on the premenstrual syndrome in relation to psychiatry. *Acta Psychiatrica Scandinavica, Supplement 203,* 261–267.

Kullander, S., and Svanberg, L. (1979). Bromocriptine treatment of the premenstrual syndrome. *Acta Obstetricia et Gynecologica Scandinavica, 58,* 375–378.

Lahmeyer, H. W. (1984). Premenstrual tension: An overview of its relationship to affective psychopathology. *Integrative Psychiatry, 2,* 106–110.

Laws, S. (1983). The sexual politics of premenstrual tension. *Women's Studies International Forum, 6,* 19–31.

Levitt, E. E., and Lubin, B. (1967). Some personality factors associated with menstrual complaints and menstrual attitude. *Journal of Psychosomatic Research, 11,* 267–270.

Luggin, R., Bernsted, L., and Petersson, B. (1984). Acute psychiatric admission related to the menstrual cycle. *Acta Psychiatrica Scandinavica, 69,* 461–465.

May, R. R. (1976). Mood shifts and the menstrual cycle. *Journal of Psychosomatic Research, 20* 125–130.

McClure, J. N., Reich, T., and Wetzel, R. D. (1971). Premenstrual symptoms as an indicator of bipolar affective disorder. *British Journal of Psychiatry, 119,* 527–528.

McNeilly, A. S., and Chard, T. (1974). Circulating levels of prolactin during the menstrual cycle. *Clinical Endocrinology, 3,* 105–112.

Menninger, K. A. (1939). Somatic correlations with the unconscious repudiation of femininity in women. *Journal of Nervous and Mental Disease, 89,* 514–527.

Moos, R. H. (1969). Typology of menstrual cycle symptoms. *American Journal of Obstetrics and Gynecology, 103,* 390–402.

Moos, R. H., and Leiderman, D. B. (1978). Toward a menstrual cycle symptom typology. *Journal of Psychosomatic Research, 22,* 31–40.

Morris, N. M., and Udry, J. R. (1972). Contraceptive pills and day by day feelings of well-being. *American Journal of Obstetrics and Gynecology, 113,* 763–765.

Morton, J. H. (1950). Premenstrual tension. *American Journal of Obstetrics and Gynecology, 60,* 343–352.

Munday, M. (1977). Hormone levels in severe premenstrual tension. *Current Medical Research and Opinion, 4,* 16–22.

Munday, M. R., Brush, M. G., and Taylor, R. W. (1981). Correlations between progesterone, oestradiol, and aldosterone levels in the premenstrual syndrome. *Clinical Endocrinology, 14,* 1–9.

O'Brien, P. M. S., Craven, D., Selby, C., and Symonds, E. M. (1979). Treatment of premenstrual syndrome by spironolactone. *British Journal of Obstetrics and Gynaecology, 86,* 142–147.

O'Brien, P. M. S., Selby, C., and Symonds,E. M. (1980). Progesterone, fluids, and electrolytes in premenstrual syndrome. *British Medical Journal, 280,* 1161–1163.

O'Brien, P. M. S., and Symonds, E. M. (1982). Prolactin levels in the premenstrual syndrome. *British Journal of Obstetrics and Gynaecology, 89,* 306–308.

Osborn, M. (1981). Physical and psychological determinants of premenstrual tension: Research issues and a proposed methodology. *Journal of Psychosomatic Research, 25,* 363–367.

Osofsky, H. J., and Fisher, S. (1967). Psychological correlates of the development of amenorrhea in a stress situation. *Psychosomatic Medicine, 29,* 15–23.

Paige, K. E. (1973). Women learn to sing the menstrual blues. *Psychology Today, 7,* 41–43.

Parlee, M. B. (1974). Stereotypic beliefs about menstruation: A methodological note on the Moos Menstrual Distress Questionnaire and some new data. *Psychosomatic Medicine, 36,* 229–240.

Paulson, M. J. (1961). Psychological concomitants of premenstrual tension. *American Journal of Obstetrics and Gynecology, 81,* 733–738.

Persky, H., O'Brien, C. P., and Kahn, M. A. (1976). Reproductive hormone levels, sexual activity and moods during the menstrual cycle. *Psychosomatic Medicine, 38,* 62–63.

Rees, L. (1953). Psychosomatic aspects of the premenstrual tension syndrome. *British Journal of Psychiatry, 99,* 62–73.

Reeves, B. D., Garvin, J. E., and McElin, T. W. (1971). Premenstrual tension: Symptoms and weight changes related to potassium therapy. *American Journal of Obstetrics and Gynecology, 109,* 1036–1041.

Reid, R. I., and Yen, S. S. C. (1981). Premenstrual syndrome. *American Journal of Obstetrics and Gynecology, 139,* 85–104.

Rubinow, D. R., and Roy-Byrne, P. (1984). Premenstrual syndromes: Overview from a methodologic perspective. *American Journal of Psychiatry, 141,* 163–172.

Ruble, D. N. (1977). Premenstrual symptoms: A reinterpretation. *Science, 197,* 291–292.

Sampson, G. A. (1979). Premenstrual syndrome: A double-blind controlled trial of progesterone and placebo. *British Journal of Psychiatry, 135,* 209–215.

Sampson, G. (1980). Progesterone, fluid, and electrolytes in premenstrual syndrome. *British Medical Journal, 281,* 227–228.

Sanders, D., Warner, P., Backstrom, T., and Bancroft, J. (1983). Mood, sexuality, hormones and the menstrual cycle I. Changes in mood and physical state: Description of subjects and method. *Psychosomatic Medicine, 45,* 487–501.

Schaumberg, H., Kaplan, T., and Windebank, A. (1983). Sensory neuropathy from pyridoxine abuse. *New England Journal of Medicine, 309,* 445–448.

Schneider, J. F., and Scheider-Duker, M. R. (1974). Conservative attitudes and reactions to menstruation. *Psychological Reports, 35,* 1304.

Schuckit, M. A., Daly, V., Herrman, G., and Hineman, S. (1975). Premenstrual symptoms and depression in a university population. *Diseases of the Nervous System, 36,* 516–517.

Shader, R. I., and Ohly, J. I. (1970). Premenstrual tension, femininity and sexual drive. *Medical Aspects of Human Sexuality, 4,* 42–49.

Shainess, N. (1961). A re-evaluation of some aspects of femininity through a study of menstruation: A preliminary report. *Comprehensive Psychiatry, 2,* 20–26.

Silbergeld, S., Brast, N., and Noble, E. P. (1971). The menstrual cycle: A double-blind study of symptoms, mood and behavior, and biochemical variables using enovid and placebo. *Psychosomatic Medicine, 33,* 411–427.

Slade, P. (1984). Premenstrual emotional changes in normal women: Fact or Fiction? *Journal of Psychosomatic Research, 28,* 1–7.

Smith, S. L. (1975). Mood and the menstrual cycle. In E. J. Sacher (ed.), *Topics in psychoendocrinology* (pp. 19–58). New York: Grune and Stratton.

Smith, S. L. (1976). The menstrual cycle and mood disturbances. *Clinical Obstetrics and Gynecology, 19,* 391–397.

Sommer, B. (1983). How does menstruation affect cognitive competence and psychophysiological response? *Women and Health, 8,* 53–90.

Spencer-Gardner, C., Dennerstein, L., and Burrows, G. D. (1983). Premenstrual tension and female role. *Journal of Psychosomatic Obstetrics and Gynaecology, 2,* 27–34.

Sutherland, H., and Stewart, I. (1965). A critical analysis of the premenstrual syndrome. *Lancet, 1,* 1180–1183.

Taylor, J. W. (1979). Plasma progesterone, oestradiol, 17B, and premenstrual symptoms. *Acta Psychiatrica Scandinavica, 60,* 76–86.

Vekemans, M., Delvoye, P., L'Hermite, M., and Robyn, C. (1977). Serum prolactin levels during the menstrual cycle. *Journal of Clinical Endocrinology and Metabolism, 44,* 989–993.

Waggener, E. L. (1981). Social and psychological influences on premenstrual tension. *Dissertation Abstracts International, 41,* 3939B.

Walker, E. A. (1974). An investigation of personality differences between women with high and low premenstrual tension. *Dissertation Abstracts International, 34,* 4675B.

Watts, S., Dennerstein, L., and Horne, D. V. (1980). The premenstrual syndrome: A psychological evaluation. *Journal of Affective Disorders, 2,* 257–266.

Wetzel, R. D., Reich, T., McClure, J. N., and Wald, J. A. (1975). Premenstrual affective syndrome and affective disorder. *British Journal of Psychiatry, 127,* 219–221.

Wood, C., Larsen, L., and Williams, R. (1979). Social and psychological factors in relation to premenstrual tension and menstrual pain. *Journal of Obstetrics and Gynaecology, 19,* 111–115.

Ylostalo, P., Kauppila, A., Puulakka, J., Ronnberg, L., and Janne, O. (1982). Bromocriptine norethisterone in the treatment of premenstrual syndrome. *Obstetrics and Gynecology, 59,* 292–298.

Zola, P., Meyerson, A. T., Reznikoff, M., Thornton, J. C., and Concool, B. M. (1979). Menstrual symptomology and psychiatric admission. *Journal of Psychosomatic Research, 23,* 241–245.

CHAPTER 5

Gender Differences in Sexual Scenarios

JOHN DeLAMATER

The empirical research on adolescent and young adult sexuality that has been conducted in the past fifteen years suggests there are few, if any, significant differences between males and females in sexual attitudes and sexual behavior. This finding is consistent with the general deemphasis on the importance of gender differences that has characterized the social science literature of the past decade. This paper argues, however, that there is a difference in male-female sexual attitudes and behavior and that this difference has important consequences.

Following the pioneering work of Reiss (1960, 1967), numerous studies have assessed premarital permissiveness—an individual's belief about the acceptability of sexual intimacy before marriage. Comparison of research conducted in the 1960s with data collected in the 1970s indicates that male-female differences in the acceptability of premarital intercourse for oneself are disappearing (Chilman 1978). Hopkins (1977) reviewed data from twenty-two surveys conducted between 1938 and 1975 regarding the incidence of premarital coitus. The review showed a clear trend toward convergence in male and female rates. Some recent studies, in fact, report virtually no differences (Bauman and Wilson 1974; Jessor and Jessor 1975; Schultz, Bohrnstedt, Borgatta, and Evans 1977). These trends have led several observers to conclude that gender is no longer a major influence on the sexuality of young single persons (King, Balswick, and Robinson 1977; DeLamater and MacCorquodale 1979).

This conclusion has generally been accepted by textbooks on human sexuality. Some of the major texts do not discuss male-female differences in premarital sexuality, implying that there are none (Crooks and Bauer 1983; Masters, Johnson, and Kolodny 1982). Several texts limit themselves to discussions of differences between men and women in masturbation and heterosexual petting (e.g., McCary and McCary 1982; Katchadourian and Lunde 1980). The one text that does devote an entire chapter to gender differences concludes, "For the most part, then, males and females are now quite similar in their sexuality" (Hyde 1982: 358).

This conclusion rests on a narrow definition of sexuality, one that emphasizes attitudes toward and the incidence of specific sexual behaviors. But an individual's sexual attitudes and expressions are embedded in a set of assumptions about the purposes of sexual behavior, a general orientation (DeLamater 1981). Orientations are embedded in the basic social institutions of religion, family, economy, and medicine (DeLamater 1986). At this more general level, the available data suggests there is a difference in the orientation held by men and women in American society. I will begin by describing some male-female differences in the development of sexuality in preadolescence. I will then describe a conceptual framework useful in understanding gender differences. Finally, I will discuss some of the consequences of these male-female differences.

MALE—FEMALE DIFFERENCES IN PREADOLESCENCE

There are several male-female differences that influence the development of preadolescent sexuality. These factors include differences in the incidence of masturbation by age thirteen, differences in the event that signals the onset of puberty, and differences in the sources of information regarding sexuality.

Masturbation

Males are much more likely to masturbate prior to adolescence. Both Hunt (1974) and Bell, Weinberg, and Hammersmith (1981) report that two-thirds of their white, heterosexual male respondents had masturbated by age thirteen, compared to one-third of the white, heterosexual females in their samples. Other studies report comparable differences (Arafat and Cotton 1974). The results of several studies are summarized in Table 1.

Table 1. Incidence of Masturbation by Age Thirteen

Source	Males	Females
Kinsey et al. (1948, 1953)	45%	15%
Simon and Gagnon (1968)	44–54%	13–19%
Hunt (1974)	63%	33%
Bell, Weinberg, and Hammersmith (1981)	63%	32%

Rook and Hammen (1977) argue that engaging in masturbation has two important consequences for the individual. First, it provides direct experience with sexual arousal and gratification. Second, it leads to the perception that arousal and gratification are under the person's own control. Since males are more likely to masturbate, they are more likely to develop a sense of personal control over their sexual expression. Because females are less likely to masturbate, they are less likely to develop the same sense of personal control.

Onset of Puberty

The events that call the adolescent's attention to his or her emerging sexuality also differ. For males, this event is ejaculation, in association with sexual arousal. For females, the event is menstruation. As a result, males are more likely to perceive their emerging sexuality as primarily behavioral and to view sexual activity as primarily a means to physical gratification. Females are more likely to perceive their emerging sexuality in the context of reproduction and in relation to the social roles of wife and mother. For them, sexuality is perceived as a means to various social rather than sexual outcomes (Gagnon and Simon 1973).

Sources of Information

There are differences in the kinds of people male and female adolescents name as sources of their information about sexuality. In a survey of 1,376 single young people, respondents were asked to name the primary source of various types of information regarding sexuality (DeLamater and MacCorquodale 1979). One information type was moral knowledge, defined as information about "what is right and what is wrong" with respect to sexual behavior. A second type was information about reproduction. The results for 861 single university students are presented in Table 2.

For moral knowledge, females were more likely to name a parent, especially the mother. Other data from this study indicate that parents held conservative premarital standards; thus, it is likely that these females were being socialized to believe that sexual intercourse is only appropriate in the context of particular relationships, that is, when one is in love or married.

A survey of 449 mother–teenage daughter dyads (Fox and Inazu 1980) found that by the age of twelve and one-half, 55 to 75 percent had discussed menstruation and reproduction, while only 24 to 35 percent had talked about sexual intercourse and morality. Thus, the earliest information girls receive from their mothers emphasizes reproduction, having babies. The results from the survey of students

Table 2. Sources of Information about Sexuality Reported by Young Single Adults[a]

| Source | Type of Information | | | |
| | Moral/Right & Wrong | | Reproduction | |
	M (432)	F (429)	M (432)	F (429)
Father	37.5[b]	48.7	20	11.8
Mother	40.8	67	14.4	57
Male Friends	48.7	49.2	37.8	18.6
Female Friends	51.5	60.5	28.5	46.2
Lover	73	72	46.5	42.9
Professionals: Doctors, Clergy	18.2	24	38.9	49.1
Sex Education Courses	15.6	18.6	48	54.3
Self-generated	83	93	_[c]	-

[a] These data are from a stratified random sample of undergraduate students at the University of Wisconsin—Madison. For additional information, see DeLamater and MacCorquodale 1979.
[b] The percentage of the group rating the source as "Very" or "Quite" important.
[c] This type of source was not included for this category.

described above indicate that mothers are the most important source of reproductive information for women, and the least important of seven such sources for men.

SEXUAL SCENARIOS

These differences in preadolescence lead to the development of different orientations toward sexuality by men and women. Males are more likely to develop a recreational or body-centered (Reiss 1960) orientation. From this perspective, the goal of sexual behavior is physical gratification. Females are more likely to develop a relational (Comfort 1973) or person-centered orientation. From this perspective, sexuality is seen as an integral part of some relationships, as a means of reinforcing emotional and psychological intimacy.

An individual's sexual behavior is governed by social norms, a sexual scenario (Simon and Gagnon 1983). A sexual scenario is a set of social definitions that specify the kinds of sexual behavior that can occur, the type(s) of persons who are appropriate partners for that behavior, and the time(s) and places in which that form of sexual expression is appropriate. Scenarios are descriptive: they tell us which behaviors are sexual and the circumstances under which these behaviors are acceptable.[1]

Scenarios are based upon orientations, thus, different orientations are associated with different sexual scenarios. For persons with a recreational orientation, sexuality is primarily physical, a set of behaviors enacted in order to experience physical pleasure. This orientation is hedonistic and is associated with few restrictions on sexual expression. To a male holding this orientation, most women are potential sexual partners, no particular social or emotional relationship is a necessary prerequisite for sexual intimacy. Any behavior that enhances physical gratification is appropriate—"If it feels good, do it."

For persons with a relational orientation, sexuality is seen as an integral part of certain relationships, as a means of reinforcing emotional and psychological intimacy. Sexuality is not primarily physical; it is intricately linked to reproduction and, thus, to the acquisition of adult social roles, especially to those of spouse and parent. For a female holding this orientation, sexual intimacy is appropriate with only a small number of persons, those with whom there is an ongoing emotional relationship. There are also restrictions on sexual behavior; here the decision rule might be, "If it feels right, do it."

MALE-FEMALE DIFFERENCES IN FIRST INTERCOURSE EXPERIENCE

If males and females are developing different sexual scenarios in late childhood and adolescence, we would expect these differences to be reflected in the nature of the person's first experience with sexual intercourse.

Relationship with Partner

Research has consistently found male-female differences in the quality of the relationship wherein one first has intercourse. The results reported by three large surveys are displayed in Table 3.

Across the three samples, 30 to 41 percent of the males reported they were in love with, engaged, or married to their first partner. The comparable percentages for women are 66 to 82 percent. Clearly, the first coital experience for women occurs in much more emotionally intimate relationships. This difference is consistent with the view that males are more likely to view sexual activity as an end in itself

Table 3. Nature of Relationship with First Coital Partner

	Source					
	Simon and Gagnon (1968)		Athanasiou et al. (1970)		DeLamater and Mac-Corquodale (1979)	
	M	F	M	F	M	F
Spouse	a	a	9%	12%	a	a
In love/engaged	30%	82%	32%	54%	36%	70%
Emotionally attached	24%	13%	b	b	31%	22%
Casual	41%	5%	34%	22%	29%	8%
Paid sexual partner	0	0	12%	0	0	0

[a] These samples were composed entirely of single persons.
[b] No equivalent of this category was employed in this study.

and do not restrict intercourse to a particular type of relationship. Women, however, seem to view coitus within the framework of romantic and marital relationships.

Reactions to First Intercourse

There are also differences between men and women in their reactions to their first intercourse experience. Sorensen (1972) surveyed about four hundred young people thirteen to nineteen years of age. Simon and Gagnon (1968) reported data from interviews with 1,100 college students. Bell, Weinberg, and Hammersmith (1981) presented findings from interviews with adults (283 white, heterosexual males and 101 white, heterosexual females). In all three studies, males reported positive reactions to the first experience. Of the men, 75 to more than 90 percent characterized it as enjoyable and satisfying. Females were less positive: 50 to 75 percent reported a favorable reaction. In addition, women were more likely than men to report feeling guilty after their first experience (Simon and Gagnon 1968).

There are two possible explanations for this differential reaction. The first is based on the assumption that males are more likely to experience an orgasm the first time they have intercourse. The greater incidence of masturbation among males means they have had more experience producing an orgasm. They are therefore more likely to engage in the behaviors necessary to produce it and to identify it accurately when it occurs. Women are less likely to have engaged in masturbation and to have experienced orgasm prior to their first coital experience. They are less likely to experience one on first intercourse because the male may not engage in the necessary behaviors. Indeed, over 80 percent of the males in Simon and Gagnon's (1968) survey of college students reported having an orgasm the first time, compared to between 7 and 22 percent of the women. Men may thus have more positive reactions because they are more likely than women to experience physical gratification.

Alternatively, the difference in reaction may be due to gender differences in sexual scenarios, in what males and females expect from the activity (Gagnon and Simon 1973). As we have seen, male scenarios focus on sexual behavior as an end in itself, on genital activity and orgasm. Since they experience an orgasm, their expectations are met, and they are satisfied. Female scenarios tie sexuality to a romantic relationship. Women might evaluate the first experience in terms of whether it occurred in a romantic setting and had the appropriate emotional tone. Such expectations are less likely to be met, and women are therefore more likely to be dissatisfied.

Reactions of Others

In an analysis of the data collected by Gagnon and Simon, Carns (1973) focused on reports of how third parties reacted. Males were more likely to tell others about their first experience. Sixty percent did so within the first month, compared to 40 percent of the females. In addition, men told a larger number of persons; over 50 percent of them told five or more friends. Only 22 percent of the women told five or more friends. Also, two-thirds of the males but only two-fifths of the women said their parents knew about their first coital experience.

The vast majority of males reported that the reactions of those they told were positive. Females were less likely to report that others approved; however, as the emotional intimacy of the relationship increased, females were more likely to report that those they confided in reacted with approval. Among the males, the intimacy of the relationship was not related to the degree to which others approved.

A related finding comes from a questionnaire study of 2,064 white high school students (Miller and Simon 1974). Among males, the incidence of sexual intercourse was positively related to involvement in male peer groups and unrelated to the intimacy of their heterosexual relationships. Among females, incidence of coitus was associated with the intimacy of their relationships and unrelated to involvement in a peer group.

The reactions of others to a person's sexual experiences reflect the social norms governing premarital sexual activity. These findings indicate that the norm communicated to women is to limit sexual intercourse to emotionally intimate relationships, relationships that may lead to marriage. This norm reinforces gender differences in sexual scenarios.

CONSEQUENCES OF GENDER DIFFERENCES IN SEXUAL SCENARIOS

Orientation toward Heterosexual Relationships

Because of gender differences in sexual scenarios, males and females differ in their orientations toward heterosexual relationships. I noted earlier that, for men, most women are perceived as potential sexual partners, including strangers. Women are likely to perceive as potential sexual partners only men with whom they already have a close relationship. An experimental study of reactions to friendliness by a member of the opposite sex yields relevant results (Abbey 1982). Male-female dyads spent five minutes in conversation about their experiences in college. Each dyad was observed by a male and a female. The observers were hidden. Males, both actors and observers, rated the female actor as more seductive and promiscuous than she or the female observer rated her. Male actors reported greater sexual attraction to the female actor than the female actors reported toward the male actor. These results indicate that men are more likely than women to perceive signs of friendliness as an indication of sexual interest. Generally, men seem to be more likely than women to perceive persons of the opposite gender in sexual terms.

Additional relevant results are reported from a study of the perceived attractiveness of a rival (White 1981). Each member of 150 heterosexual couples was asked what motives might lead his or her partner to get romantically involved with a third person. Specifically, each was asked to rate the importance of four motives: desire for sexual variety, rival's attractiveness, dissatisfaction with the current relationship, and lack of commitment in the relationship. Females rated desire for sexual variety and rival's attractiveness as most likely to lead their male partner into an involvement with another woman. Men rated their own lack of commitment as most important in leading their partners into other involvements. Thus, women believe that sexual activity is an important component of men's motivation in heterosexual relationships, while men believe that emotional commitment is most important to women.

Control over Sexual Activity

Within college-aged couples, men initiate sexual behavior and women control it. Both men and women report that the male usually initiates the specific sexual behaviors in which the couple engage, whether kissing or heterosexual intercourse (DeLamater and MacCorquodale 1979). For the 231 couples studied by Peplau, Rubin, and Hill (1977), it was the male who requested increased sexual intimacy. Females in both studies reported that they were the ones who limited the couples' sexual activity, both on particular occasions (DeLamater and MacCorquodale 1979) and in general (Peplau, Rubin, and Hill 1977). Thus, men possess and exercise proactive power and women possess and exercise reactive power in heterosexual relationships (Grauerholz and Serpe 1983).

I noted earlier that, due to their greater experience with masturbation, men are more likely than women to develop a sense of control over their sexuality. The perception that sexual arousal and gratification are under one's own control encourages men to take the initiative in sexual interactions. Furthermore, if males are taking the initiative in heterosexual activity, by implication they are responsible for the outcomes of sexual interactions. This implication contributes to the performance pressure in their sexual relationships that many men feel/complain about.

Women are less likely to masturbate and, therefore, less likely to develop a sense of control over their sexuality. This feeling makes them less likely to initiate sexual activity and more likely to let males take the initiative. Furthermore, women may be less likely to know what kind of stimulation is necessary for them to experience an orgasm and expect the male to know what to do. This expectation is the other side of the performance pressure males feel. In this context, it is interesting to note that the therapy recommended for nonorgasmic women often begins with autoerotic stimulation and masturbation. The rationale for the woman engaging in these behaviors is precisely that she learn what types of stimulation are sexually arousing.

Evaluation of Sexual Activities

Differences in sexual scenarios should lead to differences in what men and women look for in relationships and in how they evaluate sexual activity within their relationships.

Hatfield and her colleagues (n.d.) studied 131 dating and 53 newly married couples. They asked each person whether the partner was sufficiently caring and considerate during sex and whether the partner engaged in enough loving talk during sex. In general, women replied that their partners were not sufficiently caring and considerate, and that they wished the men would engage in more loving talk. Men, on the other hand, were generally satisfied with their partners on both dimensions.

In the same study (Hatfield, Traupmann, Greenberger, and Wexler, n.d.), the importance of sexual activity to each was measured by a series of questions. Respondents were asked whether they wished their partners were more or less predictable about when they wanted to have sex, more or less variable about where they had sex, and more or less "wild and sexy." Women replied that their male partners were about right on each of these dimensions. Men said they wished their partners were less predictable about timing, more variable with regard to the location of sex, and more wild and sexy.

These data are consistent with the thesis that women are more concerned about affection in their intimate relationships, whereas men are more concerned about the sexual activity itself. Hite (1976, 1981) draws similar conclusions from her studies of nonrandom samples of women and men. The chief complaint of the women she obtained questionnaires from, according to her first book, was the lack of verbal and nonverbal affection during sex. Women complained that their partners placed too much emphasis on orgasm. Men, according to her recent book, complained that sex in their heterosexual relationships is too infrequent.

Interest in Unconventional Sexuality

Finally, several studies suggest that males are more interested in novel or unconventional sexual opportunities. Weinberg (1966) reports that, for couples, usually the males are the first attracted to nudist camps. They learn about nudism from male friends or from specialized magazines. They persuade their wives to visit a camp, often over her objections. Often, males lose interest after two or three visits. Bartell (1971) found similar pattern in his study of participants in mate-swapping. It was typically the male who obtained information, made the arrangements, and persuaded the female to go. Women reported that their initial reaction was quite negative; some said their partner forced them to go the first time. After the couple got involved, the male tended to lose interest after the novelty wore off. In both nudism and mate-swapping, those couples who became regular participants reported they continued the activity because the female wanted to.

Clark and Hatfield (1982) studied receptivity to heterosexual invitations by strangers. They recruited nine students—five women and four men—to serve as confederates. The confederates were instructed to approach a person of the opposite sex outdoors on a college campus during the day. They were instructed only to approach persons they found sexually attractive. The confederates initiated interaction by saying, "I've been noticing you around campus, and I find you to be very attractive." This statement was followed by one of three invitations: Would you (1) go out with me; (2) come over to my apartment; or (3) go to bed with me? Sixteen subjects of each sex received each invitation. The results are displayed in Table 4.

Men and women were equally likely to accept the date. Men were even more likely to accept the invitation to "go to bed," while none of the women accepted that offer. In addition, the confederates reported that the men they approached were usually at ease and

Table 4. Response to Heterosexual Invitations (Percent Accepting Invitation)

Sex of Subject	Date	Type of Invitation Apartment	Bed
Male	50%	69%	75%
Female	56%	6%	0%

Source: Clark and Hatfield 1982.

responded positively for all three conditions. Women reacted negatively, particularly to the invitations to the apartment and to go to bed.

SUMMARY

Males and females differ in their orientations to sexuality—their beliefs about the purposes of sexual activity. This difference leads in turn to differences in sexual scenarios, in norms about the kinds of partners and relationships prerequisite for sexual intimacy, and in the kinds of activity considered legitimate.

There are several experiences in preadolescence that contribute to the development of these gender differences. They include differential experience with masturbation and differential reliance on parents as sources of moral knowledge. The different scenarios are reinforced by the fact that males have their first coital experience in more casual relationships and are more likely to receive approval from those they tell. As young adults, males are more likely to have a recreational orientation, and females are more likely to have a relational orientation. As a consequence, men and women differ in their perceptions of control over their sexual behavior, in their evaluations of their sexual experiences, and in their openness to novel or unconventional sexual activity.

NOTES

1. In their earlier work, Gagnon and Simon (e.g., 1973) used the term "sexual script" to refer to the social definitions about which actors, behaviors, and locales are appropriate. In their recent work (Simon and Gagnon 1983), they substituted the term "sexual scenario" and redefined a sexual script as the exact sexual interaction that occurs as persons enact a scenario.

REFERENCES

Abbey, A. (1982). Sex differences in attributions for friendly behavior: Do males misperceive females' friendliness? *Journal of Personality and Social Psychology, 42,* 830–838.

Arafat, I., and Cotton, W. (1974). Masturbation practices of males and females. *Journal of Sex Research, 10,* 293–307.

Athanasiou, R., Shaver, P., and Tavris, C. (1970). Sex. *Psychology Today,* (July), 39–52.

Bartell, G. D. (1971). *Group sex.* New York: Wyden.

Bauman, K. E., and Wilson, D. R. (1974). Sexual behavior of unmarried university students in 1968 and 1972. *Journal of Sex Research, 10,* 327–333.

Bell, A., Weinberg, M., and Hammersmith, S. (1981). *Sexual preference: Statistical appendix.* Bloomington, Ind.: Indiana University Press.

Carns, D.E. (1973). Talking about sex: Notes on first coitus and the double sexual standard. *Journal of Marriage and the Family, 35,* 677–688.

Chilman, C. (1978). *Adolescent sexuality in a changing American society: Social and psychological perspectives.* Washington, D.C.: U.S. Government Printing Office.

Clark, R., and Hatfield, E. (1982). Gender differences in receptivity to sexual offers. Reported in E. Hatfield. What do women and men want from love and sex? In E. R. Allgeier and N. B. McCormick (eds.), *Gender roles and sexual behavior: The changing boundaries.* Palo Alto, Calif.: Mayfield.

Comfort, A. (1973). Sexuality in a zero growth society. *Current, 148,* 29–34.

Crooks, R., and Bauer, K. (1983). *Our sexuality* (2nd ed.). Menlo Park, Calif.: Benjamin Cummings.

DeLamater, J. (1981). The social control of sexuality. *Annual Review of Sociology, 7,* 263–290.

DeLamater, J. (1986). Sexual desire and social norms: Sociological perspectives on human sexuality. In J. Geer, and W. Donohue (eds.), *Theories and paradigms of human sexuality,* New York: Plenum Publishing Co.

DeLamater, J., and MacCorquodale, P. (1979). *Premarital sexuality: Attitudes, relationships, behavior.* Madison: University of Wisconsin Press.

Fox, G. L., and Inazu, J. K. (1980). Patterns and outcomes of mother-daughter communication about sexuality. *Journal of Social Issues, 36*(1), 7–29.

Gagnon, J. H., and Simon, W. (1973). *Sexual conduct: The social sources of human sexuality.* Chicago: Aldine.

Grauerholz, E., and Serpe, R. T. (1983). Initiation and response: The dynamics of sexual interaction. Unpublished paper.

Hatfield, E., Traupmann, J., Greenberger, D., and Wexler, P. (n.d.). Male/female differences in sexual preferences in dating and newlywed couples.

Hite, S. (1976). *The Hite report.* New York: MacMillan.

Hite, S. (1981). *The Hite report on male sexuality.* New York: Alfred A. Knopf.

Hopkins, J. R. (1977). Sexual behavior in adolescence. *Journal of Social Issues, 33*(2), 67–85.

Hunt, M. (1974). *Sexual behavior in the 1970's.* Chicago: Playboy Press.

Hyde, J. (1982). *Understanding human sexuality* (2nd ed.). New York: McGraw-Hill.

Jessor, S., and Jessor, R. (1975). Transitions from virginity to nonvirginity among youth: A sociopsychological study over time. *Developmental Psychology, 11,* 473–484.

Katchadourian, H., and Lunde, D. (1980). *Fundamentals of human sexuality* (3rd ed.). New York: Holt, Rinehart and Winston.

King, K., Balswick, J. O., and Robinson, I. E. (1977). The continuing premarital sexual revolution among college females. *Journal of Marriage and the Family, 39,* 455–459.

Kinsey, A. C., Pomeroy, W. B., and Martin, C. E. (1948). *Sexual behavior in the human male.* Philadelphia: W.B. Saunders.

Kinsey, A. C., Pomeroy, W. B., Martin, C. E., and Gebhard, P. H. (1953). *Sexual behavior in the human female.* Philadelphia: W.B. Saunders.

Masters, W., Johnson, V., and Kolodny, R. (1982). *Human Sexuality.* Boston: Little, Brown, and Co.

McCary, J., and McCary, S. (1982). *McCary's human sexuality* (4th ed.). Belmont: Wadsworth Publishing.

Miller, P. Y., and Simon, W. (1974). Adolescent sexual behavior: Context and change. *Social Problems, 22,* 58–76.

Peplau, L. A., Rubin, Z., and Hill, C. T. (1977). Sexual intimacy in dating relationships. *Journal of Social Issues, 33*(2), 86–109.

Reiss, I. L. (1960). *Premarital sexual standards in America.* New York: Free Press.

Reiss, I. L. (1967). *The social context of premarital permissiveness.* New York: Holt, Rinehart and Winston.

Rook, K. S., and Hammen, C. L. (1977). A cognitive perspective on the experience of sexual arousal. *Journal of Social Issues, 33*(2), 7–29.

Schultz, B., Bohrnstedt, G., Borgatta, E., and Evans, R. (1977). Explaining premarital sexual intercourse among college students: A causal model. *Social Forces, 56,* 148–165.

Simon, W., and Gagnon, J. (1968). Youth cultures and aspects of the socialization process: College study marginal book. Bloomington, Ind.: Institute for Sex Research.

Simon, W., and Gagnon, J. (1983). Sexual scripts: Permanence and change. Paper presented at the American Sociological Association meetings, Detroit.

Sorensen, R. C. (1972). *Adolescent sexuality in contemporary America.* New York: World.

Weinberg, M. (1966). Becoming a nudist. *Psychiatry, 29,* 15–25.

White, G. (1981). Jealousy and partner's perceived motives for attraction to rival. *Social Psychology Quarterly, 44,* 24–30.

CHAPTER 6

Females, Males, and Sexual Responses

WILLIAM GRIFFITT

Among the most enduring beliefs about human nature are those that assume males and females differ in many important ways. The sexes have been viewed as differing not only in basic anatomy, but also in abilities, temperament, values, morality, needs, and in many other personality characteristics. The persistence and ubiquity of the assumed differences is such that they have been noted since the beginnings of recorded history and in virtually all societies studied (Staples 1973; Tavris and Wade 1984). In one view, these assumed differences have created a schism of misunderstanding, conflict, and distrust between the sexes that can best be characterized as a war (Tavris and Wade 1984).

But are the sexes really so different in the ways noted above? For a number of reasons, this question is difficult to answer. Methodological problems abound in the study of sex differences, and conclusions based on existing research must be reached with a degree of tentativeness. Maccoby and Jacklin (1974) conducted an exhaustive examination of over two thousand studies of sex differences, concluding that many assumed differences between the sexes are not supported by the available empirical evidence. The number of empirically supported differences (for example, aggressiveness or quantitative ability) was relatively small.

Nevertheless, sex stereotypes are widespread, and people continue to believe that males and females differ in many ways (Broverman, Broverman, Clarkson, and Rosenkrantz 1972; Tavris and Wade 1984). A central dimension on which men and women are widely believed to differ dramatically is in their sexual responses (Griffitt 1973; Kinsey, Pomeroy, Martin, and Gebhard 1953; Staples 1973). This chapter is an examination and discussion of sexual responses in males and females. It begins with a brief overview of common beliefs about fundamental male-female differences in sexual responses, sexual responsiveness, and sexual needs. This review is followed by a consideration of the nature of and strategies in the study of sexual responses. Next is a summary of much of the research evidence concerning sex differences and similarities in sexual responding, and the final section includes discussions of the possible bases for and consequences of sex differences in sexual responses.

CONTRADICTORY VIEWS: UNDERSEXED AND OVERSEXED FEMALES AND MALES

Throughout history and across differing cultures many contradictory beliefs about the nature of female and male sexuality can be identified. At times, females have been regarded as so oversexed and insatiable in their sexual desires that the relatively undersexed males must constantly guard against being seduced. In other historical periods, this view has been reversed—males have been thought of as strongly driven by sexual needs and females as asexual (Bullough and Bullough 1977; Tavris and Wade 1984). Similar variations in beliefs from culture to culture are not uncommon (Davenport 1978; Ford and Beach 1951; Marshall 1972). Indeed, there have been few times or places in which equality in the strength, frequency, and quality of male and female sexual responses and desires has been widely accepted.

It is generally agreed that many contemporary western beliefs about female and male sexuality are, in part, a blend of Judeo-Christian and Victorian era views and teachings (Bullough and Bullough 1977). At the risk of oversimplification, it may be said that the Judeo-Christian ethic regarding sexuality was quite restrictive, that it condemned as sinful any form of sexual expression outside of marriage and any form of sexual expression within marriage except heterosexual intercourse for the primary purpose of procreation.

Victorian views of sexuality emerged in England during the rule of Queen Alexandrina Victoria (1819–1901). Among middle-class Victorians, almost all sexual activity was regarded as disgusting and even dangerous to one's health. In spite of this attitude, however, men were seen as having strong sexual needs and as being quick to respond sexually. Most women (the good ones) were viewed as uninterested in sex and lacking in any real capacity to respond sexually. It was thought that the minority of women (the bad ones) who were interested in sex and responded sexually were moral and biological anomalies.

Victorian opinions about male and female sexuality were reinforced by some of the prominent authorities of the era, including Freud (1957–1964) and Krafft-Ebing (1965). This view of women as asexual and men as oversexed has persisted well into the twentieth century and has been accepted as fact by much of the general public and even by many purported "experts." For example, a review of gynecology texts published between 1943 and 1962 revealed that most authors assumed men inherently have stronger sex needs than women, and that some texts even implied that sexual responses are totally absent in most women (Scully and Bart 1973). In a similar review of marriage manuals, Gordon and Shankweiler (1971) reported that women were uniformly described as less interested in sex than were men. As recently as the early 1970s, similar messages could be gleaned from an enormously popular sex manual (Comfort 1972) and from the leading college-level human sexuality textbook of the time (McCary 1973).

How accurate are these widely accepted views of female and male sexuality? Are females' sexual responses weaker, less frequent, slower in appearing, and subjectively or qualitatively different than those of males? Before examining the empirical evidence concerning these questions, it is necessary first to consider the nature of sexual responses and how they may be measured and studied.

The Nature and measurement of Sexual Responses

In the most general (and possibly obvious) sense, sexual responses are those that occur in reaction to external and internal sexual stimuli. But just as there are multiple dimensions of sexual stimuli, there are multiple dimensions of sexual responses. Though other schemes are possible (Byrne 1977, 1981; Singer 1984), sexual responses can be conveniently categorized into (1) the *arousal* of a drive state; (2) *affective* or *evaluative* reactions; (3) *cognitive processes*; or (4) *sexual behaviors*. It should, of course, be emphasized that, in any complete human sexual encounter (Griffitt and Hatfield 1985), each of these dimensions of sexual responding will come into play and interact with one another in complex ways (Byrne 1977). It will also become apparent that whether females and males differ in sexual responding depends upon the specific dimensions of sexual responses being considered.

Sexual Arousal

Broadly speaking, sexual arousal can be considered a drive state based on a need for sexual release (Kelley and Byrne 1983). Sexual arousal in humans is reflected by various physiological and subjectively experienced reactions.

Physiological Arousal Though Kinsey et al. (1953) were able to describe in general terms some of the many bodily reactions to sexual stimulation, it was the work of Masters and Johnson (1966) that provided the first detailed description of physiological sexual responses in humans. Masters and Johnson identified two classes of responses to what they termed effective sexual stimulation. The first, *vasocongestion*, involves engorgement of the blood vessels of various body areas, particularly the genitals. The engorged areas become swollen, reddened, and warmed, resulting in penile erection, breast swelling, sexflush, and clitoral, labial, and vaginal changes. The second class of responses, *myotonia*, involves increases in muscular tension.

Though the observations of Masters and Johnson were relatively imprecise in a quantitative sense, their work played an important role in stimulating others to develop various approaches to more precisely measure physiological sexual responses. Some of these approaches have involved the assessment of biochemical changes in response to sexual stimulation (Barclay 1970; Pirke, Kockott, and Dittmar 1974). Still others have focused on changes in cortical, electrodermal, cardiovascular, respiratory, pupillary, and extragenital temperature as indicants of sexual arousal (Zuckerman 1971; Geer 1975). For the most part, these measures have not proven very useful, primarily because they do not record responses specific to sexual arousal. For example electrodermal, cardiac, respiratory, and many other bodily reactions occur in response to anxiety, aggression, and other types of nonsexual stimuli.

Substantially more useful are approaches that rely upon direct measures of genital responses. A number of devices have been developed to assess changes in the penis resulting from vasocongestive responses to sexual stimulation. Most widely used are various types of strain guages that attach to the penis and record changes in its circumference (Barlow, Becker, Leitenberg, and Agras 1970; Geer 1975; Rosen and Keefe 1978). These devices have been found to be sensitive indicators of sexual arousal. Another approach uses a thermistor to record penile skin temperature (Jovanovic 1971), which increases with vasocongestion of the penis.

Though a number of instruments have been developed for measuring genital responses in females, the most sensitive device appears to be the vaginal photoplethysmograph developed by Geer (1975; Sintchak and Geer 1975). It consists of a clear vaginal probe resembling a tampon. The probe contains a small light source and a photoelectric cell that indirectly measure the volume of blood in the vaginal walls by detecting the amount of light reflected back and diffused through the tissue. Vaginal pulse pressure is also measured, which along with the vasocongestion measure have been shown to be reliable indicators of female sexual arousal to erotic stimuli (Geer, Morokoff, and Greenwood 1974; Heiman 1977) and during masturbation (Geer and Quartararo 1975).

The penile and vaginal vasocongestion devices decribed above appear to be reliable indicators of sexual arousal, but they do not provide identical measures usable in female-male comparisons. Seeley,Abramson, Perry, Rothblatt, and Seeley (1980) have reported on the use of a thermograph for measuring tissue temperature changes produced by blood engorgement in both females and males. The thermogram provided by the device reliably detects genital (and nongenital) temperature changes associated with sexual arousal produced by masturbation (Seeley et al. 1980) and by erotica (Abramson, Perry, Seeley, Seeley, and Rothblatt 1981) in both sexes. This instrument has the advantage of providing measures that allow direct comparisons of female and male sexual arousal.

Subjective Arousal. Though the arousal dimension of sexual responding has very real physiological components, subjective experiences and reports of sexual arousal have more frequently been assessed. A number of factors, including the relative ease of collecting self-reports, the potential invasiveness of physiological measures, lack of instrumentation, and the reluctance of human subjects committees, account for this more common choice.

In spite of their widespread use, most measures of subjective arousal consist of rather global and gross assessments of awareness of sexual arousal. With some rather rare exceptions (Bentler and Peeler 1979; Fisher 1973; Hite 1976; Masters and Johnson 1966), the phenomenological details of arousal have not been investigated. Instead, most investigators have used nonstandardized, simple and direct self-rating scales on which subjects rated their arousal from "not at all sexually aroused" to "highly sexually aroused," usually using five-, seven- or nine-point scales (Griffitt 1973; Levitt and Brady 1965; Schmidt, Sigusch, and Schafer 1973). Most often administered following experimental treatments, these instruments reliably indicate arousal in response to erotic versus nonerotic stimuli.

Another approach to the assessment of subjective arousal uses scales on which subjects report their awareness of various physiological responses or sensations. For example, females have been asked to report on the occurrence of genital and breast sensations, vaginal lubrication, and orgasm, and males on the occurrence of erection, preejaculatory emission, and ejaculation (Przybyla and Byrne 1984; Schmidt et al. 1973). A variation on this procedure uses lists of physiological responses or sensations, graded according to the intensity of arousal. For example, Griffitt (1975) asked males to indicate their most extreme reaction from a list that included "no erection at all," "1/4 full erection," "1/2 full erection," "3/4 full erection," "full erection," "preejaculatory emission," and "ejaculation." The comparable female list included "no genital sensations at all", "mild genital sensations," "moderate genital sensations," "slightly strong genital sensations," "strong genital sensations," "vaginal lubrication," and "orgasm." These measures have been found to distinguish reliably different degrees of arousal following exposure to different erotic stimuli (Hatfield, Sprecher, and Traupmann 1978) and to be significantly related to direct self-ratings of general physical excitement (Przybyla and Byrne 1984).

Generally, the various physiological measures of arousal are significantly correlated with one another (Wincze, Hoon, and Hoon 1977), as are different subjective measures (Steinman, Wincze, Sakheim, Barlow, and Mavissakalian 1981; Przybyla and Byrne 1984). Physiological and subjective measures of arousal are, under most circumstances, significantly correlated for males and females, but, in some studies, there is greater correspondence for males (Heiman 1977; Steinman et al. 1981; Wincze and Qualls 1984). The apparent female-male differences in correspondence may, however, be due to the use of inadequate psychophysiological scaling methods (Horff and Geer 1983). An additional finding is that physiological and subjective measures correspond more closely at higher (plateau and orgasm) levels of arousal than at lower levels for both sexes (Heiman 1977).

State Arousal and Trait Arousability. As in studies of other drives and motives such as anxiety (Spielberger 1972), a useful distinction can be drawn between two aspects of the sexual arousal process— *state sexual arousal* and *trait sexual arousability.* State sexual arousal refers to a temporary condition in which sexual arousal is activated by internal or external sexual stimuli. Trait sexual arousability refers to a relatively enduring tendency, propensity, or dispositon to respond with a particular degree or intensity of arousal to sexual stimuli. Whalen (1966) suggests that an individual's sexual motivation consists of both his or her current level of state arousal and his/her degree of arousability. Theoretically, the greater a person's trait arousability, the greater the intensity of the person's state arousal will be to a given sexual stimulus or set of stimuli.

In contrast to the existence of a number of different measures of human state sexual arousal (see above), relatively few measures or indicants of trait arousability have been developed. An indirect approach has been to summate state arousal responses to a variety of different erotic stimuli (Griffitt 1973, 1975). Such indices are reliably and positively related to direct ratings of overall sexual arousal following exposure to erotic stimuli and to degree of sexual experience (Griffitt 1973, 1975), which has been positively related to sexual arousability or responsiveness (Kinsey, Pomeroy, Martin, and Gebhard 1953). A variation on this approach uses summated ratings by respondents concerning the degree to which they are sexually aroused by a variety of different sexual activities (Chambless and Lifshitz 1984; Hoon, Hoon, and Wincze 1976). Hoon et al. (1976) developed such an inventory (the Sexual Arousability Inventory) and found that high-scoring respondents reported a higher number of sexual partners, frequency of intercourse, frequency of orgasm, and degree of sex experience than did low-scoring respondents. Similar findings (Harris, Tulis, and LaCoste 1980) are available for males. Though the distinction between state arousal and trait arousability appears to be useful, substantially more research in this area is sorely needed.

Affective and Evaluative Responses

In addition to physiological and subjective sexual arousal, human reactions to sexual stimuli also include various affective and evaluative responses. Such responses, in turn, interact with and influence both cognitive and behavioral responses to sexual stimuli.

Affective Responses. The affective dimension of sexual responding has been investigated in a number of ways. Some investigators (Hain and Linton 1969; Hare, Wood, Britain, and Frazelle 1971) have assessed autonomic (electrodermal, cardiac, vascular, and respiratory) responses during exposure to sexual stimuli. Because of wide variability among people in specific patterns of autonomic responding, however, such measures have not been very useful or reliable indicators of affective responses (Zuckerman 1971).

Another approach has been to obtain self-ratings of immediate and longer-term affective or emotional responses following exposure to sexual stimuli (Byrne, Fisher, Lamberth, and Mitchell 1974; Griffitt 1973; Schmidt etal. 1973). Often a wide array of affective and emotional reactions is assessed. For example, Schmidt et al. (1973) exposed males and females to erotic written passages and obtained semantic differential ratings on twenty four feeling states before and following the exposure. Diverse emotions such as feelings of gregariousness, gentleness, concentration, anger, numbness, impulsiveness, and disgust were included. Though no formal correlational or factor analyses of these ratings were conducted, the authors grouped the reactions into categories reflecting (1) emotional activation (excitement, impulsiveness, etc.); (2) emotional instability (inner agitation, jumpiness,etc.); and (3) emotional avoidance (repulsion, disgust). Increases in each category were noted in both sexes immediately following exposure to the erotic stimuli. For some subjects, these changes persisted for twenty four hours.

Though sexual stimuli clearly evoke a number of self-reported feelings, considerable conceptual clarity and simplicity has been provided by factor analysis, which has revealed that affective responses to sexual stimuli fall along two orthogonal, positive and negative dimensions (Byrne, Fisher, Lamberth, and Mitchell 1974). Thus, for any given individual, affective responses may be predominantly positive, predominantly negative, ambivalent, or indifferent (Byrne et al. 1974; Griffitt, May, and Veitch 1974). The specific pattern of affective responding depends, among other things, upon the specific sexual stimuli to which a person is exposed (White 1979), degree of sex experience (Griffitt 1975), and dispositional tendencies to respond positively or negatively to sexuality (Byrne 1981; Griffitt 1973; Mosher and Abramson 1977).

State Affect and Trait Affect. As in the analysis of sexual arousal processes, one can distinguish between *state affect,* as the immediate pattern of affective responses evoked by sexual stimuli, and *trait affect,* as a dispositional tendency to respond in a particular affective manner to sexual stimuli. A variety of approaches for assessing state affect were described above. In contrast to trait sexual arousability, a number of different useful measures of trait affective responding to sexuality have been developed and used rather widely.The most widely used instruments—the Mosher (1966), 1968) Sex Guilt Inventories and the Byrne (Byrne and Fisher 1983; White, Fisher, Byrne, and Kingma 1977) Sexual Opinion Survey—are reliable predictors of positive and negative affective responses and approach-avoidance responses to a variety of different sexual stimuli (Byrne 1981; Griffitt and Kaiser 1978).

Evaluative Responses. Affective responses to sexual stimuli provide the mediational foundation for evaluations of sexual stimuli along a general like-dislike or positive-negative dimension. In general, one's combined positive and negative responses to a particular stimulus determines one's evaluative assessment of the stimulus (Clore and Byrne 1974). If the affect is predominantly negative, the evaluation will be negative, and if the affective response is predominantly positive, the evaluation will be a positive one.

With respect to sexuality, the affective basis for evaluative judgments has been demonstrated for reactions to erotica (Byrne et al. 1974; Griffitt 1973), sex-related words and conversations (Fisher, Miller, Byrne, and White 1980; Mosher and Greenberg 1969), and a variety of other sex-related topics such as masturbation, contraception, and homosexuality (Byrne 1981). Evaluative responses evoked by sexual stimuli are related to a number of cognitive and behavioral sexual responses. For example, individuals whose evaluations of sexual stimuli are negative tend to avoid exposure to erotic cues (Griffitt and Kaiser 1978; Schill and Chapin 1972), to retain less accurate information about sex (Fisher and Byrne 1978a; Mosher 1979b; Schwartz 1973), and to react more slowly to and avoid the sexual meaning of double-entendre words such as "screw" (Galbraith and Mosher 1968; Galbraith and Sturke 1974). Clearly the affective-evaluative dimensions of sexual responding play important roles in shaping diverse aspects of sexuality.

Cognitive Responses to Sexual Stimuli

In addition to arousal and affective-evaluative responses, sexual stimuli also evoke a class of reactions best referred to as cognitive responses. These reactions include sexual images and fantasies, information responses, and expectancies. Such responses influence and, in turn, are influenced by arousal, affective, and behavioral responses to sexual stimuli.

Sexual Images and Fantasies. Sexual stimuli of a wide variety are capable of evoking images of sexual activities. Such images can vary in detail from momentary and fleeting scenes to highly detailed and intricate plots involving multiple characters, actions, and settings. Two broad classes of sexual images activated by sexual stimuli have been investigated—*sex dreams* during sleep and *waking sexual fantasies.*

Relatively little is known about the nature and origins of sex dreams, but it is clear that they occur in the majority of individuals of both sexes at some time in their lives (Kinsey, Pomeroy, and Martin 1948; Kinsey et al. 1953). Such dreams usually coincide with sleep periods characterized by rapid eye movements (REM) and are accompanied by erections in males (Karacan, Williams, Guerrero, Salis, Thornby, and Hursch 1974) and by vaginal congestion in females (Abel, Murphy, Becker, and Bitar 1979). For both sexes, the strength of the dream imagery can sometimes be sufficient to produce orgasm.

Though the precise origins of sex dreams are not known, their contents most frequently parallel the actual experiences or preferences of the dreamers (Kinsey et al. 1948, 1953). This similarity suggests that they are evoked involuntarily by memories of past activities, of erotic stimuli to which the dreamer has been exposed during waking, or by memories of salient waking fantasies. Support for this interpretation is provided indirectly by the findings that the frequency of sex dreams is sometimes increased by exposure to erotica (Amoroso, Brown, Pruesse, Ware, and Pilkey 1971; Mosher 1971).

Waking sexual fantasies have been studied more extensively. Virtually all adult Americans report having some sort of fantasies or daydreams several times a day (Singer 1966), and a majority of both sexes report fantasizing about sex at least occasionally (Kinsey et al. 1953).

These fantasies are often triggered by everday encounters with erotic stimuli such as attractive men or women, odors, sounds, and commercially distributed photographic, literary, or auditory works (Friday 1974; Kinsey et al. 1953). Reminders or memories of previous sexual experiences also stimulate sexual fantasies, and many people deliberately rely on such memories and the resultant fantasies to enhance or elicit sexual arousal (Crepault and Couture 1980; McCauley and Swann 1978, 1980). Exposure to the sexual memories or fantasies of others can also activate one's own fantasies and produce arousal, as shown in studies demonstrating the fantasy-evoking effects of erotica (Hunt 1974; Mosher 1971; Schmidt et al. 1973). Participation in specific sexual activities such as masturbation, intercourse, and homosexual behavior is a potent source of sexual fantasy for many (Hariton and Singer 1974; Hesselund 1976; Masters and Johnson 1979; McCauley and Swann 1978, 1980). Even the mere anticipation of engaging in sexual activities can activate fantasy and arousal (Barclay 1971; Gagnon and Simon 1973). Finally, people are able to generate sexually arousing fantasies simply by being asked to do so (Byrne and Lamberth 1971; Laws and Rubin 1969) and to inhibit arousal to erotic fantasy cues by intentionally creating nonsexual fantasies (Henson and Rubin 1971).

Informational Responses. People involved in the transmission of sexual knowledge through therapy, education, or other endeavors are fully aware (sometimes painfully) that people carry with them a rather large body of information and beliefs concerning sexual topics and sexuality. Often much of this information and the beliefs associated with it are inaccurate. Indeed, a major goal is frequently to correct misinformation and erroneous beliefs that contribute to difficulties with affective and behavioral responses to sexuality (Kaplan 1974; Masters and Johnson 1979; McCary 1973).

That sexual stimuli, topics, situations, and behaviors activate informational and belief responses that, in turn, influence arousal, affect, and behavior seems obvious. Relatively little research, however, has been directed at the specific relationships involved. Much of the work that has been done involves assessing what might be regarded as "technical sexual knowledge" among teenagers and college students (e.g., Alan Guttmacher Institute 1981; Miller and Lief 1976; Mosher 1979b). Such studies regularly find an alarming degree of inaccurate information concerning sexual topics such as contraception (Delcampo, Sporakowski, and Delcampo 1976), fertility periods (Alan Guttmacher Institute 1981), sexually transmitted diseases (Griffitt 1985), masturbation (Miller and Lief 1976), and a variety of other sexual matters (female orgasm, nocturnal orgasm, sexual anatomy and physiology, and sexual technique) (Mosher 1979b). It is generally found that those with relatively negative affective orientations to sexuality and with limited sex experience have less accurate sex information than do the more positive and more experienced (Delcampo et al. 1976; Miller and Lief 1976; Mosher 1979b). In addition, when exposed to accurate information, those with high trait sex guilt retain less than do the less guilty (Schwartz 1973).

How might informational or belief responses affect other responses to sexual stimuli? Consider a female's response to a request from her sexual partner to perform fellatio. If she believes or has been taught that mouth-penis contact may lead to disease, the request will activate such information. The situation will evoke predominantly negative affective and evaluative responses to the request, to the prospects of fellatio, and possibly to her partner. The request will elicit images or fantasies of what it may be like to perform the negatively evaluated act and possibly interfere with or diminish her sexual arousal. The certainty of her belief in the fellatio-disease link will activate a probability-based expectancy concerning the likelihood of actually contracting a disease if she performs fellatio. Finally, given the conditions and mediating responses described, one could anticipate that her behavioral response to the fellatio request would be one of noncompliance. It should be apparent, of couse, that other situational variables such as her partner's insistence and persuasive efforts, her feelings about her partner, and a variety of other elements might well influence her responses.

Speculative mind problems such as the above are relatively easy to create and to solve but difficult to examine empirically. There is evidence, however, that some of the knowledge-affect-behavior relationships described occur with respect to sexual topics such as contraception (Fisher, Byrne, Edmunds, Miller, Kelley, and White 1979) and masturbation (Miller and Lief 1976). For example, Miller and Lief (1976) have shown that those who believe masturbation causes mental and emotional instability are more likely to respond with negative affect and evaluations to masturbation and less likely to engage in masturbatory behavior. Substantially more research is clearly needed concerning the role of informational responses to sexual stimuli.

Expectancies. As with informational responses, the expectancies elicited by sexual stimuli have received less study than have arousal, fantasy, affective, evaluative, and behavioral responses. Information or beliefs concerning a particular sexual stimulus, situation, or behavior are, of course, linked to expectancies regarding the conse- quences of the stimulus, situation, or performance of the behavior. Returning to the earlier example, the female who believes fellatio causes disease will also have some expectancy regarding the likelihood of her contracting a disease if she performs fellatio. If her expectancy carries a high probability estimate, she will be less likely to perform the behavior than if she views disease as a remote and rare possibility. Empirically, there is some evidence supporting this process in the realm of contraceptive behavior. For example, over 70 percent of sexually active teenage girls who do not use contraceptives do not expect to become pregnant through intercourse. Their expectancies are based on unfounded beliefs about the frequency of intercourse, about fertility cycles, or even that they are sterile (Cvetkovitch, Grote, Bjorseth, and Sarkissian 1975; Shah, Zelnick, and Kantner 1975).

Substantially more research is needed to identify the role of the specific expectancies evoked by particular sexual stimuli, situations, and behaviors (Rook and Hammen 1977). Another approach, however, is to consider individual differences in the "generalized expectancies" associated with sexual stimuli. For example, within Rotter's (1966) social learning theory framework, Mosher (1966, 1968) conceptualized sex guilt as a generalized expectancy for self-mediated (internal) punishment for the violation of, anticipated violation of, or the failure to attain internalized standards of proper sexual behavior. Using Mosher's scales for the measurement of sex guilt, it has been found that those high in sex guilt report low levels of sex experience, spend less time viewing erotic material, report more negative affective and evaluative responses to erotica, retain less information from a birth control lecture, employ less effective contraceptive techniques, and believe and transmit more sexual myths than do those low in sex guilt (Mendelsohn and Mosher 1979; Mosher 1979a, 1979b). Thus, high sex-guilt expectancies appear to shape or inhibit a wide variety of sex-related behaviors and responses.

A closely related concept is that of sex anxiety. Following the Mosher approach, Janda and O'Grady (1980) developed the Sex Anxiety Inventory to measure individual differences in generalized expectancies for *external* punishment related to various sexual responses and behaviors. Though the technique appears to be psychometrically sound, validity data for the scale are limited. It has been found, however, that high sex anxiety is associated with high sex guilt and low self-reported sexual experience (Janda and O'Grady 1980).

Locus of control (Phares 1978; Rotter 1966) is a concept referring to a generalized expectancy that the rewards, satisfactions, or reinforcements that occur in one's life are controlled by one's own behaviors or personal characteristics (internal control), or else unrelated to these variables and controlled by luck, chance, fate, or other people (external control). Catania, McDermott, and Wood (1984) have developed a measure of expectancies for control of rewards in sexual situations called the Dyadic Sexual Regulation Scale (DSR). Preliminary work with the scale indicates that increasing expectancies for internal control are associated with increasing frequencies of intercourse, receiving oral sex from partners, orgasms from intercourse, sexual satisfaction, and decreasing anxiety in dyadic sexual relations.

Given the multitude of specific sexual stimuli and situations to which people might be or have been exposed, assessment of all or even most of the specific expectancies that might be evoked would, at best, be a cumbersome task. Continued efforts to identify more dimensions of generalized sex-related expectancies such as those described might be more fruitful.

Behavioral Responses to Sexual Stimuli

Sexual functioning can be characterized as a sequential process beginning with exposure to a sexual stimulus or stimuli followed by some form of overt sex-related behavior. The stimulus-behavior link is mediated by intervening and interacting sexual arousal, affective/evaluative responses, and cognitive responses, such as those previously discussed (Byrne 1977, 1981; Griffitt and Hatfield 1985). Sexual behavior is not an inevitable consequence of exposure to sexual stimuli. Whether any overt sex-related behavior occurs, as well as the form the behavior takes, will be influenced by the intensity of the arousal produced and the nature of the affective/evaluative and cognitive responses activated by the sexual stimuli. In addition, situational factors such as the availability of sexual partners, social constraints, and so forth shape the probability and potential form of sexual behavior.

Most research investigating sexual stimulus-sexual behavior has focused on the behavioral after effects of exposure to erotic movies, photographs, or written material. In the typical experiment, the sexual behavior patterns of subjects are ascertained, they are exposed to the erotic stimuli, and their sexual behavior patterns are once again assessed. The resultant behavior is compared with preexposure behavior or with the behavior of control groups who have not been exposed to erotica, and changes in sexual behavior are attributed to the sexual stimuli.

Several such studies were conducted in the late 1960s under the auspices and funding of the Commission on Obscenity and Pornography (1970). In those studies, married and unmarried college student and noncollege student samples of males and females were exposed to various types of erotica, and postexposure changes in their sex-related behavior were assessed. Taken together, the findings of these and other studies show an increase in the probability of occurrence of several sex-related behaviors following exposure to erotica. Whether any behavior occurs and what specific behavior occurs are based on a number of factors, including previous sexual experience, partner availability, and arousal and affective responses to the erotic stimuli.

For example, unmarried college students without available sexual partners are more likely to masturbate after exposure, particularly if they are highly aroused during exposure and have previous masturbatory experience. Those married or single but coitally experienced with available sexual partners are more likely to engage in coitus following exposure if they are highly aroused, particularly if the partners are both exposed to the erotica (Davis and Braucht 1971; Kutschinsky 1971). In addition, increases in the frequency of sex conversations, sex fantasies, sexual desires, and sexual dreams following exposure have been reported (Davis and Braucht 1971; Griffitt 1975; Schmidt and Sigusch 1970; Schmidt et al. 1973).

Though significant sexual behavior changes following exposure to erotica have been noted in several studies, some aspects of these changes deserve emphasis. First, the changes occur in relatively small percentages (10 to 30 percent) of people, and the changes seem to be limited to behaviors the people engage in on a regular basis. Second, the changes are short-lived, generally subsiding in twenty-four to forty-eight hours and often limited to the day(s) of exposure (Brown, Amoroso, and Ware 1976; Mann, Berkowitz, Sidman, Starr, and West 1974). Third, there is some evidence of satiation both of the arousal and of the behavioral effects of repeated exposure to erotica (Mann et al. 1974; but, see Julien and Over 1984). Finally, whether or not changes take place and the nature of the changes are dependent on the affective responses evoked by the sexual stimuli. For example, sexual stimulation evoking positive affective responses is associated with approach behavior relevant to sexual activity (Brown et al. 1976; Griffitt and Kaiser 1978; Griffit et al. 1974), while negative affect evoked by sexual stimuli sometimes leads to avoidance behavior

(Griffitt and Kaiser 1978; Griffitt et al. 1974) and sometimes to approach behavior (Davis and Braucht 1971; Fisher and Byrne 1978a) The reasons for the inconsistent effects of negative affect are unclear.

Sexual Responses: Female-Male Comparisons

As noted earlier, regardless of the particular beliefs expressed, the sexuality of females and males has typically been characterized in very different terms. For the last century or so, however, the predominant view has been that females are undersexed and males oversexed. That is, in comparison with males, females have been characterized as less arousable by sexual stimuli, as more negative regarding sexual matters, as thinking about sex in different ways, and as behaviorally less responsive to sexual stimuli (Gordon and Shankweiler 1971; Scully and Bart 1973). The remainder of this chapter is devoted to an overview of research findings relevant to such assertions regarding arousal, affective/evaluative, cognitive, and behavioral differences between the sexes in response to sexual stimuli.

Sexual Arousal: Females and Males

Several types of evidence are seemingly consistent with views that females are less sexually aroused than males by sexual stimuli. Females become sexually active at later ages and are less likely to engage in masturbation, premarital intercourse, extramarital intercourse, and homosexual activities than are males (Kinsey et al. 1953; Hunt 1974). Females tend to avoid sex stimuli more than do males (Griffitt and Kaiser 1978), and the patrons of adult bookstores and pornographic movies are primarily male (Nawy 1971). Furthermore, *when questioned in surveys* regarding their experiences with and reactions to explicit pictorial, verbal, or written depictions of sexual activity, males exceed females in reported sexual arousal (Abelson, Cohen, Heaton, and Suder 1971; Berger, Gagnon, and Simon 1971; Kinsey et al. 1953).

During the last two decades a rather substantial amount of evidence has accumulated that sharply contrasts with views of females as relatively unresponsive to sexual stimuli. The evidence has grown out of laboratory studies in which females and males are systematically exposed to various sexual stimuli and physiological and/or subjective sexual arousal are assessed. Responses to physical sexual stimulation—masturbation, petting, coitus, and homosexual activity—to explicit erotic materials, and to sexual fantasy have been investigated.

For some time, the fundamental similarity of female and male patterns of physiological response to sexual stimuli has been recognized (Kinsey et al. 1953; Masters and Johnson 1966). As noted earlier, the primary responses include genital vasocongestion, reflected by size, color, and temperature changes in the genitals and by various myotonic or muscular reactions. When such responses are observed during physical sexual stimulation, it has repeatedly been shown that female and male response patterns are quite similar, including the rates at which they approach physiological orgasm through masturbation (Masters and Johnson 1966, 1979). Similarly, when genital vasocongestive responses are assessed, it is found that both females and males are physiologically aroused by explicit erotic stimuli (Heiman 1977; Wincze et al. 1977) and that the average intensity of arousal, as measured thermographically, is similar (Abramson et al. 1981).

As noted previously, a large number of studies have assessed reports of subjective sexual arousal to erotic stimuli. The stimulus materials have included photographs, movies, auditory tapes, literature, and fantasy-induced depictions of sexual activities. Across a wide array of college and noncollege, married and unmarried subject samples from Western Europe, the United States, and other countries, females and males have been found to be remarkably similar in their reported levels of sexual arousal to such stimuli (Byrne and Lamberth 1971; Griffitt 1973, 1975; Griffitt and Hatfield 1985; Hatfield et al. 1978; Schmidt et al. 1973).

Although gender differences in immediate arousal responses to sexual stimuli generally appear to be negligible, females and males do differ in the extent to which they are aroused by particular stimuli. For example, both sexes are more aroused by nudes of the opposite sex than nudes of their own sex (Byrne and Lamberth 1971; Griffitt 1973), by movies of an opposite-sexed person masturbating than of a same-sexed person masturbating (Schmidt 1975), and by erotic heterosexual depictions in which their own sex is characterized as dominant (Garcia, Brennan, DeCarlo, McGlennon, and Tait 1984). Similarly, both male and female homosexuals are more aroused by depictions of homosexual activity among those of their own sex than among those of the opposite sex (Wincze and Qualls 1984). It is sometimes found that females are less aroused by group sex and oral sex stimuli than are males (Byrne and Lamberth 1971; Griffitt 1973; Mosher 1971), though these differences tend to decrease as female sexual experience increases (Griffitt 1973, 1975). In contrast to the Kinsey et al. (1953) survey findings, there appear to be minimal differences between females and males in their sexual arousal to sexual stimuli that include themes of romance and affection versus those that do not (Fisher and Byrne 1978b; Heiman 1977; Schmidt et al. 1973). Males are, however, sometimes more aroused than females by stimuli depicting sexual aggression and violence (Malamuth 1984).

Earlier, a conceptual distinction between state sexual arousal and trait sexual arousability was drawn. The findings reviewed above suggest that, except for stimulus content differences, males and females differ little in their temporary or state sexual arousal in response to sexual stimuli. Similarly, viewing their summated or average degree of state arousal responses across a variety of sexual stimuli as a crude estimate of trait arousability or responsiveness, the limited evidence suggests little difference between females and males in general sexual arousability (Griffitt 1973, 1975; Veitch and Griffitt 1980). Preliminary use of the Hoon et al. (1976) Sexual Arousability Inventory with males as well as females also reveals no gender differences in arousability (Harris et al. 1980).

Affective and Evaluative Responses: Females and Males

Findings regarding female-male differences in affective and evaluative responses to sexual stimuli contrast with data pointing to substantial gender similarities in sexual arousal responses. It is, instead, rather consistently found that females' reports of affective responses to and evaluations of sexual stimuli are more negative than are those of males (Griffitt and Hatfield 1985; Kelley and Byrne 1983). Such differences are found with regard to affective responses to visual (Griffitt 1973, 1975; Schmidt and Sigusch 1970), auditory (Przybyla and Byrne 1984), and written (Garcia et al. 1984; Schmidt et al. 1973) sexual stimuli.

Following exposure to a variety of different kinds of sexual stimuli, females are more likely than males to report feelings of disgust, repulsion, irritation, anger, and nausea. Males are more likely to report positive affective feelings such as entertainment, curiosity, lack of boredom, excitement, and anxiousness (eagerness) (Fisher and Byrne 1978b; Griffitt 1973; Garcia et al. 1984; Schmidt et al. 1973). When affective responses such as those described are factor analyzed and combined into orthogonal positive and negative dimensions (Byrne et al. 1974), similar findings are obtained—females generally respond more negatively and less positively to sexual stimuli than do males (Garcia et al. 1984; Przybyla and Byrne 1984).

Most of the gender differences in affective responding reported above have been obtained in studies in which sexual stimulus content has not been systematically varied to examine stimulus-affect relationships. Relatively few such studies have, in fact, been reported.

It has, however, been found that both sexes react more negatively and less positively to same-sex than to opposite-sex masturbatory stimuli and that males tend to react more negatively to same-sex masturbation than do females (Schmidt 1975). These differences, however, are mediated by individual differences in authoritarianism, sex guilt, and attitudes toward masturbation (Kelley 1985; Mosher and Abramson 1977). In addition, both sexes react more negatively to aggressive sexual content stimuli than to nonaggressive sexual content stimuli, although female reactions are more negative than those of males (Malamuth 1984; Schmidt 1975). Females respond more negatively than males to lesbian sexual stimuli and males more negatively than females to male homosexual activity (Mann, Sidman, and Starr 1971). Finally, females respond more positively and less negatively when females rather than males are described as the dominant or central characters in sexual action, and males respond affectively in the reverse direction (Garcia et al. 1984).

The prevalence of gender differences in state affective responses to sexual stimuli, with females generally reacting more negatively than males, suggests the existence of gender differences in dispositional or state affective response tendencies. The rather limited available data concerning this issue support the notion that females are disposed to respond more negatively than are males to a wide array of sexual stimuli. Female scores on the Sexual Opinion Survey (White et al. 1977) are significantly lower (more negative) than are those of males (Gilbert and Gamache 1984). On the Janda and O'Grady (1980) Sex Anxiety Inventory, females report higher expectancies than males for negative feelings associated with a variety of sexual stimuli, and on the Mosher (1966, 1968) Sex Guilt Scales, female scores reveal more dispositional guilt than do males (Green and Mosher 1985).

Mediated, at least in part, by affective responses, evaluative responses to sexual stimuli tend to parallel affective reactions, that is, sexual stimuli that evoke negative feelings are evaluated unfavorably and those that evoke positive feelings are evaluated favorably (Byrne et al. 1974). Gender differences in affective responses to sexual stimuli are accompanied by gender differences in evaluations of the stimuli. Females generally evaluate sexual stimuli less favorably and are more likely to judge erotica as pornographic and to favor its legal restriction than are males (Griffitt 1973; Schmidt et al. 1973).

Cognitive Responses: Females and Males

Though little is known about the origins of sex dreams, it is generally thought that they are activated by sexual stimuli during sleep, such as sexual memories or thoughts (Griffitt and Hatfield

1985). The available data suggest that sex dreams are substantially more prevalent in males than in females. Nearly all males, but only 70 to 75 percent of females report dreaming about sex at some time in their lives. Around 80 percent of males and 40 percent of females report having sex dreams that result in orgasm. Most males who dream to orgasm first do so shortly following the onset of puberty, but the average female who has orgasmic dreams first does so around the age of twenty-five (Kinsey et al. 1948, 1953). Though the Kinsey data are nearly four decades old, more recent surveys continue to report comparable gender differences in sex dreams (Gravitz 1970; Wilson 1975). Though males are more likely than females to have sex dreams, the usual nature and content of male and female sex dreams appear to be similar. Generally, both sexes dream about sexual activities that they have experienced or that they might like to experience. Heterosexual dreams are more frequent in heterosexual males and females, and homosexual dreams more frequent in homosexuals. Such findings support the notion that sex dreams are activated by memories and thoughts of sexual experiences or by desires for or expectations that one might engage in particular experiences (Kinsey et al. 1948, 1953). When such thoughts, memories, or desires are activated by waking exposure to explicit sexual stimuli, sexual dream frequencies are increased in both sexes (Amoroso et al. 1971; Mosher 1971).

Early findings regarding waking sexual fantasies suggested that, though a majority of both sexes report having sexual fantasies, fewer females (69 percent) than males (84 percent) report doing so (Kinsey et al. 1948, 1953). More recent findings, however, suggest relatively few female-male differences in the prevalence of spontaneous sexual fantasies or sexual fantasies accompanying masturbation, coitus, or homosexual activities (Crépault and Couture 1980; Hesselund 1976; Hunt 1974; Knafo and Jaffe 1984; McCauley and Swann 1978, 1980). The majority of both sexes, and approximately equal percentages, report engaging in sexual fantasy under these circumstances.

Though sexual fantasies can be evoked by an array of sexually arousing stimuli, including explicit erotica (Schmidt et al. 1973), self-generated sexual fantasies are also potent sources of sexual arousal in both sexes. Self-generated sexual fantasies are capable of evoking physiological sexual arousal responses (Heiman 1977; Laws and Rubin 1969) as well as rather high levels of reported subjective sexual arousal in both sexes (Byrne and Lamberth 1971; Green and Mosher 1985).

Though contemporary findings reveal few gender differences in the prevalence of sexual fantasy or in its effectiveness as a sexual stimulant, some investigators have reported gender differences in fantasy content and fantasy function. Like the contents of sex dreams, sexual fantasy contents often parallel experience or sexual preferences—the most usual fantasies of heterosexuals are heterosexual, those of homosexuals are homosexual, and so forth (Kinsey et al. 1948, 1953; Masters and Johnson 1979)

Though the most usual sexual fantasy among heterosexuals is intercourse with a known or loved partner, male fantasies more often than those of females contain themes of group sex, sex with strangers, forcing sex on their partners, sexual irresistability, and superior sexual virility. Females are more likely than males to have fantasies of being submissive, being forced to have sex, experiencing romance and affection, and being seduced or seducing others (Arndt, Foehl, and Good 1985; Barclay 1973; Hunt 1974; Kinsey et al. 1948, 1953; Knafo and Jaffe 1984). For both sexes, frequency of sexual fantasizing, the types of fantasies used, and the degree to which fantasy is sexually arousing depend on a variety of personal characteristics such as sex guilt, frequency of daydreaming, self-centeredness, general thoughtfulness, and other factors (Arndt et al. 1985; Green and Mosher 1985; Knafo and Jaffe 1984).

For both sexes, the main functional use of sexual fantasy is to enhance sexual arousal and enjoyment, and it is demonstrably effective in doing so. In addition, the general ability to form clear and vivid images is positively related to general sexual arousability (Harris et al. 1980). There is some evidence, however, that during heterosexual activities, sexual fantasy may be employed by females and males for somewhat different purposes. Males tend to employ fantasies of ongoing sexual activity in an attempt to control and/or pace their degree of arousal and the current sexual activity. Females, on the other hand, tend to use fantasies that add to and elaborate the ongoing sexual activity in order to enhance their degree of sexual arousal (McCauley and Swann 1978, 1980).

There has been little research wherein the sexes have been compared regarding the specific information, beliefs, or expectancies brought into play by sexual stimuli or situations. Regarding information and beliefs (which are functionally equivalent as mediators of behavior), there is some evidence, however, that females have more accurate information than males. This difference has been found in studies of knowledge of contraceptive devices and techniques (Delcampo et al. 1976), awareness of sexually transmitted diseases (Griffitt 1985), and endorsement of sex myths concerning topics such as masturbation, sex during pregnancy, aphrodisiacs, conception, menopause, and other sexual matters (Mosher 1979b). Males also tend to endorse more myths regarding rape than do females (Malamuth 1984).

Though not extensively investigated, it has been suggested that sexual situations evoke fundamentally different perceptions and expectancies in females and males (Gagnon and Simon 1973), that is, sexual situations are "scripted" differently for the sexes. In heterosexual situations, males expect to play rather active roles in pursuing sexual involvement and expect females to exert controls over the sexual interaction and access to their bodies. Males expect, and are expected, to meet some resistance to their efforts but, in the absence of unambiguous "signals" of resistance, to persist. The usual female script is similar, but, of course, her own behavioral expectancies and roles are seen differently. She expects the male to push for sex and expects to behave in ways that control or limit sexual action. She expects him to persist unless her "stop" signals are unambiguous. These scripts are, to some extent, embedded in processes of self-evaluation and evaluation by others regarding masculine and feminine worth. Part of being masculine for males is sexual success, and part of being feminine for females is limited sexual accessibility (Gagnon and Simon 1973; Goodchilds and Zellman 1984).

Heterosexual situations include a complex array of stimuli, interpretations of such stimuli, and expectancies based on the interpretations that presumably influence behavior. Males push for sex, females communicate "stop" and "go" signals, males interpret and form expectancies based on the signals, and either stop or go behaviorally. There is, however, evidence that females and males differ in the expectancies they have regarding sexual signals. Males tend to attribute more sexual meaning to a wide range of behaviors than do females. More often than females, males expect that women who wear "sexy" clothing desire sex, that dating couples want to have sex, and that a variety of dating behaviors indicate a desire for and an agreement to have sex (Goodchilds and Zellman 1984). In addition, males are more likely to interpret female friendliness as sexual interest and less likely to perceive a "no" response to a request for intercourse as really meaning no (Abbey 1982). Though substantially more research in this area is needed, apparently sexual stimuli evoke stronger expectancies for sexual behavior in males than in females.

With females generally socialized to negatively value sexual activities as they relate to feminine worth, and with males positively valuing sexual activities as evidence of masculine worth (Gagnon and Simon 1973), evidence that their generalized expectancies regarding sexuality differ comes as little surprise. Females express stronger expectancies for feeling guilty regarding their sexuality than do males (Mosher 1979a). In addition, females' expectancies for and anxiety regarding external punishment for their sexuality exceed those of males (Janda and O'Grady 1980). Females and males, however, do not appear to differ in their generalized expectancies regarding their ability to exert control over the potentially rewarding outcomes of their heterosexual activities (Catania et al. 1984).

Behavioral Responses: Females and Males

In the relatively few studies wherein females' and males' sexual behavioral responses to sex stimuli have been compared, few differences have been noted. Following exposure to sexual stimuli, both sexes report increases in sexual desires and in interest in engaging in sexual activity (Griffitt 1975; Schmidt and Sigusch 1970; Schmidt et al 1973). Females and males alike report engaging in more fantasy and sexual conversations following exposure to explicit erotica (Mosher 1971; Schmidt et al. 1973). If they are single or lack an available sex partner and have previous masturbatory experience, both sexes are more likely to masturbate after rather than before exposure to sexually arousing stimuli (Amoroso et al. 1971; Schmidt and Sigusch 1970). Married and single but coitally experienced males and females with available partners are more likely to engage in coitus following sexual stimulation (Mann et al. 1971). Furthermore, when they receive signals of sexual desire such as direct requests, sexual touches, "suggestive" body movements, clothing removal, and so forth from their partners, coitally active females and males alike are likely to comply (Jesser 1978).

It appears that gender per se is not an important mediator of behavioral responses to sexual stimuli. Instead, what appear to be more important are various, within-sex dimensions of individual differences. For example, whether behavioral approach or avoidance responses to sexual stimuli occur depends for both sexes, in part, on the affective responses elicited by the stimuli. Positive affective responses tend to lead to approach behavior and negative affective responses to avoidant behavior (Brown et al. 1976; Griffitt and Kaiser 1978; Griffitt et al. 1974). Affective response tendencies are, themselves, mediated in part by variables such as authoritarianism (Griffitt 1973; Kelley 1985), sex guilt (Griffitt and Kaiser 1978; Kelley 1985), erotophobia-erotophilia (Fisher and Byrne 1978a; Sapolsky 1984), sex-role differences (Kenrick, Stringfield, Wagenhels, Dahl, and Ransdell 1980), and Type A-B personality differences (Becker and Byrne 1985).

CONCLUSIONS; FEMALES AND MALES

During the last several decades, a tremendous amount of research has been conducted in which females and males have been compared on a variety of physical, psychological, and behavioral dimensions. The results of much of this research have been confusing and contradictory. Female-male differences on particular dimensions have sometimes been found, sometimes reverse differences have been found, sometimes no differences have been found (Maccoby and Jacklin 1974; Tavris and Wade 1984). In spite of all of this controversy, long-standing stereotypes regarding differences between the sexes persist (Broverman et al. 1973; Tavris and Wade 1984).

Hopefully, this brief overview has helped clarify attempts to understand the similarities among and differences between females and males in sexual responses. It has long been assumed that the sexuality of females and males differs in many fundamental ways but particularly in the way that females and males respond to sexual stimuli. Thus, this overview has focused on female-male comparisons of arousal, affective/evaluative, cognitive, and behavioral responses to sexual stimuli. Some of the findings reviewed appear to contradict and some to confirm existing beliefs about the sexes. Others are so inconsistent or limited in scope or quantity that they offer little ground for firm conclusions.

Widely held beliefs and early survey findings (Abelson et al. 1971; Kinsey et al. 1953) that males exceed females in their sexual arousal responses to sexual stimuli and in their dispositional sexual arousability find little support in more recent studies, wherein physiological and subjective arousal responses have been studied experimentally. Instead, females and males appear to be more similar than different in the physiological and subjective arousal responses to physical as well as to psychological sexual stimuli. Most differences that occur appear to depend on the contents of the particular stimuli to which the sexes are exposed.

Do these findings mean that earlier findings and beliefs were "wrong," that earlier differences have now dissolved, or some combination of both? Though this question is impossible to answer fully, the "combination" interpretation seems most reasonable. On the one hand, the early survey research may have overstated existing differences by asking respondents to recall retrospectively their degree of arousal to various stimuli. Socialized to view sexual interests and arousability in females negatively, females may have been led to underreport their arousal responses to sexual stimuli. Laboratory settings, however, legitimize such experiences, encourage more "accurate" responses, and, therefore, female-male differences fade (Griffitt and Hatfield 1985). On the other hand, female and male sexual attitudes and practices have shown substantial convergence in the last two decades (Hunt, 1974) and, along with increases in female sexual experiences, there have been increases in female sexual responsiveness (Griffitt 1973, 1975). Taken together then, the use of experimental methodology and possible increases in female responsiveness may well account for differences between early and more recent findings.

In contrast to the apparent convergence of female and male sexual arousal responses, female affective and evaluative responses to sexual stimuli are rather consistently more negative than are those of males. Though little direct evidence is available, it seems likely that these differences are, in part, traceable to differences in sexual socialization experiences. Compared with males, females are more often socialized to be cautious in sexual matters, to avoid behaviors that might trigger sexual advances, to value negatively sexual involvements outside of loving, affectionate, exclusive, and committed relationships, to avoid pregnancy, and to guard against acquiring "loose" sexual reputations. In short, females' socialization regarding many aspects of sexuality is often quite negative compared to that of males (Gagnon and Simon 1973) and may account for their more negative responses to many sexual stimuli. Increases in female sexual experience, however, tend to reduce female-male affective response differences (Griffitt 1975).

For males, sex and sexual stimuli are more often positively valued and actively pursued, and having a successful or even "loose" sexual reputation is more often tolerated or even encouraged (Gagnon and Simon 1973). There is a potential for conflict here, since the sex males positively value and pursue may be the sex females negatively value and avoid. Sexual interactions can assume adversarial tones in which sexual signals are miscommunicated and/or misunderstood, resulting in hostility and suspiciousness that contribute to the prolonging of the "war between the sexes" (Goodchilds and Zellman 1984; Tavris and Wade 1984).

The recent evidence that exists continues to suggest that females dream less often about sex, at least to the point of orgasm, than do males but that the content of sex dreams is similar for females and males. Though it has not been verified, there is some reason to believe that differences in orgasmic dream frequency and prevalence may reflect female reluctance and inability to report such experiences. Males may be both less reluctant and more able to report such experiences because of ejaculatory evidence that orgasm has occurred (Griffitt and Hatfield 1985).

The sexes appear to differ little in the prevalence or frequency of waking sexual fantasies that occur in response to sexual stimuli, activities, or spontaneously. Both sexes are sexually aroused by such fantasies, and the usual contents of fantasies are similar in males and females. Presumably because of socialized differences in affective responses to and expectancies regarding sex activities, however, females are more likely to have fantasies of romance, submissiveness, and being seduced. Males are more likely to fantasize group sex, sex with strangers, and other activities consistent with their socialization (Gagnon and Simon 1973).

Though the sexual knowledge of both sexes is often regarded as less than adequate, some evidence suggests that females have more accurate information than do males. It is possible this difference is found because females are more likely than males to obtain their information regarding such topics as coitus, fertilization, pregnancy, menstruation, abortion, and contraception from sources such as parents or schools. Males are more likely to gain their information from less reliable sources such as peers (Gebhard 1977). Parents may well regard these topics of greater socialization importance for females since, if contraceptive practices are inadequate, only they can become pregnant and have abortions.

The differing scripts and expectancies evoked in females and males by sexual stimuli and situations were described in some detail. It is sufficient here to suggest that differing patterns of female and male sexual socialization account for these differences (Gagnon and Simon 1973) and for the potential for conflict in sexual interactions that results (Goodchilds and Zellman 1984). I might add, however, that it has been noted with some concern that relatively little change in this area has apparently occurred in recent years, the "sexual revolution" notwithstanding (Goodchilds and Zellman 1984; Tavris and Wade 1984).

Relatively few female-male differences were noted regarding behavioral responses to sexual stimuli. Depending on variables such as sexual experience, availability of sexual partners, and situational factors, both sexes are more likely to do something sexual following exposure to sex stimuli, be it fantasize, talk about sex, masturbate, or engage in coitus.

Though some rather consistent similarities and differences in female and male responses to sexual stimuli have been identified, much remains to be done in this area. Little is actually known regarding the informational and expectative responses evoked by sexual stimuli, how they may influence arousal, affective/evaluative, imagery, and behavioral responses, and how they may differ in females and males. Similarly, little is known about the precise origins of sex differences in affective responses. It has been necessary in this overview to refer to rather imprecise suggestions that sexual socialization differences account for observed differences. More detailed information regarding the processes and contents involved in the sexual socialization of females and males is sorely needed. Hopefully, future research will address these issues more directly.

REFERENCES

Abbey, A. (1982). Sex differences in attributions for friendly behavior: Do males misperceive females' friendliness? *Journal of Personality and Social Psychology. 42,* 830–838.

Abel, G. G., Murphy, W. D., Becker, J. U., and Bitar, A. (1979). Women's vaginal responses during R.E.M. sleep. *Journal of Sex and Marital Therapy, 5,* 5.

Abelson, H., Cohen, R., Heaton, E., and Suder, C. (1971). National survey of public attitudes toward and experience with erotic materials. In *Technical report of the Commission on Obscenity and Pornography* (Vol. 6). Washington, D.C.: U.S. Government Printing Office.

Abramson, P. R., Perry, L. B., Seeley, T. T., Seeley, D. M., and Rothblatt, A. B. (1981). Thermographic measurement of sexual arousal: A discriminant validity analysis. *Archives of Sexual Behavior, 10,* 171–176.

Alan Guttmacher Institute. (1981). *Teenage pregnancy: The problem that hasn't gone away.* New York: Alan Guttmacher Institute.

Amoroso, D. M., Brown, M., Pruesse, M., Ware, E. E., and Pilkey, D. W. (1971). An investigation of behavioral, psychological, and physiological reactions to pornographic stimuli. In *Technical report of the Commission on Obscenity and Pornography* (Vol. 8). Washington, D.C.: U.S. Government Printing Office.

Arndt, W. B., Foehl, J. C., and Good, F. E. (1985). Specific sexual fantasy themes: A multidimensional study. *Journal of Personality and Social Psychology, 48,* 472–480.

Barclay, A. M. (1970). Urinary acid phosphatase in sexually aroused males. *Journal of Experimental Research in Personality, 4,* 233–238.

Barclay, A. M. (1971). Information as a defensive control of sexual arousal. *Journal of Personality and Social Psychology, 17,* 244–249.

Barclay, A. M. (1973). Sexual fantasies in men and women. *Medical Aspects of Human Sexuality, 7,* 205–216.

Barlow, D. H., Becker, R., Leitenberg, H., and Agras, W. S. (1970). Mechanical strain gauge recording penile circumference change. *Journal of Applied Behavior Analysis, 3,* 73–76.

Becker, M. A., and Byrne, D. (1985). Self-regulated exposure to erotica, recall errors, and subjective reactions as a function of erotophobia and Type A coronary-prone behavior. *Journal of Personality and Social Psychology, 48,* 760–767.

Bentler, P. M., and Peeler, W. H., Jr. (1979). Models of female orgasm. *Archives of Sexual Behavior, 8,* 405–423.

Berger, A. S., Gagnon, J. H., and Simon, W. (1971). Pornography: High school and college years. In *Technical report of the Commission on Obscenity and Pornography* (Vol. 9). Washington, D.C.: U.S. Government Printing Office.

Broverman, I. K., Vogel, S. R., Broverman, D. M., Clarkson, F. E., and Rosenkrantz, P. S. (1972). Sex role stereotypes: A current appraisal. *Journal of Social Issues, 28,* 59–78.

Brown, M., Amoroso, D. M., and Ware, E. E. (1976). Behavioral effects of viewing pornography. *Journal of Social Psychology, 98,* 235–245.

Bullough, V. L., and Bullough, B. (1977). *Sin, sickness, and sanity: A history of sexual attitudes.* New York: Garland.

Byrne, D., Fisher, J. D., Lamberth, J., and Mitchell, H. E. (1974). Evaluations of erotica: Facts or feelings? *Journal of Personality and Social Psychology, 29,* 111–116.

Byrne, D. (1977). Social psychology and the study of sexual behavior. *Personality and Social Psychology Bulletin, 3,* 3–30.

Byrne, D. (1981). *Predicting human sexual behavior.* G. Stanley Hall Lecture. American Psychological Association, Los Angeles.

Byrne, D., and Fisher, W. A. (eds.). (1983). *Adolescents, sex, and contraception.* Hillsdale, N.J.: Erlbaum.

Byrne, D., and Lamberth, J. (1971). The effect of erotic stimuli on sex arousal, evaluative responses, and subsequent behavior. In *Technical report of the Commission on Obscenity and Pornography* (Vol. 8). Washington, D.C.: U.S. Government Printing Office.

Catania, J. A., McDermott, L. J., and Wood, J. A. (1984). Assessment of locus of control: Situational specificity in the sexual context. *Journal of Sex Research, 20,* 310–324.

Chambless, D. L., and Lifshitz, J. L. (1984). Self reported sexual anxiety and arousal: The expanded Sexual Arousability Inventory. *Journal of Sex Research, 20,* 241–254.

Clore, G. L., and Byrne, D. (1974). A reinforcement-affect model of attraction. In T. Huston (ed.), *Foundations of interpersonal attraction,* New York: Academic Press.

Comfort, A. (1972). *The joy of sex.* New York: Crown.

Commission on Obscenity and Pornography. (1970). *The report of the Commission on Obscenity and Pornography.* Washington, D.C.: U.S. Government Printing Office.

Crépault, C., and Couture, M. (1980). Men's erotic fantasies. *Archives of Sexual Behavior, 9,* 565–581.

Cvetkovich, G., Grote, B., Bjorseth, A., and Sarkissian, J. (1975). On the psychology of adolescents' use of contraceptives. *Journal of Sex Research, 11,* 256–270.

Davenport, W. H. (1978). Sex in cross-cultural perpsective. In F. A. Beach (ed.), *Human sexuality in four perspectives.* Baltimore: Johns Hopkins University Press.

Davis, K. E., and Braucht, G. N. (1971). Reactions to viewing films of erotically realistic heterosexual behavior. In *Technical report of the Commission on Obscenity and Pornography* (Vol. 8). Washington, D.C.: U.S. Government Printing Office.

DelCampo, R. L, Sporakowski, M. J. and DelCampo, D. S. (1976). Premarital sexual permissiveness and contraceptive knowledge: A biracial comparison of college students. *Journal of Sex Research, 12,* 180–192.

Fisher, S. (1973). *The female orgasm: Psychology, physiology, fantasy.* New York: Basic Books.

Fisher, W. A., and Byrne, D. (1978a). Individual differences in affective, evaluative, and behavioral responses to an erotic film. *Journal of Applied Social Psychology, 8,* 355–365.

Fisher, W. A., and Byrne, D. (1978b). Sex differences in response to erotica? Love versus lust. *Journal of Personality and Social Psychology, 36,* 117–125.

Fisher, W. A., Byrne, D., Edmunds, M., Miller, C. T., Kelley, K., and White, L. A. (1979). Psychological and situation-specific correlates of contraceptive behavior among university women. *Journal of Sex Research, 15,* 38–55.

Fisher, W. A., Miller, C. T., Byrne, D., and White, L. A. (1980). Talking dirty: Responses to communicating a sexual message as a function of situational and personality factors. *Basic and Applied Social Psychology, 1,* 115–126.

Ford, C., and Beach, F. A. (1951). *Patterns of sexual behavior.* New York: Harper & Row.

Freud, S. (1957–1964). Three essays on the theory of sexuality. In J. Strachey (ed.), *The standard edition of the complete psychological works of Sigmund Freud* (Vol. 7). London: Hogarth Press. (originally published, 1905).

Friday, N. (1974). *My secret garden: Women's sexual fantasies.* New York: Pocket Books.

Gagnon, J. H., and Simon, W. (1973). *Sexual conduct.* Chicago: Aldine.

Galbraith, G. G., and Mosher, D. L. (1968). Associative sexual responses in relation to sexual arousal, guilt, and external approval contingencies. *Journal of Personality and Social Psychology, 10,* 142–147.

Galbraith, G. G., and Sturke, R. W. (1974). Effects of stimulus sexuality, order of presentation, and sex guilt on free association latencies. *Journal of Consulting and Clinical Psychology, 42,* 828–832.

Garcia, L. T., Brennan, K., DeCarlo, M., McGlennon, R., and Tait, S. (1984). Sex differences in sexual arousal to different erotic stories. *Journal of Sex Research, 20,* 391–402.

Gebhard, P. H. (1977). The acquisition of basic sex information. *Journal of Sex Research, 13,* 148–169.

Geer, J. H. (1975). Direct measurement of genital responding. *American Psychologist, 30,1* 415–418.

Geer, J. H., Morokoff, P., and Greenwood, P. (1974). Sexual arousal in women: The development of a measurement device for vaginal blood volume. *Archives of Sexual Behavior, 3,* 559–564.

Geer, J. H., and Quartararo, J. D. (1976). Vaginal blood volume responses during masturbation. *Archives of Sexual Behavior, 5,* 403–413.

Gilbert, F. S., and Gamache, M. P. (1984). The Sexual Opinion Survey: Structure and use. *Journal of Sex Research, 20,* 293–309.

Goodchilds, J. D., and Zellman, G. L. (1984). Sexual signalling and sexual aggression in adolescent relationships. In N. M. Malamuth and E. Donnerstein (eds.), *Pornography and sexual aggression.* New York: Academic Press.

Gordon, M., and Shankweiler, P. J. (1971). Different equals less: Female sexuality in recent marriage manuals. *Journal of Marriage and the Family, 33,* 459–466.

Gravitz, M. A. (1970). Large scale normal adult base-rates for MMPI "privacy" items: I. Sexual attitudes and experiences. *Journal of General Psychology, 82,* 153–156.

Green, S. E., and Mosher, D. L. (1985). A causal model of sexual arousal to erotic fantasies. *Journal of Sex Research, 21,* 1–23.

Griffitt, W. (1973). Response to erotica and the projection of response to erotica in the opposite sex. *Journal of Experimental Research in Personality, 6,* 330–338.

Griffitt, W. (1975). Sexual experience and sexual responsiveness: Sex differences. *Archives of Sexual Behavior, 4,* 529–540.

Griffitt, W. (1985). [Sexually transmitted diseases: Knowledge, attitudes, and intentions]. Unpublished raw data.

Griffitt, W., and Hatfield, E. (1985). *Human sexual behavior.* Glenview, Ill.: Scott, Foresman, and Company.

Griffitt, W., and Kaiser, D. L. (1978). Affect, sex guilt, gender, and the rewarding-punishing effects of erotic stimuli. *Journal of Personality and Social Psychology, 36,* 850–858.

Griffitt, W., May, J., and Veitch, R. (1974). Sexual stimulation and interpersonal behavior: Heterosexual evaluative responses, visual behavior, and physical proximity. *Journal of Personality and Social Psychology, 30,* 367–377.

Hain, J. D., and Linton, P. H. (1969). Physiological response to visual sexual stimuli. *Journal of Sex Research, 5,* 292–302.

Hare, R., Wood, K., Britain, S., and Frazelle, J. (1971). Autonomic responses to affective visual stimulation: Sex differences. *Journal of Experimental Research in Personality, 5,* 14–22.

Hariton, E. B., and Singer, J. L. (1974). Women's fantasies during sexual intercourse: Normative and theoretical implications. *Journal of consulting and Clinical Psychology, 42,* 313–322.

Harris, R., Tulis, S., and LaCoste, D. (1980). Relationships among sexual arousability, imagery ability, and introversion-extraversion. *Journal of Sex Research, 16,* 72–86.

Hatfield, E., Sprecher, S., and Traupman, J. (1978). Men's and women's reactions to sexually explicit films: A serendipitous finding. *Archives of Sexual Behavior, 7,* 583–592.

Heiman, J. R. (1977). A psychophysiological exploration of sexual arousal patterns in females and males. *Psychophysiology, 14,* 266–274.

Henson, D. E., and Rubin, H. B. (1971). Voluntary control of eroticism. *Journal of Applied Behavior Analysis, 4,* 37–44.

Hessellund, H. (1976). Masturbation and sexual fantasies in married couples. *Archives of Sexual Behavior, 5,* 133–147.

Hite, S. (1976). *The Hite report.* New York: Dell.

Hoon, E. F., Hoon, P. W., and Wincze, J. P. (1976). An inventory for the measurement of female sexual arousability: The SAI. *Archives of Sexual Behavior, 5,* 291–300.

Hunt, M. (1974). *Sexual behavior in the 1970's.* Chicago: Playboy Press.

Janda, L. H., and O'Grady, K. E. (1980). Development of a sex anxiety inventory. *Journal of Consulting and Clinical Psychology, 48,* 169–175.

Jesser, C. J. (1978). Male responses to direct sexual initiatives of females. *Journal of Sex Research, 14,* 118–128.

Jovanovic, U. J. (1971). The recording of physiological evidence of genital arousal in human males and females. *Archives of Sexual Behavior, 1,* 309–320.

Julien, E., and Over, R. (1984). Male sexual arousal with repeated exposure to erotic stimuli. *Archives of Sexual Behavior, 13,* 211–222.

Kaplan, H. S. (1974). *The new sex therapy.* New York: Brunner/Mazel.

Karacan, I., Williams, R. L., Guerrero, M. W., Salis, P. J., Thornby, J. I., and Hursch, C. J. (1974). Nocturnal penile tumescence and sleep of convicted rapists and other prisoners. *Archives of Sexual Behavior, 3,* 19–26.

Kelley, K. (1985). Sex, sex guilt, and authoritarianism: Differences in responses to explicit heterosexual and masturbatory slides. *Journal of Sex Research, 21,* 68–85.

Kelley, K., and Byrne, D. (1983). Assessment of sexual responding: Arousal, affect, and behavior. In J. Cacioppo and R. Petty (eds.), *Social psychophysiology.* New York: Guilford.

Kenrick, D. T., Stringfield, D. O., Wagenhals, W. L., Dahl, R. H., and Ransdell, H. J. (1980). Sex differences, androgyny, and approach responses to erotica: A new variation on the old volunteer problem. *Journal of Personality and Social Psychology, 38,* 317–324.

Kinsey, A., Pomeroy, W., and Martin, C. (1948). *Sexual behavior in the human male.* Philadelphia: Saunders.

Kinsey, A., Pomeroy, W., Martin, C., and Gebhard, P. (1953). *Sexual behavior in the human female.* Philadelphia: Saunders.

Knafo, D., and Jaffe, Y. (1984). Sexual fantasizing in males and females. *Journal of Research in Personality, 18,* 451–462.

Korff, J., and Geer, J. (1983). The relationship between sexual arousal experience and genital response. *Psychophysiology, 20,* 121–127.

Krafft-Ebing, R. V. (1965). *Psychopathia sexualis* (H. E. Wedeck, Trans.). New York: G. P. Putnam's Sons. (Originally published, 1886)).

Kutschinsky, B. (1971). The effect of pornography: A pilot experiment on perception, behavior, and attitudes. In *Technical report of the Commission on Obscenity and Pornography* (Vol. 8). Washington, D.C.: U.S. Government Printing Office.

Laws, D. R., and Rubin, H. B. (1969). Instructional control of an autonomic sexual response. *Journal of Applied Behavior Analysis, 2,* 93–99.

Levitt, E. E., and Brady, J. P. (1965). Sexual preferences in young adult males and some correlates. *Journal of Clinical Psychology, 21,* 347–354.

Maccoby, E. E., and Jacklin, C. N. (1974). *The psychology of sex differences.* Stanford: Stanford University Press.

Malamuth, N. M. (1984). Aggression against women: Cultural and individual causes. In N. M. Malamuth and E. Donnerstein (eds.), *Pornography and sexual aggression.* New York: Academic Press.

Mann, J., Berkowitz, L., Sidman, J., Starr, S., and West, S. (1974). Satiation of the transient stimulating effect of erotic films. *Journal of Personality and Social Psychology, 30,* 729–735.

Mann, J., Sidman, J., and Starr, S. (1971). Effects of erotic films on the sexual behavior of married couples. In *Technical report of the Commission on Obscenity and Pornography* (Vol. 8). Washington, D.C.: U.S. Government Printing Office.

Marshall, D. S. (1972). Sexual behavior on Mangaia. In D. S. Marshall and R. C. Suggs (eds.), *Human sexual behavior: Variations in the ethnographic spectrum.* Englewood Cliffs, N.J.: Prentice-Hall.

Masters, W. H., and Johnson, V. E. (1979). *Homosexuality in perspective.* Boston: Little, Brown, & Co.

McCary, J. L. (1973). *Human sexuality* (2nd ed.). New York: D. Van Nostrand.

McCauley, C., and Swann, C. P. (1978). Male-female differences in sexual fantasy. *Journal of Research in Personality, 12,* 76–86.

McCauley, C., and Swann, C. P. (1980). Sex differences in the fequency and functions of fantasies during sexual activity. *Journal of Research in Personality, 14,* 400–411.

Mendelsohn, M. J., and Mosher, D. L. (1979). Effects of sex guilt and premarital sexual permissiveness on role-played sex education and moral attitudes. *Journal of Sex Research, 15,* 174–183.

Miller, W. R., and Lief, H. I. (1976). Masturbatory attitudes, knowledge, and experience: Data from the Sex Knowledge and Attitude Test (SKAT). *Archives of Sexual Behavior, 5,* 447–467.

Mosher, D. L. (1966). The development and multitrait-multimethod matrix analysis of three measures of three aspects of guilt. *Journal of Consulting Psychology, 30,* 25–29.

Mosher, D. L. (1968). Measurement of guilt in females by self-report inventories. *Journal of Consulting and Clinical Psychology, 32,* 690–695.

Mosher, D. L. (1971). Psychological reactions to pornographic films. *Technical report of the Commission on Obscenity and Pornography* (Vol. 8). Washington, D.C.: U.S. Government Printing Office.

Mosher, D. L. (1979a). The meaning and measurement of guilt. In C. E. Izard (ed.), *Emotions in personality and psychopathology.* New York: Plenum Press.

Mosher, D. L. (1979b). Sex guilt and sex myths in college men and women. *Journal of Sex Research, 15,* 224–234.

Mosher, D. L., and Abramson, P. R. (1977). Subjective sexual arousal to films of masturbation. *Journal of Consulting and Clinical Psychology, 45,* 796–807.

Mosher, D. L., and Greenberg, I. (1969). Females' affective responses to reading erotic literature. *Journal of Consulting and Clinical Psychology, 33,* 472–477.

Nawy, H. (1971). The San Francisco erotic marketplace. In *Technical report of the Commission on Obscenity and Pornography* (Vol. 4). Washington, D.C.: U.S. Government Printing Office.

Phares, E. J. (1978). Locus of control. In H. London and J. E. Exner, Jr. (eds.), *Dimensions of personality.* New York: John Wiley & Sons.

Pirke, K. M., Kockott, G., and Dittmar, F. (1974). Psychosexual stimulation and plasma testosterone in man. *Archives of Sexual Behavior, 3,* 577–584.

Przybyla, D. P. J., and Byrne, D. (1984). The mediating role of cognitive processes in self-reported sexual arousal. *Journal of Research in Personality, 18,* 54–63.

Rook, K. S., and Hammen, C. L. (1977). A cognitive perspective on the experience of sexual arousal. *Journal of Social Issues, 33,* 7–29.

Rosen, R. C., and Keefe, F. J. (1978). The measurement of human penile tumescence. *Psychophysiology, 15,* 366–376.

Rotter, J. B. (1966). Generalized expectancies for internal versus external control of reinforcement. *Psychological Monographs, 80,* (1, Whole No. 609).

Sapolsky, B. S. (1984). Arousal, affect, and the aggression-moderating effect of erotica. In N. M. Malamuth and E. Donnerstein (eds.), *Pornography and sexual aggression.* New York: Academic Press.

Schill, T., and Chapin, J. (1972). Sex guilt and males' preference for reading erotic magazines. *Journal of Consulting and Clinical P:sychology, 39,* 516.

Schmidt, G. (1975). Male-female differences in sexual arousal and behavior during and after exposure to sexually explicit stimuli. *Archives of Sexual Behavior, 4,* 353–364.

Schmidt, G., and Sigusch, V. (1970). Sex differences in responses to psychosexual stimulation by films and slides. *Journal of Sex Research, 6,* 268–283.

Schmidt, G., Sigusch, V., and Schafer, S. (1973). Responses to reading erotic stories: Male-female differences. *Archives of Sexual Behavior, 2,* 181–199.

Schwartz, S. (1973). Effects of sex guilt and sexual arousal on the retention of birth control information. *Journal of Consulting and Clinical Psychology, 41,* 61–64.

Scully, D., and Bart, P. (1973). A funny thing happened on the way to the orifice: Women in gynecology textbooks. In J. Huber (ed.), *Changing women in a changing society* (pp. 283–288). Chicago: University of Chicago Press.

Seeley, T. T., Abramson, P. R., Perry, L. B., Rothblatt, A. B., and Seeley, D. M. (1980). Thermographic measurement of sexual arousal: A methodological note. *Archives of Sexual Behavior, 9,* 77–85.

Shah, F., Zelnick, M., and Kantner, J. F. (1975). Unprotected intercourse among unwed teenagers. *Family Planning Perspectives, 7,* 39–44.

Singer, B. (1984). Conceptualizing sexual arousal and attraction. *Journal of Sex Research, 20,* 230–240.

Singer, J. L. (1966). *Daydreaming.* New York: Random House.

Sintchak, G., and Geer, J. H. (1975). A vaginal plethysmograph system. *Psychophysiology, 12,* 113–115.

Spielberger, C. D. (1972). *Anxiety: Current trends in theory and research* (Vol. 1). New York: Academic Press.

Staples, R. (1973). Male-female sexual variations: Functions of biology or culture. *Journal of Sex Research, 9,* 11–20.

Steinman, D., Wincze, J., Sakheim, D., Barlow, D., and Mavissakalian, M. (1981). A comparison of male and female patterns of sexual arousal. *Archives of Sexual Behavior, 10,* 529–547.

Tavris, C., and Wade, C. (1984). *The longest war: Sex differences in perspective* (2nd ed.). San Diego.

Veitch, R., and Griffitt, W. (1980). The perception of erotic arousal in men and women by their same and opposite sex peers. *Sex Roles, 6,* 723–733.

Whalen, R. E. (1966). Sexual motivation. *Psychological Review, 73,* 151–163.

White, L. A. (1979). Erotica and aggression: The influence of sexual arousal, positive affect, and negative affect on aggressive behavior. *Journal of Personality and Social Psychology, 37,* 591–601.

White, L. A., Fisher, W. A., Byrne, D., and Kingma, R. (1977). *Development and validation of a measure of affective orientation to erotic stimuli: The Sexual Opinion Survey.* Paper presented at the Midwestern Psychological Association, Chicago.

Wilson, W. C. (1975). The distribution of selected sexual attitudes and behaviors among the adult population of the United States. *Journal of Sex Research, 11,* 46–64.

Wincze, J. P., Hoon, P., and Hoon, E. G. (1977). Sexual arousal in women: A comparison of cognitive and physiological responses by continuous measurement. *Archives of Sexual Behavior, 6,* 121–133.

Wincze, J. P., and Qualls, C. B. (1984). A comparison of structural patterns of sexual arousal in male and female homosexuals. *Archives of Sexual Behavior, 13,* 361–370.

Zuckerman, M. (1971). Physiological measures of sexual arousal in the human. *Psychological Bulletin, 75,* 297–329.

CHAPTER 7

Sexuality: A Feminist Perspective*

BERNICE LOTT

Sex is a good gift, a delight; . . . It participates in the fullness of fruit, wine, music, amity, the vitality of the senses.

Kate Millett (1978:80)

Lydia had thought of the sex act . . . as something the man "took" and the woman "gave." "He took her quickly," the books would say; or, "She gave herself to him." If anything in these verbal images aroused Lydia, it was the idea of making a present of her virginity to the man to whom she could then "belong."

Gail Godwin (1983:141)

The quotations opening this chapter describe sexual experiences as they might be and as they actually are for many women. Sexual interaction with a man often proves to be a disappointment to a young woman because her anticipations may differ greatly from those of her partner. For example, one woman's bitter and angry reactions to the realities of "love making" are expressed in this remarkable poem by Alta:

> penus envy, they call it
> think how handy to have a thing
> that poked out; you could just shove
> it in any body, whang whang & come,
> wouldn't have to give a shit.
> you *know* you'd come!

---

* This chapter is taken from the author's book, *Women's Lives: Themes and Variations in Gender Learning*, 2d edition, Monterey, California, Brooks/Cole, in press (first edition, Charles Thomas, 1981).

wouldn't have to love that person,
trust that person,
whang, whang & come.
if you couldn't get relief for free,
pay a little $, whang whang & come.
you wouldn't have to keep, or abort.
wouldn't have to care about the kid.
wouldn't fear sexual violation.
penus envy, they call it.
the man is sick in his heart,
that's what I call it (1973:295)

Alta's words reflect what social scientists have been validating through more systematic and objective means, the existence of two human cultures divided by gender. Girls and boys not only learn different role expectations and different motives and behaviors, but also divergent meanings of sexuality.

William Simon and John Gagnon (1977) have pointed out that, although adolescent boys are committed to sexuality and are encouraged to seek gratification, they receive little training in "the language and actions of romantic love," whereas adolescent girls are "committed to romantic love and relatively untrained in sexuality." In the process of dating, each gender must train "the other in what each wants and expects," but this exchange system does not always proceed smoothly.

Investigators continue to document gender differences in the meaning and expectations of sexuality. Patricia Miller and Martha Fowlkes have noted that "whereas males are encouraged to give full expression to their sexuality as an indication and demonstration of their masculinity, female sexual response has traditionally been thought to be appropriately derived from relationships with men and their needs" (1980:786). This traditional ideology remains dominant and descriptive generally of the behavior of contemporary adults. Thus, a recent study of sexual attitudes (Hendrick, Hendrick, Slapion-Foote, and Foote, 1985) reported substantial and significant gender differences, with college women expressing less support than college men for sexual permissiveness and more support for sexual responsibility. Philip Blumstein and Pepper Schwartz studied 12,000 American couples from varied geographical backgrounds, including heterosexual and homosexual married and cohabiting pairs. Their conclusions support the proposition that gender plays a primary organizing role in sexuality. "Our data," they write, "have compelled us to see that men and women represent two very distinct modes of behavior" (1983:302), regardless of sexual orientation. With respect to sexual motivation and attitudes, for example, "lesbians are more like heterosexual women than either is like gay or heterosexual men" (1983:303).

Women's experiences of sexuality (arousal and gratification) were, until relatively recently, not much discussed or researched, nor described in literature by women themselves. It was primarily men who attempted descriptions of women's sexual feelings in fiction and in psychiatric and medical texts, basing their descriptions on their own assumptions. William Masters told Mary Hall (1969) in an interview for *Psychology Today* that when he had reviewed the literature in 1954, he found that "everything said about female orgasm was written by males." The situation is considerably changed today, although a search of the social science literature through the 1970s still revealed little material on "the sexuality of adult women in the context of their normative social roles and relationships" (Miller and Fowlkes 1980).

Currently, women are talking about their sexual experiences and describing their behavior in autobiography, fiction, poetry, and in response to questions asked by researchers engaged in empirical investigation. Comparisons between the new information and the older assumptions reveal significant discrepancies. For those unfamiliar with the work of early sex education pioneers like Havelock Ellis or Margaret Sanger, the findings reported in the famous "Kinsey Report," *The Sexual Behavior of the Human Female* (Kinsey, Pomeroy, Martin, and Gebhard, 1953), provided many surprises. The book was a landmark—the data it presented had come from women themselves. Almost eight thousand women had been interviewed (albeit by men) and had responded to a variety of questions that women had not typically been asked before. More recently, valuable information about women's sexual behavior and erotic fantasies has come from the work of William Masters and Virginia Johnson (1966) and from the inquiries of journalists like Nancy Friday (1973) and Shere Hite (1976). Women fiction writers have also been speaking about sexuality: Erica Jong's *Fear of Flying* (1973) and *Parachutes and Kisses* (1984), Judith Rossner's *Looking for Mr. Goodbar* (19760, and Marge Piercy's *Braided Lives* (1983), to name just a few, have jolted readers into recognizing that typical differences between women and men in sexual attitudes and responses are a consequence of culture or social learning, and that, among women and men with similar experiences and perspectives, there is a remarkable similarity in their sexuality.

Basic Concepts: Sex as Motive and Behavior

Human beings do not restrict their sexual behavior to times when females are "in heat" and when the probability of conception is maximal. Our closest mammalian relatives, primates like apes and monkeys, also engage in sexual play when the female is not in estrus. In general, however, the sexual behavior of lower animals is tied to physiological signs of readiness for mating, when a series of typically stereotyped, relatively inflexible, and unlearned (instinctive) responses are triggered by appropriate stimuli. "As one moves up the evolutionary scale," according to Frank Beach (1969), "there is a gradual loosening of the tie between mating [sexual behavior] and reproduction." Whereas the sexual behavior of lower mammals is controlled by hormones, "in higher mammals, the balance of power shifts toward the central nervous system—and especially toward the neocortex." The erotic responsiveness of human beings, then, depends upon the highest brain center, the cortex (the center for flexible behavior, for learning and memory), which constitutes 90 percent of the volume of brain tissue.

The influence of learning and experience on sexuality can be seen among our closest animal relatives, the primates. Harry and Margaret Harlow (1966) found that monkeys raised in social isolation or with surrogate wire mothers were not sexually competent when they became physically mature. They did not seem to know what to do and did not exhibit what is generally considered to be "natural" sexual behavior.

Like other mammals, humans have *biological needs* that must be satisfied if the individual is to survive. These unlearned (primary or biogenic) needs are related to human physiology and to the maintenance of a stable internal environment (homeostasis). These needs include those for oxygen, for food and water, for waste elimination, and for pain avoidance. Deprivation of nutritional needs or continued exposure to an excessively aversive state (pain, for example) produces a general state of arousal characterized by intense and persistent stimulation, referred to as *drive*, that typically activates an organism and evokes behavior. Only some of this behavior is innate (for example, reflex movements). In humans, most of the behavior exhibited in response to a state of arousal is behavior that we have learned will successfully reduce the drive (the persistent and intense stimulation) because it is instrumental in obtaining what is "needed" (such as food to relieve hunger). In Figure 1, these concepts are diagrammatically related.

In addition to needs originating from the nature of human physiology, there is a second category of needs acquired during the course

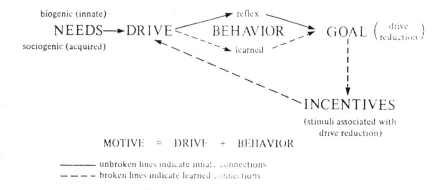

of a person's life. These needs result from experiences common to all human beings; from experiences common to groups of individuals (in particular cultures, for example); or from experiences specific to a particular person. These needs are variously described as sociogenic, psychological, secondary, or *acquired* and may be illustrated by desires for approval, for love, for affiliation or friendship, for power, for money, and so on. These needs, too, when aroused, result in a state of tension or drive and will elicit behavior. Again, the behavior most successful or instrumental in reducing the person's intense state of arousal (drive) will be learned and strengthened and will tend to be elicited again. Where do sexual desires stand in this dichotomy between innate/biogenic and acquired/sociogenic needs?

Some human needs appear to be closely tied to physiological functions but do not require satisfaction for biological survival. Their satisfaction may simply enhance physical well-being or health, or promote more efficient or optimum functioning. One such need is for sensory and physical stimulation. We know that infants who lack such stimulation are not as healthy as those who receive it, perhaps because, as Margaret Ribble (1944) long ago suggested, blood circulation is improved with physical stimulation, exercise, and movement. Adults find sensory deprivation aversive and disorienting (which is why solitary confinement is such a severe and effective punishment). Sexual stimulation may be a variant of this more general need category and, when satisfied, may also have the effect of promoting optimum functioning without being biologically essential. Thus, after surveying the sexual behavior of one hundred thousand women who responded to a *Redbook* questionnaire, Carol Tavris (one of the investigators) told an interviewer (Hahn, 1977) that female sexuality is "just plain fun . . . . It's jolly. . . . A good, happy sex life is like having good health."

Hormonal changes at puberty appear to be associated in all cultures with increased attention to, and desire for, sexual experience, supporting the proposition that there is a physiological component in sexual motivation. On the other hand, sexual satisfaction is not necessary for the maintenance of either homeostatic equilibrium or life, and it may continue as a strong motivator in individuals with low levels of sex hormones, for example, in postmenopausal women and persons whose sex glands have been surgically removed. In normal adults, there is no reliable correlation between frequency of sexual behavior or the experience of sexual arousal (drive) and level of either androgen or estrogen. Miron Zuckerman (1971) concluded, after reviewing the literature, that "most cases of impotence in males and frigidity in women are not expressions of hormonal insufficiencies and do not respond to treatment with additional exogenous hormone." Only in some special instances (e.g., hypogonadal men who have underdeveloped testes) has hormone therapy been effective in increasing the frequency of sexual arousal.

Sexual arousal is primarily a psychological phenomenon. It can occur under a vast variety of conditions. It is affected by general physical contact or by stimulation of specific body parts, such as the clitoris, or of certain especially sensitive erogenous areas of the skin. Sexual arousal can also occur in response to any stimulus physically present or present in fantasy or imagination. Learning theorists assume that such motivational stimuli, called *incentives* (see Figure 1), acquire their motivational properties through previous association with gratification or pleasure. For many poeple of either gender, there is some special song, situation, look, or memory that has acquired erotic meaning and will be sexually arousing. This approach to sexual arousal, somtimes referred to as the "appetitional theory of sexual motivation," contrasts sharply with Freud's libido theory, which postulates a fixed sexual drive. Ethel Person has distinguished between these two positions simply and succinctly, as follows: "In libido theory sexuality is both a motor force in culture and an innate force [in individuals] with which culture must contend. In appetitional theory the content of sexuality is formed by culture" (1980:607). In other words, as expressed by Ruth Bleier (1984), "our consciousness, our world, shapes our libido."

Given a state of sexual arousal, individuals will behave in a variety of ways, depending upon their particular learning experiences. Among humans, all aspects of sexual *behavior*, that is, what we do to achieve satisfaction or pleasure, is acquired or learned. Just as the arousal stimuli will vary, so too will the specific acts we engage in, the time and the place for the behavior, and the person(s) with whom we interact, if any. All these factors are subject to variation, depending upon one's cultural group and one's particular individual experiences as influenced by family, friends, special circumstances, and so on.

These variations have been well documented by social scientists and complement our own experiences and observations of other persons.

In this view of sexuality, homosexual and heterosexual are adjectives referring to same- or other-sex erotic attraction and require no major separation in a general discussion of sexual motivation. Philip Blumstein and Pepper Schwartz (1977) studied a sample of women and men who viewed themselves as bisexual and concluded that adult sexual preferences are not immutable and that either gender can be eroticized under particular circumstances. The investigators found that, especially among the women, sexual involvement followed "intense emotional attachment," which served as the "prerequisite for sexual attraction, sexual behavior, or a change in sexual identity." Alice Walker's (1982) novel *The Color Purple* is a compelling fictional account of just such an experience. As Carole Vance and Ann Snitow have pointed out:

> There are examples of both persistence and fluidity in sexual desire: for example, individuals who "knew" they were gay at an early age and remained so despite aversion therapy and incarcertion, and others who "became" lesbian or gay at different stages of the life cycle in a manner suggesting internal change rather than belated expression of "repressed" desire (1984:128).

PSYCHOPHYSIOLOGY OF SEXUAL EXPERIENCE AND BEHAVIOR

Sexuality can be considered a dimension of personality—a more or less consistent way of responding to a particular class of stimuli—and sexual response can be defined in both physiological and psychological terms. According to Virginia Johnson (cf. Hall 1969), "there is no such thing as the pure physiology of sexual response . . . . From a functional point of view, the correct terminology is . . . psychophysiology."

William Masters and Virginia Johnson (1966), who gathered data on female sexuality from observations and interviews with 387 women, learned that sexual arousal can occur in response to anything present or imagined that has sexual meaning for a woman, from general body stimulation, from indirect stimulation of the clitoris through pressure in the vagina, or from direct clitoral stimulation. They also concluded that orgasm (sexual gratification) for women is a complete body phenomenon involving more than just the vagina or the clitoris. Orgasmic experiences vary in duration and in intensity, in extent of body involvement, and in degree of pleasure. Although simple neural reflexes for orgasmic release are involved, orgasm is not an all-or-none phenomenon. This conclusion is reinforced by the experiences reported by approximately three thousand women who responded to Shere Hite's (1976) questionnaire, and by the over two hundred women studied by Michael Newcomb and P. M. Bentler (1983).

The clitoris is a woman's primary erogenous or sexually arousing portion of the body. Sigmund Freud (1905) considered the clitoris to be an analogue of the male penis and believed that clitoral pleasure represented a childish masculinity. With maturity, Freud insisted, the vagina becomes the prime focus of a woman's sexual experience and the locus of a more mature orgasm for normal, feminine women. Freud's assumptions, however, have been challenged by data from physiology, by reports of women's experiences, and by feminist critics. The title of a now classic paper by Anne Koedt (1973), "The Myth of the Vaginal Orgasm," became a challenging call to debate on this issue and a feminist slogan. There is now little question that the clitoris is the major organ involved in the physiology of female sexual response. It is, in fact, a unique human organ in that its sole function appears to be sexual. It is unlike the penis in this way, although these organs are anatomically related. Both organs originate from the same embryonic tissue and are similar in structure and function. The clitoris can become erect and enlarged (tumescence), its size changing both in diameter and in length, and its tip (glans), packed with nerve endings, is extremely sensitive to stimulation and has the greatest erotogenic potential.

Physiologically, more is involved in sexual response, however, than just clitoral tumescence. The muscles in the lower half of the vagina also participate in sexual response by rhythmically contracting. There is a thick layer of veins (venous plexus) in the vagina that becomes engorged, thereby narrowing the vaginal passageway so that a penetrating penis, for example, will provide stimulation for the walls of the vagina, which also contain nerve endings. The clitoris and lower third of the vagina function, to a very large extent, as an integrated unit. In addition, vaginal lubricants are released during sexual arousal. This physiological sign of a human female's sexual arousal is not hormonal but results from dilation of the venous plexus (Zuckerman 1971).

Vaginal lubricants and clitoral erection indicate sexual arousal in females, and penile erection signifies arousal in males. Are there differences between the two sexes in their subjective experiences and in sexual gratification or orgasm? William Wiest (1977) asked a group of college students to rate their experiences of orgasm on six bipolar, adjective scales. No significant differences were found between the responses of the women and those of the men. Wiest also cites an earlier study by other investigators in which judges were unable to distinguish reliably between reports written by women and those written by men of "what an orgasm feels like." Shere Hite (1976) reported that most of her informants described sexual arousal as involving sensations all over their bodies. They used such words as: "tingly," "alive," "warm," "happy," "feelings of wanting to touch and be touched," while descriptions of orgasm were more genitally localized.

Women can experience sequential orgasm more easily than men, and retain this ability over most of their lives. This multiorgasmic potential in women has a physiological basis. The engorgement or accumulation of blood (vasocongestion) in the vaginal wall and in the clitoris is reduced with orgasm, but is promptly followed, reflexively, by re-engorgement or refilling of the blood vessels. Each orgasm, therefore, produces increased vasocongestion and arousal. Sexual experience thus increases the physiological capacity of females for greater sexual pleasure. The frequency of multiple orgasms as well as sexual gratification have been found to increase with age and pregnancies, and also seem to be potentially greatest when pelvic congestion is maximal during the menstrual cycle (the postovulatory and premenstrual days).

Mary Jane Sherfey (1970) has proposed that women "could go on having orgasms indefinitely if physical exhaustion did not intervene" and that a woman must will herself to be satisfied. Sherfey refers to this phenomenon as "the paradoxical state of sexual insatiation in the presence of the utmost sexual satiation." She suggests that primitive men took steps to supress women because, unless women were confined and restricted, there could be no family life, agriculture, or civilization. (The assumption that civilization rests on the suppression of primitive urges or "instincts" is very much in the Freudian tradition. Freud, however, tended to ignore women and emphasized the destructive impulses of men.) According to Sherfey, men gradually (over thousands of years) forced women to accept monogamy, accepting it themselves only in principle in order to have knowledge of children's paternity and to ensure the care of children and the stability of the family, essential for property ownership and inheritance.

Regardless of the historical merits or validity of Sherfey's hypothesis, its basis in female physiology serves to counter the claim of men's insistent sexual needs and the popular denial of sexuality to women. The view that women are less sexual than men has not always been prevalent. The ancient Hebrews, for example, assumed that a woman's sexual desires were at least equal to those of a man's, and the marriage contract, therefore, provided not only for the wife's financial security but also for her sexual satisfaction. In the *Book of*

Women compiled in the twelfth century by the physician and rabbi Maimonides (cf. *Intellectual Digest*) the rules governing a woman's "conjugal rights" were presented in detail.

> For men who are healthy and live in comfortable and pleasurable circumstances without having to perform work that would weaken their strength, and do nought but eat and drink and sit idly in their houses, the conjugal schedule is every night. For laborers, such as tailors, weavers, masons, and the like, the conjugal schedule is twice a week if their work is in the same city, and once a week if their work is in another city. For ass drivers, the schedule is once a week; for camel drivers once in thirty days; for sailors, once in six months; for disciples of the wise, once a week, because the study of *Torah* weakens their strength (1972:53).

Men, it was believed, had to satisfy women's sexual needs, not vice versa. The early Hebrew practice of rigid separation between men and women and the imposition of strict standards of modesty for women may have been imposed because of men's fear of women's sexuality and to avoid being tempted into lust.

> It was considered immoral, for example, for a [Hebrew] man to listen to a woman sing, to look at her hair, or to walk behind her on the street. Thus, the most pious men shunned all contact with women other than their wives, would not look directly at women, and avoided hearing their voices by refusing to address them by name or ask them questions ("for the voice of woman leads to lewdness") (Baum, Hyman, and Michel 1975:9f).

Susan Griffin (1981) has suggested that a dominant idea in Judeo-Christian culture is that "the sight of a woman's body calls a man back to his own animal nature, and that this animal nature soon destroys him." It was Eve, we are told, who tempted Adam; and the belief in witchcraft was closely associated with the belief that carnal lust was insatiable in women. There is some evidence that women in pre-Christian England had considerable sexual freedom, that virginity was considered shameful, that marriage was temporary, and that women took lovers freely (Staples 1977). According to Carolyn Heilbrun, the Roman poet Ovid (who believed that women's lust was uncontrollable) recounted a story about Teiresias (the "blind prophet of Thebes") who had been both a man and a woman and was asked to mediate a dispute between the gods Jove and Juno about which sex enjoyed love-making more. "He agreed with Jove that women had greater pleasure, and Juno, in a fit of temper at the decision, struck Teiresias blind" (1973:11)

Contrary to such beliefs, we have been taught that it is male sexuality that is overwhelming and powerful and more insistent than female sexuality. Women are urged to sympathize with men's sexual needs. Ross Wetzsteon, in an analysis of the humor of Woody Allen, suggested the following:

> The jokes seem to be saying that Woody Allen always wants to get laid, but that women keep rejecting him, so he feels like a schlemiel. But notice how they all assume male sexuality and female indifference—what they're actually saying then, and what men actually identify with, is that men are sex maniacs and that women don't like sex . . . Woody Allen tells us that although we [men] have trouble with women (and we all feel we do) we don't have trouble with our sexuality . . . we're still ever-ready cocksmen. Men identify . . . not with his incompetence but with his libido (1977:14)

To Freud, the libido was masculine, an assumption he accepted from his own time and place and then maintained and proclaimed as biological certainly. Sexuality is still typically presented as being more crucial to men than to women, as an index of gender identity and a measure of self-worth. Ethel Person (1980) has suggested that for women "sexual expression is not critical to personality develop-ment," but for men, for whom "sexuality represents domination," it is essential. Philip Blumstein and Pepper Schwartz (1983) have con-cluded from their large-scale study of American couples that it is the man who is attributed with "greater appetite" and "greater license." "Women," they write, "often feel restrained and not in control of their own experience, and men feel pressed to perform." This same imagery, Blumstein and Schwartz assert, is shared by homosexual as well as by heterosexual couples.

There are, of course, women and men whose personal histories have reinforced sexual behavior that does not conform to the dom-inant gender ideology. In addition, the ideology itself does not present a simple, uncomplicated set of prescriptions. There are contradictory expectations, and we receive mixed messages about the sexuality of women and men. Molly Haskell (1973) has pointed out, for example, that in movies from the 1960s, a spinster like Joanne Woodward in *Rachel, Rachel* or Maggie Smith in *The Prime of Miss Jean Brodie* was depicted as suffering from "sexual malnutrition," looking "pinched and bloodless as a prune, the objective correlative of her unlubricated vagina." The message seemed to be that women really need sex whether they know it or not! In films of the 1980s, sexual overtures are still primarily made by men, but women are shown as acquiescing with little hesitation and their sexual pleasure is detailed and highlighted by cameras at close range.

The contradictions in historical and contemporary views of male and female sexuality, and in beliefs about which sex has the greater "need," illustrate the significance of learning (and culture) in defining sexual behavior and in affecting sexual experience. The human brain is the guardian and regulator of the body's hormones. Cognitive processes (thoughts, fantasies, fears, expectations, and beliefs) function in sexual arousal and nonarousal, in sexual satiation and nonsatiation; and the behaviors used to achieve gratification are learned. All aspects of human sexuality involve the interplay of psychological and physiological factors, and learning and experience are dominant. The biologist Ruth Bleier has compared sexuality with intelligence.

> Sexuality, like intelligence, is a learned relationship to the world, with an important and necessary, but not in itself determinate, biological component. For intelligence, it is not enough to have a brain and billions of neurons and synapses. Intelligence develops out of experience and learning . . . . So in sexuality, there is a real biological substrate for a range of sexual responses that involve the brain, hormones, muscles, and blood vessels. . . . But whatever or whoever arouses us . . . are . . . part of one's history of experiences and interactions with the external world. . . . [T]here is nothing about desire, arousal, orgasms, or feeling of transcendant oneness that "comes naturally."(1984:167)

PSYCHOLOGICAL CUES FOR SEXUAL AROUSAL

Alfred Kinsey and his associates (1953) reported that women are less apt to be sexually stimulated by visual (or ideational) cues than are men, and this belief has long been part of our general folklore about male-female differences in sexuality. Recently, a considerable amount of interest has been shown in this issue. Surveys have asked women and men about their exposure to, and enjoyment of, sexual material, and experimental investigations have tested responses to such material in laboratory settings.

The anonymous responses of twenty thousand readers of *Psychology Today* to a questionnaire on sexuality were analyzed by Robert Athamasion, Phillip Shaver, and Carol Tavris (1970). The respondents tended to be liberal politically and in their sexual attitudes; the majority were young (under 30), well educated (median level was college graduate), and of relatively high socioeconomic status. Among this highly selective sample, the voluntary exposure of men to "erotic or pornographic books, movies, magazines, etc." differed considerably from the voluntary exposure of women. Among the women, 72 percent had viewed such materials at some time, compared to 92 percent of the men, while 8 percent of the women and 25 percent of the men viewed such materials "frequently." Also of interest is the reported response to the materials. Among the women, 51 percent said they were aroused "occasionally" or "greatly," compared to 73 percent of the men.

Experimental studies, on the other hand, have failed to validate differences between men and women in objectively measured reactions to sexually explicit stimuli. Donn Byrne and John Lamberth (1971) tested a sample of married couples who volunteered to participate in a study described as "dealing with opinions about pornography." They were exposed to slides and literary selections depicting heterosexual, homosexual, and autosexual acts and were asked to imagine specific sexual scenes. The reactions of women and men were not reliably different, although there were wide individual differences within each group. For both women and men, instructions to imagine sexual acts produced greater arousal than exposure to either pictorial or printed presentations of the same themes. Byrne and Lamberth attempted to reconcile the survey data with their findings.

> The long accepted Kinsey finding with respect to sex differences in response to erotic material has either disappeared in the years following his study or . . . the survey method simply answers a different question than does the experimental method. That is, women are relatively less likely to purchase hard-core pornographic pictures or books, attend stag movies, etc., because of social pressures and custom. When asked whether they are frequently stimulated by such material, they indicate that they are not—because they are seldom exposed to these stimuli. On the other hand, when they are presented with erotic stimuli, as in an experiment, they are as sexually aroused as the males. In fact, the females in the present experiment were significantly more aroused than were the males by the various masculine stimuli such as male nudity, male masturbation, and even homosexual fellatio. (1971:26f)

Support for the findings of Byrne and Lamberth has come from
the work of other investigators. In one study (Schmidt, Sigusch, and
Schafer 1977), single men and women in a German university were
found to exhibit similar verbal and physiological responses to both
a purely sexual story and an affectionate sexual one. Julia Heiman
(1975) carefully measured physiological reactions to sexual materials
with a penile strain gauge and an instrument called a photoplethysmograph, which detects blood volume and pressure pulse in the
penis and vagina. College student volunteers listened to tapes of
heterosexual interaction that varied in sexual context. Heiman found
that "women like erotica as much as men do, that they are turned
on by sexual descriptions, that their fantasies are as vivid and self-
arousing."

There appear to be two separate questions at issue: the first is, To
what extent do women seek erotic stimulation in pictures, books,
etc.? The second question is, To what degree can women be aroused
by such material? With respect to the second issue, findings such as
those cited above support the conclusion that any stimulus with
sexual significance for an individual can be arousing and that this
fact is no less true for women than for men. However, women in
general do not seem to actively pursue sexual titillation in this way
as much as men do.

In one study, William Griffitt and Donn Kaiser (1978) asked women
and men to perform a discrimination task for which correct responses
were followed (rewarded) by a slide of a "sexually explicit act" or
by a neutral slide. Compared to persons rewarded with slides of a
nonsexual nature, the performance of men was found to be "positively
influenced" and that of women, "negatively influenced when correct
responses [in the discrimination task] were followed by exposure to
erotic stimuli." A peek at a "sexually explicit act" did not, apparently,
function as a positive reinforcement for women, whereas it did for
men. Perhaps this result reflects the fact that women have learned
to expect censure (or other punishment) from the pursuit of sexual
interests. Sexually explicit material, therefore, may be guilt arousing,
and the most likely response will be avoidance. Griffitt and Kaiser
found that persons of both genders who scored low on a measure
of "sex guilt" were more likely to repeat responses that were followed
by a sexually explicit slide than were individuals who scored high
on "sex guilt." On the other hand, Patricia Morokoff (1985) found
that although a sample of women who scored high in sex-guilt self-
reported less arousal to an erotic videotape than low sex-guilt women,
the former showed significantly greater physiological arousal than
the latter.

Some researchers have suggested that women do not actively seek sexually explicit material because such material omits romance. Generally, women in our culture are assumed to be more romantic than men, more concerned with relationships and less interested in sexual satisfaction that does not include love. Some evidence supports this view. One group of college women who were interviewed after seeing a series of sexually explicit films indicated that their ideal erotic film was one in which an attractive heterosexual pair romantically and affectionately engages in prolonged foreplay leading gradually to coitus (Steele and Walker 1976). Another investigation (Kenrick, Stringfield, Wagenhals, Dahl, and Ransdell 1980) found that a sample of college women chose to view a "loving" erotic film as opposed to hard-core "lustful" film significantly more often than did a sample of college men. On the other hand, William Fisher and Donn Byrne (1978) found that college women and men responded very similarly to both love and lust themes in erotic films, and they concluded that affectional or romantic emphases are not preconditions for women's arousal by erotic stimuli.

An alternative explanation of gender differences in the pursuit of sexual imagery focuses on the nature or quality of that material. Although many writers and social science researchers fail to distinguish between erotica and pornography and use the terms interchangeably, feminists have been asserting that these terms refer to very different kinds of visual and prose materials. Gloria Steinem has reminded us that the word pornography stems from the Greek *porné*, which means prostitute. Pornography, Steinem maintains, is not about sexual love or passion but about "dominance and violence against women"; it involves the depiction of women being coerced or conquered, degraded, humiliated, or beaten, but always dominated.

> It may be very blatant, with weapons of torture or bondage, wounds and bruises, some clear humiliation, or an adult's sexual power being used over a child. It may be much more subtle: a physical attitude of conqueror and victim, the use of race or class differences to imply the same thing, perhaps a very unequal nudity, with one person exposed and vulnerable while the other is clothed. In either case, there is no sense of equal choice or equal power (1978:54).

In pornography, men are at war against women; sexual acts are used, like weapons, to inflict pain and to defeat the enemy. In pornography, writes Maureen Howard (1983), a woman "becomes no more than a word for a part of her body, a mechanical device acted upon by a male thrust; if not willing to submit, brought to submission." Susan Griffin has argued that pornography is the antithesis of eroticism and, ultimately, antisexual and antinature. "The pornographer reduces a woman to a mere thing, to an entirely material object without a soul." The woman, as object, "shows her goods," and, "like a piece of furniture, she must be pictured from the side, and particular parts of her body, those intended for use . . . must be carefully examined . . . . There is no person there . . . this objectification of a whole being into a thing is the central metaphor" (1981:36). Griffin notes that some pornography debases and humiliates men, but these men are always smaller, weaker, and more "feminine" than their sexual dominators.

In erotica, unlike pornography, sexual behavior is instrumental to mutual pleasure. Steinem (1978) has pointed out that erotica comes from the root word *eros*, that it pertains "to passionate love or sexual desire" and is defined by the depiction of sexual love. It implies positive choice, acceptance, shared pleasure, communication, and, as Maureen Howard (1983) suggests, it may "reveal to us the wonders . . . of our sexuality" and encourage "personal revelation."

Pornography is not about the sexual pleasure of women. Recently, an unsolicited package of illustrated materials advertising "premier discount erotica" (films and magazines) came by mail to a young man who had been a guest in my home several years earlier. The featured materials, graphically and unambiguously illustrated, were on "incest, animals, and young girls" and carried titles such as "Mammaries," "Shaved Naked Twats," "Anal Lust," and "Dominate Women." Such material is pornographic not because it is sexually explicit but because its primary message is the physical or psychological humiliation of women, which, tragically, stimulates sexual arousal in large numbers of men.

It is probable that many women avoid pornography for these reasons. Also, for these reasons, most feminists actively discourage the distribution of such material. Research that distinguishes between erotica and pornography and that examines women's (and men's) reactions to each should provide important information. Other questions about the effect of pornography on men's attitudes and interactions with women have been asked repeatedly over the past several decades and are currently being investigated (e.g., Donnerstein 1980).

SEXUAL BEHAVIOR IN THE SERVICE OF OTHER GOALS

Sexual behavior serves a number of functions beyond the primary one of being instrumental to sexual gratification (arousal and orgasm). Some of these secondary functions are discussed below.

Sex as a Symbol of Autonomy

Some writers (e.g., Person 1980) have argued that women are less likely than men to use sexuality to achieve self-identity. Ann Snitow (1980), in reviewing how women novelists have treated sex in their works, concluded that although sex is sometimes presented as a reward for being daring and liberated, it is not presented (as in men's fiction) as a testing ground for the ego, as a way to assert oneself, or as a "symbol of . . . triumph or defeat." Yet, such themes have appeared in recent novels by women (e.g., *Braided Lives* by Marge Piercy [1983], *August* by Judith Rossner [1983], and Gail Godwin's *A Mother and Two Daughters* [1983]). The heroine in *Fly Away Home*, for example, recalls the beginning of her relationship with her husband as follows: "She had slept with Ross, not out of passionate desire, not because she felt swept away, but because she was annoyed with herself for being twenty-one, graduated from college and still a virgin. . . . She was celebrating her independence of body, life, of judgment" (Piercy 1984:170). Similar reports come from women's descriptions of their own experiences. Sarah Crichton, for example, in an article about college women, began with a disclosure about herself: "About all I can remember from spring in sophomore year is that I got myself a double bed. . . . For me, that bed was the ultimate symbol of adulthood—an advertisement that I was not only 'sexually active,' but that my body was my own, to do with as I pleased." (1983:68). For this young woman, sex was a "means of defining yourself."

Maggie Scarf (1980) has suggested that such an objective can sometimes boomerang. For some of the women she met during the course of her research on depression, the sexual relationships they initiated served "to ward off feelings of isolation" and to heighten activity or excitement, but only temporarily. Sexual interaction proved to be a poor substitute for intimacy and was not effective in increasing feelings of autonomy or control. In writing about the attitudes of black women, Toni Bambara has distinguished between "control" and indiscriminate sexual behavior. Among the older women she remembers as influential in her own life, lip service was paid to virginity, but "a greater premium was placed on sexual expertise; you were a 'real woman' when you had knowledge of and control of your sensual gifts. However, if a woman indiscriminately flaunted these gifts, she was either a loose woman or a fool. . . . So you learned growing up that . . . healthy liaisons . . . should be based on partnership and sexual competency on both sides" (1974:41).

Sex as Status Symbol

Men boast of their sexual conquests, and women boast of the number of men who find them attractive and who make sexual overtures. Reporting these to friends is an attempt to gain social recognition and to enhance one's social status.

For Sylvia Plath (1972), speaking through fictional heroines, the world in the 1950s was "divided into people who had slept with somebody and people who hadn't, and this seemed the only really significant difference between one person and another." Several decades later, the same issue remains salient, at least for the college women who have been most studied. Since middle-class, college-educated women tend to marry later than working-class women, sexual experience outside of marriage may be a more compelling, status-relevant issue for the former. Writing from the perspective of a college woman, Sarah Crichton (1983) has talked about the "pressure" felt by sexually inexperienced women, to whom virginity "simply means nobody wants you and you feel like shit." She quotes a junior at a midwestern university who echoes Plath's heroine of the 1950s: " 'I've got to get rid ot it,' that's all you can think about."

Sex as a Commodity

Women have been purchased, won, conquered, taken, traded, or been part of the victor's booty in war. During the war in Bangladesh between East and West Pakistan, according to reporter Joyce Goldman (1972), "as many as 200,000 Bengali women, victims of rape by West Pakistani soldiers" were "abandoned by their husbands, because no Moslem will live with a wife who has been touched by another man." A woman, in this view, has one owner; to be used by another man is to render her unclean and unworthy of her husband. In protest of this belief (which extends beyond the Moslem world), a group of mad and marvelous Israeli women in a novel by E. M. Broner (1978) perform a hymenotomy on the eight-day-old daughter of one of them, saying: "May she not be delivered intact to her bridegroom or judged by her hymen but by the energies of her life."

Women are used to attract the attention of men and to sell products. For example, an ad for a centrifuge in a prestigious science journal reads, "the first beautiful centrifuge," and shows a beautiful blonde woman in a lab coat standing next to the item. Hi-fi equipment is advertised in a newspaper by showing a stereo cylinder surrounded by a nude woman in four different poses and asks the question, "Going 4 channel?" A magazine ad attempts to convince a prospective male buyer that "you can fit a lot of important things in Toyota's . . . Wagon" by showing it filled with six lovely young women. A major airline attempts to lure customers by presenting a bathing-suit clad young woman under a giant caption that reads, "What's your pleasure?" Women are thus used as "incentives" for men of varied background, education, and interests. A newspaper story described how private companies "use sex to win government contracts" (Providence Evening Bulletin, June 26, 1980). Since this occurrence is common in our culture, the story was relegated to a midsection of the paper and informed us that sex is "routine in the world of government contracting" and business in general.

That sex can be exchanged for goods and services is a lesson learned across ethnic groups and is part of the experience of both black and white women. Thus, Gloria Joseph, writing about the childhood and adolescence of black women in America, noted that in our society "sex is the dominant commodity for monetary profit, personal gains and gratifications, and human exploitation" (1981:205). Many adolescent girls are taught to "cash in" on their sex appeal, to use it to manipulate boys for material advantage. Ossie Guffy and Caryl Ledner have told the story of a black woman who grew up in the "usual world of lower-middle-class America, in the period from 1931 to the present," and who received this advice about sex from her smart big sister:

> Boys lust even more than girls. . . . When a boy lusts after you, that's when you get him to do what you want. You've got to make them feel you're going to let them, and then when they're so horny they can't see straight, you kind of pull back and whisper you're afraid. Then . . . you start talking about how you'd love to have a charm bracelet, or a new scarf, or see a certain movie, and they'll fall all over themselves getting you what you want, 'cause they figure once you've got what *you* want, you'll give them what *they* want (1971:63).

This advice is straight talk, direct and clear. Other girls receive similar messages from peers, parents, or the media, but they are more subtle, ambiguous, unspoken. In the real life story of Teresa Cardenas told by Robert and Jane Coles (1978) we learn that her father, a strict, traditional patriarch, responded to knowledge of his daughter's well-paying job in a dance hall at the age of fifteen by reminding her that "money is not an evil thing." When Teresa considered consulting the priest, her father said, "no—there are some things it's best not to tell priests."

The message that sex is exchangeable for goodies is so well accepted in our culture that we treat with good humor even the portrayal of very young girls in this role. One full-page, *New York Times Magazine* ad, for example, showed a seductive little girl with a sexy look dressed as half-adult, half-child with an enormous fur coat under the caption, "Get what you've always wanted."

Sex as Sport

Sexual responses can be viewed as acts requiring skill, expertise, and training; like gourmet chefs, persons boast of themselves or others as expert lovers, or, like players of a game, they "score" or win. This attitude is reflected in the extraordinary popularity of "how to" sex manuals and in the concern that has been expressed among some mental health practitioners about the "demands" experienced by individuals for sexual "performance."

The idea that sex is something a person can do well or badly seems to be an old one, however, and has provided both men and women with a source of humor about each other's vulnerabilities. Rayna Green, in an article about "bawdy lore of southern women," has shared some of the tales told by the women among whom she grew up about the sexual errors of men. "Usually the subject for laughter is men's boasts, failures or inadequacies ('comeuppance for lack of uppcomance,' as one of my aunts would say)" (1977:31). Sexual disappointments, frustrations, humiliations, and anxieties may be partially relieved by humor. Funny stores help women react against their cultural definitions and provide a safe and in-group outlet for hostility against men. They can put men down and laugh at their pretensions. Bawdy lore, according to Green, also provides sex education for young girls; what they do not understand in the joke (which they are both supposed to hear and not supposed to hear) they will inquire about from friends or relatives. Tony Bambara has presented a similar picture of the sex education of young black girls by older women. There is bound to be an aunt, she writes, who will "encourage you to hang out in the beauty parlor or her living room with her and her friends and eavesdrop." There, some woman is bound to look you straight in the eye and warn, "If he don't know what he's doing, pitch him out the bed on his head." For, "while the church ladies daily castigated the run-around men and adulterers, they were equally adamant about men who . . . withheld themselves or could not or would not deliver. For that was sinful, an abuse of nature" (1974:40).

When sex with other persons falls short of our expectations and their or our own expertise is found wanting, we invent pleasure machines. William Masters and Virginia Johnson popularized the vibrator and, according to a recent report (Ehrenriech, Hess, and

Jacobs 1982), "A growing number of housewives can choose between a Tupperware party and a Tupper-style party where the wares are exotic sex paraphernalia instead of plastic containers." In his film *Sleeper*, a science fiction view of the future, Woody Allen presented the ultimate sensual device, an orgasmic box for one.

Recent indications that sadomasochistic sex is now "popular" with a portion of the population can be viewed as another extension of sex-as-sport. The influence of "S & M" can be seen in women's fashions, as illustrated in a magazine like *Vogue* that presented an entire section on steel accessories worn by wide-eyed, frightened models; arm shackles as bracelets, steel belts, and neck leashes were featured. The matching clothing, described in fashion jargon as "hard-edged" and "rough," was shown with jagged edges and pieces cut out, as though ripped (Howard 1983). The sexual innuendoes are clear from the body postures, sultry lips, and tousled hair of the models.

Sex in the Maintenance of Gender Inequality

A rather well-known ad for men's shoes (withdrawn after publicized protests by women's groups) showed a lovely nude woman lying contentedly next to her man's shoe under the message, "Keep her where she belongs." Although we might be inclined to laugh at this rather old cliché, it appears to be remarkably sturdy. In the late 1970s and early 1980s, for example a top-selling manufacturer of women's underwear produced a series of full-page, glossy ads, in color, for the *New York Times Magazine* that showed women in bikini underpants and bras in outrageous places and in various roles: in telephone booths, in the subway, in an airplane cockpit, conducting an orchestra, playing basketball, as a physician talking with a patient, as a lawyer pleading a case, as a chef, as a businesswoman, as a tourist, as a musician, etc. In every case, the only other persons in the ad were fully clothed, appropriately dressed men who functioned as obvious counterpoints to the ridiculous (but sexy) women.

This sexual put-down of women, thereby elevating men's image, is also evident in writing that emerged from the politically passionate period of the 1960s and 1970s, when sizable numbers of black and white women worked together to achieve common social objectives. Even within these groups, sex with men functioned to maintain women's lesser status: Stokeley Carmichael's comment about women in the civil rights movement, that their "only position" within it was "prone," has been widely quoted (cf. Morgan, 1970). We have paid less attention, however, to how women saw themselves in this arena of revolutionary, political activity. Marge Piercy's Vida tells us, "She would sometimes in the middle of a serious conversation catch herself looking at a man in a certain way she had learned over the years as apology to men for being smart, aggressive, political, for being a competitor in the real things. Putting out a certain sexual buzz was a way of apologizing for being herself" (1979:124). Similarly, in Rosellen Brown's *Civil Wars*, Jessie remembers herself as a northern college girl working in the civil rights movement in Mississippi:

> She was Teddy's girl . . . They made room for her, but not for herself; they respected her because they must; she walked in his aura. She was exhilirated and depressed in the same instant; then Teddy would come up behind her, turn her to him, no matter where they were, and suck a kiss so sweetly from her lips (right in the middle of conversation, as her lips formed an important word) that speech and opinion, hers at least, were put in their place. (1984:237)

Other novels about the 1960s, such as Alice Walker's *Meridian* (1976) and Sara Davidson's *Loose Change* (1978), relate how sexual relationships with men served to neutralize and diminish women's bids for leadership in radical political groups and to prevent their equal participation in decision making. Sexual involvement with a politically active man was viewed as a contribution by the woman to the "movement," just as in other times and places sexual relationships with men have been seen as contributing to their successes and progress by promoting their health and welfare.

A somewhat different motive for sexual behavior, but one that also serves to maintain gender inequality, is to obtain male protection against the demands made by other men. I experienced that clear "click" of recognition feminists talk about when I read Alice Walker's (1976) description of her heroine's high school years. Sex was "not pleasure, but a sanctuary in which her mind was freed of any consideration for all the other males in the universe who might want anything of her. It was resting from pursuit" (1976:62).

Sex as a Means of Communication

Sexual play with another person involves a unique closeness, achievable in no other way; it permits and provides the opportunity for the most intimate nonverbal communication. Sometimes, what a person cannot verbalize—the tenderest and most gentle of feelings— can be expressed sexually. (Or, a sexual encounter can communicate the most violent and hostile of feelings, short of murder.) A classic study of working-class wives (Rainwater, Coleman, and Handel, 1962) found many to be alienated from their husbands; and the lives of men and women were seen as highly segregated. It is not surprising. then, to find that these women also reported little enjoyment from sexual relations with their husbands and expressed little desire for them.

Many women find it difficult to relate sexually to their husbands after an argument; their husbands, on the other hand, may feel they can "make up" by "making love." Lillian Rubin has provided examples of this kind of conflict among both working-class and middle-class couples.

> He says, "I want to make love." She says, "It doesn't feel like love." Neither quite knows whan the other is talking about; both feel vaguely guilty and uncomfortable—aware only that somehow they're passing each other, not connecting . . . Split off, as he is, from the rest of the expressive-emotional side of himself, sex may be the one place where he can allow himself the expression of deep feelings. . . . His wife, on the other hand . . . finds it difficult to be comfortable with her feelings in the very area in which he has the greatest—sometimes the only—ease (1976:147f.).

With great frequency, the women who responded to Shere Hite's (1976) questionnaire told her how important body contact and physical closeness were to them. Communication through touching and proximity were valued "just for their own sakes—rather than only as a prelude to intercourse or orgasm." In addition by providing pleasure for another person, we also communicate our caring and concern.

Ambivalent Attitudes Toward Sexuality

Women derive pleasure from sexual arousal and orgasm. The experience of sexual gratification, both psychologically and physiologically, appears to be extremely comparable in women and men. Ample data support these conclusions, some of which have been cited and discussed above. Examination of the social context in which sexual behavior is learned, however, reveals important differences in the conditions or circumstances for women and men and in their resultant attitudes toward sexuality. Because of gender differences in social conditions, sex is almost always a positive goal for men, but for women it has both positive and negative aspects.

Boys typically learn that sexual activity is desirable, that it is pleasurable (and even necessary for good health). Heterosexual experience confers high status and is a sign of maturity and manhood. Girls, however, are taught opposite or unclear values in relation to sexuality. Many girls still learn that sexual activity is primarily a means to attract and keep a boyfriend; that a girl should engage in sexual behavior only to the extent necessary to satisfy her boyfriend's needs, not her own. Girls are still given the responsibility of restraining and tempering the sexual demands of boys, whose needs, they are taught, are greater and more insistent than their own. Naomi McCormick (1979), for example, found among a group of college students that sex is regarded "as a male goal and avoiding sex as a female goal." A subsequent study (McCormick, Brannigan, and LaPlante 1984) supported the earlier findings and obtained evidence that women and men behave in accordance with these stereotypes. Thus, a sample of men college students "reported using strategies more to have sex," while "women reported using strategies more to avoid sex." Other investigators (Grauerholz and Serpe 1985) have also found that women are less comfortable than men in initiating sex and more comfortable refusing it, thus acting as "gatekeepers." Some women did report initiating sexual intimacies; these women were likely to have many sexual partners and to be aware of sexual inequalities. In general, however, the data indicated that "rising sexual intercourse rates . . . do not suggest a fundamental change in sex roles."

Sexual relations with boys, though instrumental in keeping their attention, reduce an adolescent girl's status, besmirch her reputation, and mark her as a "bad girl." Lillian Rubin's study of married couples led her to conclude that although

> the media tell us that the double standard of sexual morality
> is dead . . . women don't believe it. They know from
> experience that it is alive and well, that it exists side by side
> with the new ideology that heralds their sexual liberation.
> They know all about who are the "bad girls" in school, in the
> neighborhood; who are the "good girls." Everybody knows!
> . . . The definitions of "good girl" and "bad girl" may vary
> somewhat according to class, but the fundamental ideas those
> words encompass are not yet gone either from our culture or
> our consciousness at any class level (1976:136f).

Adolescent boys may gain respect from sexual exploits, but among girls such behavior is still considered a sign of deviance or low status. Sexual offenses define delinquency for girls, but not for boys, and this difference is maintained in the legal approach to prostitution. In most states, it is the seller (typically a woman) and not the buyer (typically a man) who is considered more reprehensible, threatening to society, and criminal.

The research literature indicates that women's sexuality is now more freely and frequently expressed in behavior than during our parent's and grandparents' young adulthoods, but that attitudes have changed more slowly. Women's magazines have polled their readers about sexual behavior and attitudes, and among *Cosmopolitan* readers, for example, 82 percent said they had "seduced a man" at least once (cf. *Providence Evening Bulletin,* July 30, 1980), while among readers of *Glamour* magazine, premarital sex is acceptable to two-thirds of the women between eighteen and twenty-four and to one-third of the women over fifty-five (cf. *Providence Evening Bulletin,* December 14, 1983). J. Ray Hopkins (1977) examined surveys conducted prior to 1965 and compared their results with those obtained from surveys in the 1970s. He concluded that among young adolescents (aged thirteen to fifteen) there "is some evidence for earlier experimentation with intercourse," but that the actual incidences have been exaggerated and that more is talked about than is actually done. Among college-aged women and men, the data point to a "discontinuous," dramatic increase in sexual activity and to "intergender *convergence* in sexual behavior." Compared to earlier college surveys in which fifty-five percent of the men and twenty-five percent of the women had reported premarital coitus, those conducted after 1965 found at least sixty percent of the men and at least forty percent of the women reporting such behavior, with some recent studies citing even greater incidences for both genders. A national survey of single women in their 20s (cf. *Providence Evening Bulletin,* June 2, 1986) reported that four out of five have had several relations with a man at least once and, on the average, with 4.5 men; one in three have lived with a man.

Despite the increased frequency of sexual behavior by women, researchers seem to agree that conventional gender relationships persist. One group of investigators (Peplau, Rubin, and Hill 1977) concluded, after studying 231 heterosexual couples who had been dating for a median period of eight months, that as *individuals* there was "considerable similarity in the attitudes and sexual experiences of men and women"; however, when the pattern of interaction in *couples* is examined, what emerges is "clear evidence that traditional sexual role playing persists." This same conclusion was reached from the large-scale and more recent investigation of couples by Philip Blumstein and Pepper Schwartz (1983) and is complemented by other evidence. One study (Keller, Elliott, and Gunberg 1982) of over 400 college students of varied sexual experience examined relationships between psychological characteristics and sexual behavior. Although reiterating the often-cited finding that "male and female single college students are moving toward an equal standard," important differences between the genders were found. Not only were women more likely than men to have just one sexual partner, but no support was found for a movement by men "toward sex with affection." Dominance factors were characteristic of sexually active men, while affection factors were more descriptive of the women.

In general, then, women are expressing sexuality more openly, but in the context of intimate love relationships in which the traditional power inequalities between the genders still persist. Although losing one's virginity appears to have become a powerful motive among college women (and perhaps among women in general), sexual experience does not confer general likability. Luis Garcia (1982) found that women designated as being well experienced sexually were evaluated less positively by a sample of unmarried college men and women than were women with less sexual experience. In another study (Garcia and Derfel 1983), women shown in slides as interacting with men in nontraditional ways (e.g., staring directly at a man rather than looking down) were judged as being more sexually experienced than women whose nonverbal behavior was traditional. Sexual experience, therefore, may bring a young, unmarried woman a positive feeling of maturity and independence, while, at the same time, it may produce negative consequences—she may be evaluated less highly and be more apt to be associated with nontraditional ("unfeminine") attributes. Such a double-bind does not exist for her male peers. A study by Meg Gerrard (1982) documents the disparity between what women *do* and how they feel. Comparing a sample of college women in 1973 with one in 1978, Gerrard found that among the latter there was a lower correlation between sexual activity and sex guilt (defined as self-punishment for "violating standards of proper sexual conduct"). In other words, in 1978, single college women were sexually active *even if* such behavior produced feelings of guilt or psychological discomfort.

There are other factors that contribute to women's ambivalence about sex. Men experience pleasure in the use of their penises—for urination, masturbation, and fornication. Even little boys who may be told horrible tales by their parents about the evils that will befall them if they "play with themselves" have ample opportunities to find out otherwise from peers, older boys, and personal trial and error. By and large, boys will acquire positive associations for that part of their body that is the focus of male sexuality. Girls, on the other hand, learn to expect aversive consequences from their sexuality—to anticipate pain or problems during menstruation, pregnancy, childbirth, and during their first sexual intercourse. A recent study (Gartrell and Mosbacher 1984) has documented differences in what little girls and boys learn about their sexuality. From the retrospective responses of adults to questions about their first learning of words for genitalia, the investigators found that boys were far more likely than girls to have learned the correct anatomical names for their own genitalia as children, that both boys and girls learned "penis" significantly earlier than they learned any correct name for female genitals, and that the incorrect words taught for the latter were more euphemistic and pejorative than the nonanatomical words learned for male genitals. Thus, while "peenee" or "peter," for example, were learned by little boys instead of "penis," the former terms may be considered derivatives of the latter, whereas "privates," "shame," "nasty," or "down there," words learned by the girls, have no linguistic relationship to "vagina" or "clitoris." These data indicate that our culture regards the sexuality of boys and men, not only as more important, but as nicer, cleaner, and less embarrassing than the sexuality of girls and women.

Sexuality to many women means being a "sex object." While this concept has been translated into humorous images for cartoons, films, and fiction, it is of utmost seriousness to women, who learn from all areas of the culture that we have "utility." One cartoon given to me by a student shows a sexily dressed woman clerk behind a drugstore counter. A sign on the counter reads, "If You Don't See It, Ask for It." The customer, a genial, well-dressed gentleman, smiles and asks, "Can I see your tits?"

We learn that women can be bought (by favors, by being "wined and dined," or by cash), exchanged, treasured, or manhandled. I suspect that only rarely has a young woman not questioned at some point whether she was "being used" in a sexual relationship. The interchangeability of women (as bodies) is the subject of a cartoon (another student donation) in which a movie "love scene" is about to be filmed. The leading man lies waiting on the bed. The male director has his arm around the voluptuous, naked woman who will also play in the scene; she is faceless, and the director shouts, "Makeup!"

Related to this still prevalent view of women as "curves and orifices, or tits 'n ass with a bit of class," as Ross Wetzsteon has put it (1977), is another problem that contributes to the ambivalent nature of sexuality for women—our deeply felt fear of rape and the frequency with which we experience sexual harassment. Girls learn at an early age that we are vulnerable and largely unprotected from male predators. We try to separate the bad men (who openly leer, catcall, or follow us on the street) from the good ones (our fathers, brothers, and boyfriends), but such a classification becomes increasingly difficult as we encounter more and more men who are fathers or brothers to some other women but pinchers, leerers, or propositioners to us.

In a report prepared by the Project on the Status and Education of Women, some myths about sexual harassment were countered by facts. For example, it is not true that only a few women are affected by sexual harassment; surveys have documented its widespread nature, from on the job to college campuses. Male college professors and business executives may be more subtle than the often stereotyped (and probably maligned) blue-collar construction worker, but their sexual allusions and unwanted advances are no less insistent and demeaning. The authors of the report concluded:

> Fear of ridicule, and a sense of helplessness about the problem and a feeling that it's a personal dilemma have kept the problem concealed. . . . Many men believe a woman's "no" is really "yes," and therefore do not accept her refusal. Additionally, when a man is in a position of power, such as employer or teacher, the woman may be coerced or feel forced to submit. . . . Women who openly charge harassment are often not believed, may be ridiculed, may lose their job, be given a bad grade or be mistreated in some way (1978:1).

The ubiquitous nature of the sexual harassment of women has been amply documented in contemporary social science surveys, women's literature, and reports by journalists. Lin Farley (1978) found that 70 percent of the women she surveyed had personally experienced sexual harassment on the job. A study of the federal workplace, involving the largest number of randomly sampled respondents (Tangri, Burt, and Johnson 1982), found that 42 percent of the women reported having been sexually harassed at work within the past two years, primarily by older married men. Karen Lindsey (1977) has related the experiences of women who have worked as waitresses, in assembly lines, in advertising, in hospitals, on Capital Hill, and so on, all of whom have been approached for "sexual favors" by their male employers or coworkers. The women vary in age, position, and background, but all share the common experience of having been demeaned, frightened, and treated as a sexual commodity. A cartoon from *Playboy* tells it "like it is." The leering, obviously satisfied boss is getting into his clothes (complete with vest and tie), while his secretary is zipping up her skimpy outfit. "By the way," says the boss, "for your raise, you have to ask Mr. Peacock."

Sexual harassment has been reported by patients and clients in medical and legal settings and by students in secondary and college environments. The literature on this subject is sizable and continues to grow. In the introduction to an annotated bibliography on sexual harassment in education, Phyllis Crocker has written, "Sexual harassment in education is a frighteningly pervasive problem. For a woman, the injury . . . occurs when she is confronted by an educator whose concern is not with her intellectual growth but with the satisfaction of his own sexual needs and a desire for power" (1982:91).

In two studies of women and men at my own university (Lott, Reilly, and Howard 1982; Reilly, Lott, and Gallogly, in press), responses were obtained to ten statements dealing with sexually harassing behavior (e.g., "An attractive woman has to expect sexual advances and should learn how to handle them"). Women and men differed significantly in their level of agreement with every one of the statements, with the men showing greater tolerance for sexual harassment. The men, in other words, viewed sexually related behavior on the job and at school as expected and less problematic and serious than did the women.

When women experience sexual harassment, they are often not quite certain that they have not somehow been at fault. Have we enticed the men by our manner or our dress, been too friendly or forward? Women are sometimes reluctant to discuss sexual harassment because of the common belief that they have provoked it. Consider how difficult it is to reconcile the humiliation experienced by receiving the unwanted attentions of a man with the feeling of flattery that comes from being found attractive by him. Among the lessons learned by adolescent girls is that to attract a man is highest on the list of achievements. "Cosmetic sexuality" is a goal acquired by women in our culture. As noted by Judith Laws and Pepper Schwartz:

> those parts of the body which are sexualized in our culture—
> legs, face, breasts, and to a lesser extent buttocks—are
> subjected to special routines of display and enhancement . . .
> A socialization of the young woman for the role of sex object
> takes place during puberty. A great deal of attention is
> focused on the way she looks, and she receives a lot of
> feedback on her "good points" and "figure faults." . . . She
> learns the techniques of enhancement, display and
> artifice. . . . The dialectic between display and concealment,
> or permissible flaunting and taboo, can be seen clearly in the
> conventions of dress (1977:42f.).

The results of one study (Edmonds and Cahoon 1984) indicated that college women and men agree substantially in their ratings of women's clothing on "how sexually arousing" they appear to men. Other evidence suggests, however, that men tend to perceive the same cues as more explicitly sexual in meaning than do women. A group of investigators (Zellman, Johnson, Giarusso, and Goodchilds 1979) studied a large sample of adolescents in Los Angeles and found that the young women were significantly less likely than the men to interpret behavioral cues and clothing in sexual terms. In an experimental study, Antonia Abbey (1982) had pairs of mixed-gender observers watch pairs of mixed-gender actors (all college students) carry on a five-minute discussion. The observers then rated the actors on various dimensions. The men were found to "interpret women's friendliness as an indication of sexual interest" and to see themselves and other men, as well as women, in a sexual context. The investigator concluded that "men are more likely to perceive the world in sexual terms and to make sexual judgments than women are." Future research should focus on how much the greater salience of sex in men's lives contributes to the sexual harassment of women and adds to men's conviction that women who say "no" are merely being coy and hoping to be pursued further.

Although our culture strongly encourages women to be attractive to men, it also promises that we will make decisions about which man to accept, that we will have choices. Boys and men, on the other hand, experience a reality of higher status and power, and learn that women (no matter what else they may be or what skills they may have) are fundamentally sexual objects for men to use. (Many men may find it difficult to reconcile this cultural message with the realities of their own self-doubts, fears of incompetence, and needs for affection and acceptance.) For men, sex and the aggressive pursuit of sex may be difficult to separate; and the pursuit of women may range from a benign visual ogling to a whistle, from verbal comments about a woman's body to casual physical contact or to violent assault.

Changing expectations for women's sexual behavior may have added to women's ambivalence about sexuality, as increasingly greater demands are made of us by husbands or boyfriends. Lillian Rubin has pointed out that

> until recently, women were expected to submit passively to
> sex; now they are told their passivity diminishes their
> husband's enjoyment. Until recently, especially among the
> less-educated working class, orgasm was an unexpected gift;
> now it is a requirement of adequate sexual performance. These
> new definitions of adequacy have many women feeling "under
> the gun"—fearful and anxious if they do not achieve orgasm;

if it does not happen at the "right" moment—that is, at the instant of their husband's ejaculation; or if they are uncomfortable about engaging in behaviors that feel alien or aberrant to them. (1976:150)

One woman told Rubin that "it's really important for him [her husband] that I reach a climax and I try to everytime. He says it just doesn't make him feel good if I don't. But it's hard enough to do it once! What'll happen if he finds out about these women who have lots of climaxes?" A woman's orgasm signifies to a man that he has performed well and he may, therefore, require it of his partner as a validation of his sexual skill or competence.

Despite the ready availability of oral and other contraceptives, the fear of an unwanted pregnancy still contributes to women's ambivalence about sex. In *Meridian*, Alice Walker described a southern college for black women in which one common experience brought women from different social backgrounds together. "Any girl who had ever prayed for her period to come was welcome to the commemoration, which was held in the guise of a slow May Day dance. . . . It was the only time in all the many social activities at Saxon that every girl was considered equal. On that day, they held each other's hands tightly" (1976:45). It is the unusual woman who has not experienced, at some time in her life, that indescribable anxiety associated with "being late."

Given the present social conditions under which young women learn sexual behavior, it seems inevitable that conflict with respect to sexuality will result for both lesbian and heterosexual women. All women in our culture experience or observe similar consequences for sexual behavior. There is the positive anticipation of pleasure from body arousal, sensual excitement and orgasm, and the gratification to be derived from human physical contact and affection. At the same time, however, there are considerations of possible aversive consequences: concern about sexual exploitation; uncertainty about one's adequacy; fear of pregnancy; social rejection for having (or for not having) a sexual relationship; and concern about the meaning of the relationship. Judith Laws and Pepper Schwartz have suggested that most young women today have been exposed to a sexual standard that emerged during the 1960s—sex is permissible if love is present. "But *when is love present?* . . . [The new standard] that both partners should love in order for sex to be acceptable . . . provides no way to tell if your partner feels the same way you do" (1977:48f.).

Ambivalence about sexuality should become progressively lessened as women experience primarily positive outcomes and communicate this experience to other women (and to men). A study of two generations of college women from upper- and middle-class families (Yalom, Estler, and Brewster 1982) found a largely comfortable and substantial amount of inter-generational sexual communication reported by both daughters and mothers. In addition, as women grow older, the pleasure derived from sexual experience and close physical contact with another person probably becomes more potent, as the negative associations of badness, of pain, and of being used weakens. Positive outcomes may also increase as women explore more varied "sexual scripts," and experience sexuality with other women. Judith Laws and Pepper Schwartz (1977) have suggested that women are becoming more accepting of autoeroticism, "are receiving permission, instruction, and support in learning about their own bodies and the patterns of their own sexual response," and are also becoming more sexually assertive and "less reactive or passive in sexual situations," taking more responsibility for contraception and for talking about what maximizes their sexual pleasure.

Sexual conflict for young women, however, is unlikely to become substantially less intense until girls and boys are socialized to expect the same outcomes from their sexual experiences and to give similar meaning and value to them. This change, in turn, is not likely to occur while men and women continue to be unequal in social status. Changes in sexual standards and greater tolerance for sexuality in an otherwise unchanged world, in which women have less value and power than men, will merely compound the pressure on women, increase the chances for exploitation, and enhance the probability of conflict.

As noted by Barbara Ehrenreich, Elizabeth Hess, and Gloria Jacobs (1982), feminism is "the first political movement in history to address itself to sensual desire, . . . to personal eroticism as *political issues;*" and there is currently intense discussion and debate among feminists about sexual morality and the dangers and pleasures inherent in contemporary sexual practices (cf. Ferguson 1984; Philipson 1984). Despite the lack of consensus about what women's sexuality *should be*, most feminists would, I believe, subscribe to the values expressed by Charlotte Bunch (see Ehrenreich, et al. 1982) and prefer "a sexuality that is based on exploration and freedom of choice, but that also values the human being, soul, body, and intellect . . . [and] the quality of interaction of people."

An important first step is understanding that women and men are fundamentally similar in sexuality in terms of psychophysiological processes and the acquisition of learned motives and responses to sexual cues. Though necessary, however, this knowledge is not sufficient to eliminate either the ambivalence from women's sexual attitudes or sexual exploitation. We must dispel old myths about the nature of women (and men) and work toward elimination of the differences in status, power, and expectations that currently separate the genders.

References

Abbey, A. (1982). Sex differences in attributions for friendly behavior: Do males misperceive females' friendliness? *Journal of Personality and Social Psychology, 42,* 830–838.

Alta (1973). penus envy, they call it. In F. Howe and E. Bass (eds.), *No more masks! An anthology of poems by women.* New York: Anchor, p. 295.

Athamasion, R., Shaver, P., and Tavris, C. (1970). Sex. *Psychology Today,* July, pp. 39–52.

Bambara, T. C. (1974). Commentary: Sexuality of black women. In L. Gross (ed.), *Sexual behavior: Current issues.* Flushing, N.Y.: Spectrum.

Baum, C., Hyman, P., and Michel, S. (1975). *The Jewish woman in America.* New York: New American Library.

Beach, F. (1969). It's all in your mind. *Psychology Today,* July, pp. 33–35, 60.

Bleier, R. (1984). *Science and gender: A critique of biology and its theories on women.* New York: Pergamon.

Blumstein, P., and Schwartz, P. (1977). Bisexuality: Some psychological issues. *Journal of Social Issues, 33* (2), 30–45.

Blumstein, P., and Schwartz, P. (1983). *American couples: Money, work, sex.* New York: Morrow.

Broner, E. M. (1978). *A weave of women.* New York: Holt, Rinehart, & Winston.

Brown, R. (1984). *Civil wars.* New York: Knopf.

Byrne, D., and Lamberth, J. (1971). The effect of erotic stimuli on sex arousal, evaluative responses, and subsequent behvior. In *Technical report of the Commission on Obscenity and Pornography* (Vol. 8). Washington, D.C.: U.S. Government Printing Office.

Coles, R., and Coles, J. H. (1978). *Women of crisis.* New York: Delacorte.

Crichton, S. (1983). Sex and self-discovery. *Ms.,* October, pp. 68–69.

Crocker, P. L. (1982). Annotated bibliography on sexual harassment in education. *Women's Rights Law Reporter, Z,* 91–106.

Davidson, S. (1978). *Loose change.* New York: Pocket Books.

Donnerstein, E. (1980). Pornography and violence against women: Experimental studies. *Annals of the New York Academy of Sciences, 347,* 277–288.

Edmonds, E. M., and Cahoon, D. D. (1984). Female clothes preference related to male sexual interest. *Bulletin of the Psychonomic Society, 22,* 171–173.

Ehrenreich, B., Hess, E., and Jacobs, G. (1982). A report on the sex crisis. *Ms,* March, pp. 61–64, 87–88.

Farley, L. (1978). *Sexual shakedown.* New York: McGraw-Hill.

208   BERNICE LOTT

Ferguson, A. (1984). Sex war: The debate between radical and liberatarian feminists. *Signs, 10,* 106–112.

Fisher, W. A., and Byrne, D. (1978). Sex differences in response to erotica? Love versus lust. *Journal of Personality and Social Psychology, 36,* 117–125.

Freud, S. (1905). Three essays on the theory of sexuality. In A. A. Brill (ed.), *The basic writings of Sigmund Freud.* New York: Modern Library, 1938.

Friday, N. (1973). *My secret garden.* New York: Pocket Books.

Garcia, L. T. (1982). Sex-role orientation and stereotypes about male-female sexuality. *Sex Roles, 8,* 863–876.

Garcia, L. T., and Derfel, B. (1983). Perception of sexual experience: The impact of non-verbal behavior. *Sex Roles, 9,* 871–878.

Gartrell, N., and Mosbacher, D. (1984). Sex differences in the naming of children's genitalia. *Sex Roles, 10,* 869–876.

Gerrard, M. (1982). Sex, sex guilt, and contraceptive use. *Journal of Personality and Social Psychology, 42,* 153–158.

Godwin, G. (1983). *A mother and two daughters.* New York: Avon.

Goldman, J. (1972). The women of Bangladesh. *Ms.,* August.

Grauerholz, E., and Serpe, R. T. (1985). Initiation and response: The dynamics of sexual interaction. *Sex Roles, 12,* 1041–1059.

Green, R. (1977). Magnolias grow in dirt. *Southern Exposure, 4* (4), 29–33.

Griffin, S. (1981). *Pornography and silence.* New York: Harper Colophon.

Griffitt, W., and Kaiser, D. L. (1978). Affect, sex guilt, gender and the rewarding-punishing effects of erotic stimuli. *Journal of Personality and Social Psychology, 36,* 850–858.

Guffy, O., and Ledner, C. (1971). *Ossie: The autobiography of a black woman.* New York: Norton.

Hahn, J. (1977). Sex if fun; so is more, report says. *Providence Evening Bulletin,* November 2.

Hall, M. H. (1969). A conversation with Masters and Johnson. *Psychology Today,* July, pp. 50–58.

Harlow, H., and Harlow, M. K. (1966). Learning to love. *American Scientist, 54,* 244–272.

Haskell, M. (1973). *From reverence to rape: The treatment of women in the movies.* New York: Holt, Rinehart & Winston.

Heilbrun, C. G. (1973). *Toward a recognition of androgyny.* New York: Harper & Row.

Heiman, J. R. (1975). Women's sexual arousal: The physiology of erotica. *Psychology Today,* April, pp. 91–94.

Hendrick, S., Hendrick, C., Slapion-Foote, H. J., and Foote, F. H. (1985). Gender differences in sexual attitudes. *Journal of Personality and Social Psychology, 48,* 1630–1642.

Hite, S. (1976). *The Hite report.* New York: Dell.

Hopkins, J. R. (1977). Sexual behavior in adolescence. *Journal of Social Issues, 33*(2), 67–86.

Howard, M. (1983). Forbidden fruits. *Vogue,* March, pp. 385–386, 428.

Intellectual Digest. (1972). Holy or wholly wedlock: Maimonides 1174 A.D. November, p. 53.

Jong, E. (1973). *Fear of flying.* New York: Signet.

Jong, E. (1984). *Parachutes and kisses*. New York: Signet.

Joseph, G. I. (1981). Styling, profiling, and pretending: The games before the fall. In G. I. Joseph and J. Lewis, *Common differences*. Garden City, New York: Anchor, pp. 178–230.

Keller, J. F., Elliott, S. S., and Gunberg, E. (1982). Premarital sexual intercourse among single college students: A discriminant analysis. *Sex Roles, 8,* 21–32.

Kenrick, D. T., Stringfield, D. O., Wagenhals, W. L., Dahl, R. H., and Ransdell, H. J. (1980). Sex differences, androgyny, and approach responses to erotica: A new variation on the old volunteer problem. *Journal of Personality and Social Psychology, 38,* 517–524.

Kinsey, A. C., Pomeroy, W. B., Martin, C. E., and Gebhard, P. H. (1953). *Sexual behavior in the human female*. Philadelphia: Saunders.

Koedt, A. (1973). The myth of the vaginal orgasm. In A. Koedt, E. Levine & A. Rapone (eds.), *Radical feminism*. New York: Qaudrangle, pp. 198–207.

Laws, J. L., and Schwartz, P. (1977). *Sexual scripts: The social construction of female sexuality*. New York: Dryden.

Lindsey, K. (1977). Sexual harassment on the job, and how to stop it. *Ms.,* November, pp. 47–51, 74–78.

Lott, B., Reilly, M. E., and Howard, D. (1982). Sexual assault and harassment: A campus community case study. *Signs, 8,* 296–319.

Masters, W., and Johnson, V. (1966). *Human sexual response*. Boston: Little, Brown.

McCormick, N. B. (1979). Come-ons and put-offs: Unmarried students' strategies for having and avoiding sexual intercourse. *Psychology of Women Quarterly, 4,* 194–211.

McCormick, N. B., Brannigan, G. G., and LaPlante, M. N. (1984). Social desirability in the bedroom: Role of approval motivation in sexual relationships. *Sex Roles, 11,* 303–314.

Miller, P. Y., and Fowlkes, M. R. (1980). Social and behavioral constructions of female sexuality. *Signs, 5,* 783–800.

Millett, K. (1978). Reply to "What do you think is erotic?" *Ms.,* November, p. 80.

Morgan, R. (1970). *Sisterhood is powerful*. New York: Vintage, p. 35.

Morokoff, P. J. (1985). Effects of sex guilt, repression, sexual "arousability," and sexual experience on female sexual arousal during erotica and fantasy. *Journal of Personality and Social Psychology, 49,* 177–187.

Newcomb, M. D., and Bentler, P. M. (1983). Dimensions of subjective female orgasmic responsiveness. *Journal of Personality and Social Psychology, 44,* 862–873.

Peplau, L. A., Rubin, Z., and Hill, C. T. (1977). Sexual intimacy in dating relationships. *Journal of Social Issues, 33*(2), 86–109.

Person, E. S. (1980). Sexuality as the mainstay of identity: Psychoanalytic perspectives. *Signs, 5,* 605–630.

Philipson, I. (1984). The repression of history and gender: A critical perspective on the feminist sexuality debate. *Signs, 10,* 113–118.

Piercy, M. (1979). *Vida*. New York: Summit.

Piercy, M. (1983). *Braided lives*. New York: Fawcett.

Piercy, M. (1984). *Fly away home*. New York: Summit.

Plath, S. (1972). *The bell jar*. New York: Bantam.

Project on the Status and Education of Women. (1978). *Sexual harassment: A hidden issue*. Washington, D.C.: Association of American Colleges, June.

Providence Evening Bulletin. (1980). How firms use sex to win government contracts. June 26.

Providence Evening Bulletin. (1980). Women in poll tell of seducing men. July 30.

Providence Evening Bulletin. (1983). Poll says women are more tolerant of premarital sex. December 14.

Providence Evening Bulletin. (1986). Sex habits of single women detailed in national survey, June 2, p. A-4.

Rainwater, L., Coleman, R. P., and Handel, G. (1962). *Workingman's wife*. New York: MacFadden.

Reilly, M. E., Lott, B., and Gallogly, S. M. (in press). Sexual harassment of university students. *Sex Roles*.

Ribble, M. A. (1944). Infantile experience in relation to personality development. In J. McV. Hunt (ed.), *Personality and the behavior disorders* (Vol. 2). New York: Ronald.

Rossner, J. (1976). *Looking for Mr. Goodbar*. New York: Pocket Books.

Rossner, J. (1983). *August*. New York: Houghton Mifflin.

Rubin, L. (1976). *Worlds of pain: Life in the working class family*. New York: Basic Books.

Scarf, M. (1980). The promiscuous woman. *Psychology Today*, July, pp. 78–87.

Schmidt, G., Sigusch, V., and Schafer, S. (1977). Responses to reading erotic stories: Male-female differences. In D. Byrne and L. A. Byrne (eds.), *Exploring human sexuality*. New York: Crowell.

Sherfey, M. J. (1970). A theory on female sexuality. In R. Morgan (ed.), *Sisterhood is powerful*. New York: Random House.

Simon, W., and Gagnon, J. (1977). Psychosexual development. In D. Byrne and L. A. Byrne (eds.), *Exploring human sexuality*. New York: Crowell.

Snitow, A. B. (1980). The front line: Notes on sex in novels by women. *Signs*, 5, 702–718.

Staples, R. (1977). Male-female sexual variations: Functions of biology or culture? In D. Byrne and L. A. Byrne (eds.), *Exploring human sexuality*. New York: Crowell.

Steele, D. G., and Walker, C. E. (1976). Female responsiveness to erotic films from a feminine perspective. *Journal of Nervous and Mental Disease*, 162, 266–273.

Steinem, G. (1978). Erotica and pornography: A clear and present difference. *Ms.*, November, pp. 53–54, 75–76.

Tangri, S. S., Burt, M. R., and Johnson, L. B. (1982). Sexual harassment at work: Three explanatory models. *Journal of Social Issues*, 38 (4), 33–54.

Vance, C. S., and Snitow, A. B. (1984). Toward a conversation about sex in feminism: A modest proposal. *Signs*, 10, 126–135.

Walker, A. (1976). *Meridian*. New York: Washington Square Press.

Walker, A. (1982). *The color purple.* New York: Washington Square Press.

Wetzsteon, R. (1977). Woody Allen: Schlemiel as sex maniac. *Ms.,* November, pp. 14–15.

Wiest, W. M. (1977). Semantic differential profiles of orgasm and other experiences among men and women. *Sex Roles, 3,* 399–403.

Yalom, M., Estler, S., and Brewster, W. (1982). Changes in female sexuality: A study of mother/daughter communication and generational differences. *Psychology of Women Quarterly, 7,* 141–154.

Zellman, G. L., Johnson, P. B., Giarusso, R., and Goodchilds, J. D. (1979). *Adolescent expectations for dating relationships: Consensus and conflict between the sexes.* Paper read at the meeting of the American Psychological Association, September, New York, N.Y.

Zuckerman, M. (1971). Physiological measures of sexual arousal in the human. *Psychological Bulletin, 75,* 297–329.

CHAPTER 8

Emotional and Cognitive Barriers to Effective Contraception: Are Males and Females Really Different?

MEG GERRARD

It has been twenty-five years since the oral contraceptive pill and antiseptic plastic and stainless steel intrauterine devices were introduced, marking the beginning of the contraceptive revolution. Never before have men and women had such control over their fertility. Options now include a broad array of contraceptives: tubal ligation, vasectomy, plastic and hormone-releasing intrauterine devices (IUDs), fertility awareness techniques such as calendar, basal body temperature, and natural rhythm, diaphragms, spermicidal foams, suppositories, sponges, creams, condoms, and a wide choice of oral contraceptive pills. This variety allows everyone, regardless of aesthetic or religious preferences or health history, to enjoy protection from unplanned pregnancy.

In spite of the wide availability of this sophisticated contraceptive technology, unplanned pregnancy continues to be a significant problem. Premarital sexual activity increased dramatically during the 1970s; by 1979, 50 percent of all fifteen to nineteen-year-old females reported sexual activity, and 53 percent of never-married twenty to twenty-nine-year-old females reported having engaged in sexual intercourse within the last month (Tanfer and Horn 1985; Zelnick and Shah 1983). The second half of that decade, however, saw a sharp decline in the use of reliable methods of birth control (Gerrard 1982; Zelnick and Kantner 1980). Between 1976 and 1979 there was a 41 percent *decline* in the use of the most effective methods, the pill and IUD, and an 86 percent *increase* in the use of the less effective methods of withdrawal and rhythm among teenagers (Zelnick and

Kantner 1980).[1] Even among married women, the use of rhythm, a relatively ineffective method of contraception, increased from 17 percent in 1974 to 25 percent in 1981.

Given these shifts in sexual activity and in contraceptive use, it is not surprising that current statistics indicate that 36 percent of sexually active teenagers become pregnant during their first two years of sexual activity (Koenig and Zelnick 1982), and that 33 percent of never-married women aged twenty to twenty-nine have conceived at least once (Tanfer and Horn 1985). It is also not surprising that the abortion rate rose each year from 1973 to 1980 (Grimes 1984; Henshaw, Forrest, and Blaine 1984; Zelnick and Kantner 1980). These dramatic shifts in the pattern of sexual activity, contraceptive use, and pregnancy rates have generated a great deal of research aimed at identifying the antecedents of poor contraception and unplanned pregnancy. As a result, a relatively clear profile of the female contraceptive risk taker has emerged. In this chapter, I will examine the literature generated by this research and compare what we know about the ineffective female contraceptor with what we know about the ineffective male contraceptor. In addition, I will discuss current trends in contraceptive use.

THE HIGH-RISK FEMALE

Rational or Irrational Behavior

Engaging in unprotected sexual intercourse when pregnancy is not desired is clearly irrational behavior. Even Luker, who argues that "unwanted pregnancy is the result of an informed decision making process," allows for the possibility that this process is guided by irrational beliefs (1975:32). Luker suggests that contraceptive behavior results from a rational decision-making process in which the costs of contraception (e.g., medical side effects, loss of spontaneity) are weighed against the potential costs and benefits of pregnancy (e.g., proof of femininity and fertility). Conversely, the rewards of contraception (e.g., freedom from worry about conception) are weighed against the costs of contraceptive failure (e.g., psychological strain resulting from an unplanned child, abortion). Thus, although Luker hypothesizes a rational decision-making process, she does suggest that this process may be based on irrational beliefs and/or misinformation.

Fishbein and his colleagues (Ajzen and Fishbein 1980; Fishbein 1972; Fishbein and Ajzen 1975; Fishbein and Jaccard 1973; Jaccard and Davidson 1972) have also presented a model of contraceptive use that incorporates both rational and irrational beliefs into the decision-making process. According to this model, a woman's intention to use contraception is a function of (1) her attitudes and beliefs about the consequences of contracepting or not contracepting (i.e., her subjective judgment of the probability that practicing birth control will lead to certain consequences and that not practicing birth control will lead to certain other consequences); and (2) her beliefs about what others expect her to do and her desire to comply with these expectations. The model thus incorporates a belief such as "the pill causes cancer" into the decision-making process. In a number of successful tests of this model (e.g., Davidson and Jaccard 1975; Fishbein and Jaccard 1973; Jaccard and Davidson 1972), birth control intentions and behavior have been predicted by a formula that multiplies beliefs about the consequences of birth control by the evaluation of these consequences, and beliefs about the norms for contraception by the motivation to comply with these norms.

One of the central assumptions of this model is that women are rational and base their birth control behavior on the available information. "We do not subscribe to the view that human social behavior is controlled by unconscious motives or over-powering desires, nor do we believe that it can be characterized as capricious or thoughtless. Rather we argue that people consider the implications of their actions before they decide to engage or not engage in a given behavior." (Ajzen and Fishbein 1980:5).

If Fishbein and Luker are correct and the contraceptive decision-making process is rational, then the high rate of unplanned pregnancies suggests that the *information* many women use in this decision-making process is incorrect. Horowitz (1980) provides data that support this suggestion. She reports that discontinuation of contraception among pregnant teenagers is related to exaggerated fears and irrational beliefs about the possibility of serious medical risks from the use of the pill and IUD. Her sample consisted of young women who had a second, unwanted pregnancy after they had participated in an intensive contraceptive educational program aimed at promoting the use of the pill, IUD, and diaphragm. While nearly three-quarters of these young women used contraception after their first pregnancy, the median time it was used was only three months. Nearly 50 percent of these ineffective contraceptors had discontinued the use of the pill or IUD sometime after their first pregnancy because of fears related to minor physical side effects attributed to these methods of birth control.

In our own research (Gerrard, McCann, and Fortini 1983), we also found that irrational beliefs and exaggerated fears about the medical risks of contraception were related to contraceptive risk taking. In our first study, we interviewed effective and ineffective contraceptors and discovered that the sexually active women using rhythm, withdrawal, or no contraception held more negative attitudes and irrational fears about specific contraceptives than did women using the pill, IUD, or diaphragm. In a second study conducted with poor contraceptors, we compared the effectiveness of two types of intervention—one designed to use cognitive restructuring to alter the irrational beliefs and exaggerated fears discovered in the interview study, and a second designed only to provide contraceptive information. The educational content of both interventions consisted of information regarding contraceptive use and effectiveness and was designed to increase the women's knowledge of the risk of conception and the available means of preventing it. In addition to this information, the cognitive restructuring intervention also focused on common negative attitudes and beliefs about effective contraceptive methods and actively challenged these attitudes and beliefs. The results of this study complement the Horowitz data. One month after the intervention, subjects in both the informational and the restructuring intervention groups had increased their use of effective methods significantly more than had the subjects in a no treatment control group. Three months after the intervention, however, only those women who had participated in the cognitive restructuring intervention were maintaining significantly better contraceptive behavior than were those in the control group.

Both of these studies thus implicate irrational beliefs and exaggerated reactions to side effects in ineffective contraception. This conclusion suggests that, if contraceptive behavior is the result of a rational decision-making process, this process is not based on accurate information about the potential medical risks of various birth control methods and the potential medical risks of pregnancy and abortion. In fact, there is ample evidence that women who use ineffective methods of contraception, or use no contraception at all, are less planful and future oriented than are women who use effective methods. In particular, effective contraceptors have been shown to differ from ineffective contraceptors on measures of planfulness, future time perspective (Keller, Sims, Henry, and Crawford 1970; Mindick, Oskamp, and Berger 1977; Mindick, Oskamp, and Berger 1978; Oskamp et al. 1976). In addition, Harvey (1976) reports that pill and IUD users demonstrate more achievement concerns for both the present and the future than do women who use less effective methods of birth control or no contraception. Taken together, these studies suggest that the process of choosing a birth control method and using it effectively and consistently may not always be as planful and rational as Luker and Fishbein have suggested. Regardless of the accuracy of their information, at least some, and perhaps quite a number, of women apparently do not apply thoughtful and careful logic to this important area of decision making. In this vein, a number of recent studies have explored the possibility that contraceptive behavior is mediated by emotional factors.

Emotional Inhibition of Contraception

One of the most consistent findings in the literature on personality and cognitive determinants of contraceptive behavior is a relationship between negative emotional orientation toward sexuality and ineffective contraception. Numerous studies have demonstrated that a negative emotional orientation toward sexuality inhibits sexual intimacy and the frequency of sexual intercourse (e.g., D'Augelli and Cross 1975; Langston 1973; Mosher and Cross 1971). Moreover, other studies have indicated that women who maintain a negative emotional predisposition toward sex, but nonetheless engage in sexual intercourse, generally tend to use either inadequate contraceptive methods or use no birth control method at all. In general, the results of this body of literature indicate that personality factors such as sex guilt, sex anxiety, and erotophobia are strongly associated with contraceptive risk taking and contraceptive failure.[2]

Sex Guilt. Mosher and Cross define sex guilt as "a personality disposition characterized by a generalized expectance of self monitored punishment for violating or anticipating violating standards of proper sexual conduct" (1971:27). This disposition is manifested by resistance to sexual temptation, inhibited sexual behavior, and/or the disruption of cognitive processes in sex-related situations. For example, scores on Mosher's sex guilt scales (Mosher 1966, 1968) are associated with changes in the episodic state of guilt after reading an erotic literary passage (Mosher and Greenberg 1969) and with sexual responses to double-entendre words like "screw" and "rubber" (Galbraith, Hahn, and Lieberman 1968; Galbraith and Mosher 1968). Subjects with high sex guilt also report limiting their sexual practices to less intimate forms of expression (D'Augelli and Cross 1975; Langston 1973; Mosher 1973; Mosher and Cross 1971), engaging in intercourse less often (Love, Sloan, and Schmidt 1976; Mosher 1973), and limiting the number of sexual partners (Mosher 1973).

More pertinent to the current review, however, is the association between sex guilt and contraceptive risk. In particular, women who are high in sex guilt appear to be misinformed or confused about sexual matters. They are more likely than low sex guilt women to believe in contraceptive myths such as "conception is most likely to occur if the man and the woman experience simultaneous climax" (Mosher 1979). They are also more likely to communicate sexual misinformation than are low sex guilt women (Mendelsohn and Mosher 1979). Given these deficits in their knowledge and ability to communicate about sex and contraception, it is not surprising that high sex guilt women are more likely than low sex guilt women to use either ineffective methods of birth control or no method at all (Geis and Gerrard 1984; Gerrard 1977, 1982; Mosher 1973). In sum, although sex guilt does not always inhibit sexual activity, it does inhibit effective contraception.

Erotophobia. In a closely related line of research, Byrne and his colleagues have suggested that people develop a persistent and general tendency to respond to sexual cues with positive or negative emotions. This learned disposition then mediates approach-avoidance responses to and evaluations of sexual situations and affects one's responses to both intercourse and contraception. The scale developed to measure this construct, the Sexual Opinion Survey (SOS) (White, Fisher, Byrne, and Kingma 1977), places respondents on a continuum of emotional responses to sexual stimuli ranging from negative emotional reactions (erotophobic) to positive emotional reactions (erotophilic). Erotophobic individuals have been found to dream less about sex, masturbate less, and have fewer premarital sexual partners than do erotophilic individuals (Fisher, Byrne, and White 1983). Erotophobics also react to erotic slides more negatively, are less interested in viewing erotica, and are more likely to favor restricting erotic materials than are erotophilics (Fisher and Byrne 1978). Like sex guilt, the Sexual Opinion Survey predicts use of effective contraceptive methods. It should be noted, however, that use of effective methods of contraception is not the same as consistent use of contraceptive methods.

Consistency of Contraception. A relationship between consistent use of birth control and sex guilt was found in a study in which I compared women who were successfully using contraceptives with those who had failed to avoid unplanned pregnancy (Gerrard 1977). In this study, abortion patients, who could be considered ineffective contraceptors, and equally sexually active, nonpregnant women were divided into groups based on the effectiveness of the contraceptives they reported using. The abortion patients who reported being on the pill at the time of conception were thus compared with the nonpregnant women who reported using the pill the last time they had intercourse. Within each contraceptive classification, the abortion patients (i.e., the ineffective contraceptors) had higher sex guilt scores than did the nonpregnant patients (i.e., the effective contraceptors). Though it could be argued that unplanned pregnancy or abortion increases a woman's guilt about sex, thereby explaining this difference in sex guilt, a study by Fisher et al. (1979) suggests that this explanation is too simple. In their study of the relationship between erotophobia and contraceptive use, they found that the Sexual Opinion Survey significantly differentiated between consistent and inconsistent nonpregnant contraceptors. Women who reported regularly using birth control scored lower on the SOS than did women who reported irregular use of contraceptive protection. These two studies, then, suggest that when sex guilt (and/or erotophobia) is not sufficient to inhibit sexual intercourse, and not sufficient to inhibit the choice of an effective contraceptive method, it can still have an effect on the success of the chosen method.

Some additional support for this hypothesis is found in a study that examined changes in sex guilt, sexual activity, and contraceptive use among college women between 1973 and 1978 (Gerrard 1982). This study revealed a rather dramatic increase in sexual activity among college women over this period of time (from 35 percent reporting having sexual intercourse at least once a month in 1973 to 51 percent in 1978); there was, however, no corresponding change in the mean level of sex guilt over this same period of time. Given that sex guilt was related to sexual activity in both of these samples, it would appear that the level of sex guilt sufficient to inhibit sexual intercourse in 1973 was no longer sufficient in 1978. In other words, more women with moderate and high levels of sex guilt were sexually active in 1978 than were in 1973. Even more pertinent to the current discussion is the fact that the use of effective contraception *decreased* significantly over this period of time. This decrease would suggest that although the level of sex guilt necessary to inhibit sexual activity increased, its power to inhibit contraceptive activity did not diminish. That is, while a given level of sex guilt was no longer sufficient to inhibit sexual activity in 1978, it did appear to inhibit the use of contraceptives.

To summarize the research reviewed thus far, there is evidence that a women's emotional orientation toward sexuality (sex guilt, erotophobia, or sex anxiety) is associated with her knowledge of contraception, her choice of contraceptive methods, and her ability or motivation to effectively use the contraceptives she chooses. Negative attitudes toward sex predict lack of knowledge about birth control, selection of ineffective contraceptives, and inconsistent use of the contraceptive methods chosen. These relationships are hardly intuitive, however, and they raise several interesting questions: Why are women who are sexually active but uncomfortable with their sexuality apparently *less* motivated to avoid pregnancy than those comfortable with their sexual behavior? One would think that those women feeling most guilty about having sexual intercourse would be more careful and more effective contraceptors than those who treat sex more casually. But this is not the case. The basic question, then, is: How do sex guilt, erotophobia, and sex anxiety inhibit effective contraception?

How Does a Negative Emotional Orientation toward Sex Interfere with Effective Contraception?

Avoiding pregnancy requires that a woman negotiate a complex sequence of psychological and behavioral events. First, she must accept that she is sexually active and be aware that unprotected sexual activity places her at high risk for becoming pregnant. Second, she must obtain adequate information to make an informed decision about which methods of birth control best fit her needs. Third, she must acquire the contraceptive devices and/or knowledge necessary to prevent pregnancy. Finally, she must use these devices and/or knowledge consistently and effectively.

A breakdown at any step in this sequence of events results in a high risk of pregnancy. For example, a woman can be unaware of the potential risk of pregnancy and assume she is safer than she actually is. Medical statisticians report that a young woman in good health has a 90 percent chance of conceiving during a year of unprotected sexual activity of average frequency (two to three times per week) (MacLeod and Gold 1953). Numerous studies have indicated that most young women are unaware of the high probability that pregnancy will result from unprotected intercourse (Zelnick and Kantner 1979). Moreover, women who pass this first step are often either unaware of the contraceptive options available to them or misinformed about the side effects of the more effective methods. They consequently make uninformed decisions about contraceptives. Even if the woman has acquired adequate knowledge about the options and chooses to use an effective method, an active commitment to avoiding pregnancy is required in order to use the method consistently and effectively. It is reasonable to suggest that negative attitudes toward sexuality could interfere with this complex sequence of events in a variety of ways.

Emotional orientation and self-perception. First, negative attitudes toward sexuality might interfere with a woman's ability to see herself as someone likely to engage in sexual intercourse. In fact, there is evidence suggesting that unsuccessful contraceptors are less accepting of their sexuality than are successful contraceptors (Goldsmith, Gabrielson, Gabrielson, Matthews, and Potts 1972). There is, however, no evidence that directly relates negative emotional orientation to this lack of acceptance of sexuality in women. Evidence of the relationship between negative attitudes and males' acceptance of their sexuality is available, however, and will be discussed later in this chapter. (Interestingly, this area is one place where the data are stronger for men than for women.) Although there is no direct evidence, then, that sexually active women with a negative orientation toward sex are less accepting of their own sexuality, this assumption seems to be self-evident. If a woman feels that engaging in sexual intercourse has negative connotations, she is not likely to define herself as a sexual person and therefore is unlikely to plan for contraception.

Interference with Learning.   In contrast to the lack of evidence regarding a relationship between attitudes and self-definition in women, there is direct evidence that negative attitudes or orientation toward sexuality interfere with obtaining and retaining information about contraception. Fisher (1980) found that erotophobic students of both sexes did poorer than erotophilic students on a midterm examination in a human sexuality class. This relationship held even when past educational achievement was statistically controlled.

In a more systematic laboratory examination of this issue, Schwartz (1973) tested the relationships between sex guilt, sexual arousal, and retention of birth control information. High and low sex guilt subjects either read sexually arousing (erotic) passages or neutral passages. They then listened to a twenty-minute lecture on relatively little-known biological and medical aspects of contraception. As was expected, high sex guilt subjects of both sexes remembered less of the lecture information than did low guilt subjects. Though Schwartz did not get the interaction between sex guilt and arousal that he had predicted, he did get the predicted learning effects for both sex guilt and arousal. He concludes that both sexual arousal and negative disposition toward sex have potentially disruptive effects on the retention of contraceptive information.

Cognitive Inconsistency.   Two recent studies (Gerrard and Gibbons 1982; Breda 1985) offer another interesting suggestion about how sex guilt interferes with effective contraception. In a study of the relationship between sexual experience, sex guilt, and sexual-specific moral reasoning, Frederick X. Gibbons and I asked high and low guilt men and women to articulate, in three or four sentences, their opinions of six sexual activities (e.g., "Do you favor premarital sex or oppose it, and why do you feel that way?"). They were then presented with a set of three of these activities, each accompanied by two lists: one comprised of six statements in favor of the activity, the other, six statements opposed to the activity. Each statement was designed to represent a different stage of moral reasoning as suggested

222 MEG GERRARD

by Kohlberg (1964) and had been rated as to stage by four raters trained in the Kohlberg method (e.g., the favorable response for prostitution at stage I was, "Okay if the chances of being punished are very small"; the unfavorable response at stage I was, "Wrong because you could be prosecuted and sentenced"). After the subjects provided their open-ended responses to the six activities, they were asked to read through the two lists of statements accompanying each of the three activities and endorse the statement (either pro or con) they most agreed with. Each subject thus provided us with two measures: (1) an articulated opinion about each activity that was subsequently rated for level of moral reasoning, and (2) their choice from a list of six statements representing Kohlberg's six levels of moral reasoning.

The results of this study indicated that the high guilt females were less "sophisticated" in terms of their *articulated* moral reasoning than were the low guilt women, or the men. In contrast, high guilt women's moral *preferences* were the highest of any group. This discrepancy between what high sex guilt women articulate as their opinions about sex and what they endorse when written opinions are presented to them suggests that their sexual standards are not clearly defined and may be only tentatively held.

In another recent study, Breda (1985) performed a more direct test of the strength of women's moral standards. She had dating individuals respond to moral issues independently and then as a couple (i.e., each partner first provided his or her individual responses to the issues, then the two partners worked together to form a joint response). The results of this study indicate that the couples' moral reasoning level is more affected by the males' level of moral reasoning than by the females', and that this imbalance is especially true in couples where the female has high sex guilt. Given that these high sex guilt women follow their partners' lead in moral reasoning, it follows that their moral standards may be only loosely related to their actual sexual and contraceptive behavior.

This interpretation is consistent with the data on couples' sex guilt, moral reasoning, and sexual behavior presented by D'Augelli and Cross (1975). In this study, sixty-five dating college couples completed the Mosher Sex Guilt Inventory, a Kohlberg Moral Dilemmas questionnaire, and a sexual experience inventory that measured the intimacy of the couples' sexual activities. A stepwise multiple regression analysis revealed that the couple's level of sexual intimacy was best predicted by the male's sex guilt and moral reasoning level. The female's sex guilt contributed only weakly to the prediction equation, whereas her level of moral reasoning did not contribute at all. Apparently, then, the males set the sexual standards for these couples, especially when there was disagreement on what the standards should be. Combining the results of the two studies (Gerrard and Gibbons 1982; D'Augelli and Cross 1975) leads to the conclusion that high guilt women who happen to be in a relationship with a male with lower sex guilt will often abandon their personal (inhibitory) sexual standards in response to pressure from their boyfriends, and will engage in more intimate forms of sexual expression than they find comfortable. It would appear, then, that negative attitudes toward sexuality are associated with moral standards about sexual behavior that are rather tenuously held. Moreover, though neither of the studies examined contraceptive behavior directly, the lack of strong commitment to standards observed in the high guilt woman makes it very likely that their contraceptive behavior will be erratic.

Fortunately, more direct evidence of the crucial link between cognitive consistency and contraceptive use has been presented in another study of the consistency of attitudes and beliefs about contraception (Insko, Blake, Cialdini, and Mulaik 1970). These authors interviewed 256 black and white, married and unmarried women to assess their attitudes toward family planning. This study demonstrated that women who were not using contraception not only had less positive attitudes about birth control, as might be expected, but, more importantly, they also had less consistent attitude and belief systems about birth control than did women using contraceptives. The authors' interpretation of this finding is that the nonusers had not "sorted out or attended to the rewards or costs that can be achieved or avoided through the use of birth control" (1970:236).

Passivity.   The final connection between ineffective contraception and emotional orientation was first suggested by D'Augelli and Cross (1975), and later by Geis and Gerrard (1984). These authors raise the possibility that women with a strong negative emotional orientation toward sexuality are passive in sexual decision making. In their study of dating couples, D'Augelli and Cross found that women defer to their partners' preferences about the level of sexual intimacy the couple engages in. The Geis and Gerrard study found that single college women who reported using the condom during their last sexual encounter scored higher on both sex guilt and sex anxiety than did women who used other methods of birth control. Given that the condom is a method usually initiated by the male and is the male's responsibility, Geis and Gerrard concluded that this group of women tend to rely on their partners for contraception. In sum, these two studies suggest that women with negative emotional orientations toward sex do not actively participate in decision making regarding contraception. Given that the most effective, nonsurgical birth control methods available today (the pill and the IUD) usually require female initiative and female responsibility, being passive about contraception or relying on the male partner to provide it typically means less effective protection.

Summary

Though some have made theoretical arguments and provided data to the effect that women's contraceptive behavior is planned and rational even though it may be based on misinformation and irrational beliefs, the evidence reviewed here does not always support this argument. There is a large body of research consistent with the hypothesis that, at least for many women, effective contraceptive behavior is inhibited by their negative emotional orientation toward sex. Specifically, this emotional orientation is related to inhibited forms of sexual expression, misinformation about sex and contraception, choice of ineffective methods of birth control, and inconsistent use of chosen birth control methods.

The literature also suggests a number of mechanisms that may link this emotional orientation to actual contraceptive behavior. It suggests, for example, that women with a negative emotional orientation toward sex (1) have difficulty processing information about sex and contraception, (2) have internally inconsistent attitudes and beliefs about contraception, and (3) maintain their birth control preferences so tenuously that they are often passive in sexual decision-making situations. In short, these women often rely on their male partners for contraceptive decisions. Whether this passivity and reliance on the male is actually good or bad depends, of course, on their partner's behavior. I will now turn to an examination of the literature on the emotional cognitive antecedents of male contraceptive use.

Male Contraception

Problems with Measurement and Interpretation

In contrast to the vast literature on female contraceptive behavior, there is very little to be found on male contraceptive behavior. Before reviewing the literature, it is appropriate to ask why so much less research has been conducted on male contraception than on female contraception.

The first major obstacle to the examination of male contraceptive behavior is the difficulty in interpreting the data. If, for example, a man reports that he and his partner use the pill or an IUD, he is likely to be classified as an effective contraceptor. It is very difficult in such cases, however, for the investigator to determine if the man is indeed motivated to avoid conception, or if he just happens to be involved with a woman who is motivated to avoid pregnancy.

An example of this problem can be found in a recent study of variables that discriminate between effective and ineffective contraceptors (Geis and Gerrard 1984). In the study, we were better able to describe the personalities of effective male contraceptors than the personalities of effective female contraceptors. Men who reported using effective contraception were more open-minded, more informed about birth control, less dogmatic, more likely to be involved in a stable relationship, and older when they started engaging in sexual intercourse than were less effective male contraceptors. Given the previously outlined methodological problems in measuring male contraceptive effectiveness, however, it is dangerous to conclude that this profile is of men who initiate and practice effective contraception. In this study, as in many others, to be classified as effective contraceptors, men had to be in relationships with women who used the pill or IUD. This definition of male "effective contraception" makes it difficult to determine if the men who fit this description are really dedicated to effective contraception.

Another difficulty in exploring male contraceptive use is that men may not know if their partner was protected the last time they engaged in sexual intercourse. In fact, they may be generally unaware of their partner's use of the pill, IUD, or even the diaphragm. Though it may be tempting to simply blame men for their ignorance and lack of initiative, the issue is much more complex and warrants examination.

Male Responsibility

Perhaps the primary characteristic of modern contraceptive technology is that, with the exception of vasectomy, the most effective medical methods of birth control are designed for use by women rather than by men. As such, they usually necessitate female initiative and female responsibility. Use of the pill, IUD, and diaphragm, for example, all require the woman to visit a physician for a pelvic examination, something the man, of course, cannot do. In addition, and perhaps just as important, a woman can utilize these methods without her partner's involvement, even without his knowledge. Even when the man does take an active part in the decision, shares the expense, and, in the case of the pill and diaphragm, shares the reponsibility for using the method conscientiously, it is still the woman who faces the risk of potential medical side effects. The most effective, single methods of birth control, therefore—the pill and IUD—and even the relatively less effective diaphragm, are designed for women's bodies and require female initiation. Given these facts of modern medical technology, it is not surprising that many men allow their partners to make the decisions and to take most of the responsibility for contraception.

There are also strong cultural norms that decrease the male's feelings of responsibility about birth control. For example, the historical tendency for men to have more sexual partners and more casual sexual encounters than women still persists. Since a man is more likely than a woman to engage in a number of sexual liaisons, yet is not able to bring highly effective methods of contraception with him to these encounters, it makes sense that he would develop a reliance on his partners' use of contraceptive devices and medications.

Consider the male who is seriously concerned about the possibility of pregnancy and wants to take an active role in avoiding conception. What are his options? What can he suggest to his partner?

Male-initiated nonsurgical methods (i.e., the condom and withdrawal) are considerably less effective than the most effective female-initiated nonsurgical methods (i.e., the pill and IUD). For a man to implement any of the most effective birth control strategies, he must ask his partner to at least share the responsibility for using the method, and he must ask her to bear the medical risks associated with the methods. It is not unlikely, then, that a man might feel impotent in implementing an *effective* contraceptive strategy, and this feeling of impotence might lead him to abdicate responsibility for contraception and perhaps even ignore the possibility of conception.

To summarize, men are often inhibited from initiating effective contraception because the technology of birth control is designed for women's bodies, because the risks associated with these methods affect women's bodies, because the consequences of pregnancy and abortion are greater for women than for men, and because men are more likely than women to be engaging in sex in the context of casual relationships. It is not surprising, then, that men are more likely than women to report that they do not know what method of birth control was used the last time they had intercourse. This lack of knowledge makes tracing the antecedents of effective male contraception difficult. With this qualification of the definition of male "effective contraception" in mind, I will now turn to the literature on the emotional and cognitive antecedents of male contraception.

The High-risk Male

Two studies have provided evidence of a relationship between a negative emotional orientation toward sex and poor contraceptive practices in men, very similar to that demonstrated in women. In one of these studies, Fisher (1984) surveyed 145 university men to examine the relationship between their scores on the Sexual Opinion Survey and their use of condoms. He reports a moderate correlation ($r = .33$, $p < .05$), with erotophobic men less likely than erotophilic men to use condoms consistently. In a similar study of 142 university men, Przybyla (cited in Fisher, Byrne, and White 1983) found that erotophilic men were more likely than erotophobic men to report that they, or their partners, always used some method of contraception. The Fisher and Przybyla studies also provide us with evidence about *how* erotophobia is related to poor contraception in men. Przybyla reports that erotophobics think that using birth control will result in guilt feelings or in decreased sexual pleasure, and that they are less convinced than erotophilics that contraception is good, right, or effective.

Planning for Intercourse. To explore another aspect of effective contraception, Fisher (1984) asked erotophobic and erotophilic men to predict whether they would have sexual intercourse during the coming month. Even when past sexual frequency was statistically controlled, erotophilics were more likely than erotophobics to predict that they would have sexual intercourse. Next, Fisher checked the accuracy of these men's predictions at the end of the month. He reports that 17 percent of the erotophobic men who had not anticipated having sexual intercourse did, in fact, have intercourse. None of the erotophilic men had made this error in prediction. The erotophilic men were thus more likely than erotophobics to consider sex to be a part of their lives. That is, men with negative emotional orientations toward sex were less likely than men with positive orientations to view themselves as sexual beings. Though the small number of subjects in this study (only forty-two men reported that they had sex during the month) did not permit a statistical comparison of the contraceptive behaviors of the sexually active erotophobes and erotophiles, Fisher reports that all of these erotophobes reported using either rhythm or the pill. It is notable that both these methods are usually the female's responsibility. It is very likely, then, that all the erotophobic men who had "unanticipated" intercourse relied on their partners for contraception. These two studies suggest that for men, as for women, a negative emotional orientation toward sex is related to the choice of ineffective contraceptive methods, inconsistent use of methods, and generally negative attitudes toward birth control. In

addition, they suggest that this predisposition is related to lack of
planning for sexual intercourse and possibly to lack of planning for
contraception.

Three additional studies, discussed earlier in this chapter with
regard to women, provide evidence that the ineffective male contraceptor experiences the same problems with retaining sexual and
contraceptive information and with communicating about sex that
women experience. Both the Schwartz (1973) and Fisher (1980) studies
of retention of sexual information included male as well as female
subjects. In both studies, the findings were comparable for men and
women: both men and women with negative orientations toward sex
experienced more difficulty retaining sexual information than did
those with positive orientations. In a related study, Fisher, Miller,
Byrne, and White (1980) demonstrated that emotional orientation is
related to both males' and females' feelings regarding communication
about sex.

This body of literature suggests, then, that many of the dynamics
of effective contraceptive behavior are similar for men and women.
In both sexes, there is a reliable relationship between a negative
emotional orientation toward sex and (1) contraceptive risk taking,
(2) retention of sexual material, (3) attitudes toward contraception,
and (4) discomfort in communicating about sex. Nonetheless, there
is evidence in the literature of some differences between the antecedents of male contraceptive behavior and the antecedents of female
contraceptive behavior.

Cognitive Consistency. In the review of the literature on women's
contraceptive behavior presented earlier, it was suggested that high-
risk women evidence cognitive inconsistency regarding sexual attitudes and contraception. This hypothesis was supported by data on
the consistency of women's attitudes toward family planning and
contraceptive behavior (Insko et al. 1970), and by data indicating a
discrepancy between the moral reasoning levels high guilt women
can articulate and those they prefer (Gerrard and Gibbons 1982).
Though there is no study comparable to the Insko et al. study that
can provide evidence of the consistency of males' attitudes toward
family planning, the Gerrard and Gibbons study did include male
subjects and thus provides some basis for a comparison between the
sexes. In this study, both high and low sex guilt males articulated
sexual moral reasoning that was very close to the level of moral
reasoning they chose from a list of opinions. This outcome suggests
that, unlike the high guilt women for whom a discrepancy existed,
males' moral reasoning is generally (internally) consistent. One interpretation from these data is that, with regard to moral reasoning,

high guilt men appear to hold firmer attitude and belief systems about sex than do women. Though it is risky to extrapolate from these specific findings to contraceptive attitudes and beliefs, these data raise the possibility that men have more internally consistent attitudes about contraception that women do.

Acceptance of Sexuality.   It is noteworthy that Fisher and his colleagues have provided evidence of two important links between men's emotional orientation toward sex and contraceptive behavior that are not available for women. The first of these relationships is the connection between emotional orientation and acceptance of sexuality. The Fisher (1984) study cited above reports that erotophobic men are less accurate than erotophilic men in predicting whether they will have sexual intercourse and that their error was that they underestimated their sexual activity. This result suggests that erotophobic men are less comfortable with their sexual behavior than are erotophilic men.

Obtaining Contraceptives.   The second piece of evidence available for men but not for women concerns the relationship between negative emotional orientation toward sex and the act of obtaining contraceptive protection. Fisher, Fisher, and Byrne (1977) instructed forty single male subjects to purchase a pack of three lubricated condoms in a pharmacy, in a situation that required the subjects to make the purchase directly from the male pharmacist. After the sale was completed, the subjects' affective reactions to the process were measured. A negative reaction to the process was associated with a relative disdain for condoms, a perception that the pharmacist was making negative attributions about the subject, and apparently even negative judgments about the reliability of condoms. Since the design of this study does not allow causal interpretations, it is possible that the negative reaction to the process of buying the condoms created the attitudes about the condoms, pharmacist, and reliability of the method. Regardless, this study demonstrates a relationship between negative emotional reactions and the process of acquiring contraceptives that has serious implications for the contraceptive behavior of erotophobics.

Males' Effect on the Couples' Decision Making

Before leaving this review of the literature, it is appropriate to turn to the contraceptive decision-making processes of couples. The D'Augelli and Cross (1975) and Breda (1985) studies cited earlier in this chapter are two of the few studies that have examined this process. D'Augelli and Cross surveyed men and women enrolled in an introductory psychology class and their partners, that is those people they were dating casually, "pinned" or engaged to, or living with. Multiple regression was used to predict couples' sexual activities from both partners' sex guilt and moral reasoning scores. As noted earlier, the couple's level of sexual intimacy was best predicted by the male's sex guilt score (simple $r = -.38$, R^2 change $= .14$), next by the male's moral reasoning score (simple $r = -.29$, R^2 change $= .05$), and then by the female's sex guilt score (simple $r = -.34$, R^2 change $= .03$) (all $ps < .05$). D'Augelli and Cross concluded,

> in order to maintain a relationship, female partners might participate in sexual liaisons to a degree that is in excess of their personal preference, or they might inhibit sexual liaisons despite their preference. . . . This interpretation . . . is supported by the findings of earlier studies indicating that women will transgress their standards if the relationship is important enough to them. . . . This suggests that the male is more influential in setting standards than the female. (1975:46–47)

The D'Augelli and Cross study suggests, then, that the men do have the power to control the sexual situation. But since D'Augelli and Cross did not examine the contraceptive use of the couples they studied, we can only infer from their results that contraceptive decision making is also dominated by the male.

Breda, however, did examine the relationship between sex guilt, moral reasoning, and contraceptive use. She reports evidence consistent with the inference that contraceptive behavior in a couple is strongly influenced by the male partner. Her regression analyses indicated that the couples' contraceptive *behavior* was best predicted by the female's contraceptive preferences. When predictors of the females' *preferences* were examines, it became obvious that the best predictors were the *partner's preference*, his level of moral reasoning, and her sex guilt.

Earlier in this chapter, I argued that ineffective female contraceptors are likely to have high sex guilt, be passive, and exhibit cognitively inconsistent attitudes and beliefs about birth control. The D'Augelli and Cross study indicates that men control the sexual situation, and the Breda study suggests that men also have a very powerful influence on the contraceptive preferences of women with high sex guilt and, thus, on their contraceptive behavior.

Summary

A number of the important relationships between emotional orientation toward sexuality and contraceptive use apparently hold for both men and women. There are, however, two important differences suggested by the literature. The first is that, although women with negative emotional orientations or women who report ineffective contraception have inconsistent attitude and belief systems regarding sex or contraception, there is no evidence of this kind of cognitive inconsistency in men. This result suggests that men are less likely to be burdened with inconsistent and confusing attitudes and belief systems about contraception. In other words, whatever their cognitions, these cognitions are more likely to be both internally consistent and congruent with the man's behavior. The second important difference is that whereas there is evidence that women with negative attitudes toward sex tend to abdicate responsibility for sexual decisions to their partners, men with similarly negative attitudes apparently do not abdicate their responsibility. In fact, it appears that, regardless of the male's attitudes toward sex, his opinions are likely to be very influential in the decision-making process. One can only speculate about whether the strength of the males' influence is related to the interaction between their consistent, stable attitudes and their female partners' lack of consistency.

CONTRACEPTION IN THE 1980s

The vast majority of the literature I have reviewed in this chapter was written in the 1970s or based on data collected in the 1970s. Recent evidence suggests that there was a definite trend in the 1980s toward less sexual activity (Gerrard in press) and decreases in fertility among young women (O'Connell and Rogers 1984). Given this trend, are the conclusions presented thus far in this chapter still valid? To test the applicability of the 1970s data and conclusions to the early 1980s, I will examine data I collected at the University of Texas since the early 1970s.

The 1970s

During the 1973–74, 1978–79, and 1983–84 academic years, I collected data on the sexual activity, sex guilt, and contraceptive habits of female undergraduates at the University of Texas. Each year, the subjects (approximately one hundred per year) were unmarried women in a large, required, sophomore-level government class who volunteered to complete the questionnaires anonymously.[3] This data collection yielded three comparable samples separated by five years, which enabled me to examine changes in the sexual behavior and attitudes of college women over a span of ten years. I will first summarize the comparisons of the first two samples, and then discuss the most recent sample.

As can be seen in Table 1, there was a significant increase in the number of women reporting sexual activity between 1973 and 1978. In 1973, 35 percent reported having sexual intercourse once a month or more, whereas in 1978, the percentage of sexually active women increased to 51 percent. A 2 (1973 versus 1978) x 2 (active, inactive) analysis of variance of sex guilt scores demonstrated that, as would be expected, sexually active women had lower sex guilt scores than did sexually inactive women (16.39 versus 26.14, $F[1,216] = 59.29$, $p < .01$). More importantly, this analysis also indicated that although the women in the 1978 sample were more sexually active, their sex guilt scores were not lower than those of the women in the 1973 sample (22.47 versus 21.48 respectively, $F[1,216] = .63$, $p > .40$). Given this absence of change in the mean sex guilt score, it is not surprising that maximum likelihood logistic regression revealed differences between the sex guilt score that predicted sexual activity in 1973 and the score that predicted sexual activity in 1978. The thresholds estimated by this analysis were 14 for 1973 and 23 for 1978. The threshold in this case is the score on the sex guilt scale below which individuals are estimated to have a greater than 50 percent chance of being sexually experienced, above which they have less than a 50 percent chance of being sexually experienced. Comparison of these thresholds for sexual activity revealed that the difference was significant, X^2 ($df = 1$) $= 9.4$, $p < .005$.[4] It thus appears that the level of sex guilt sufficient to inhibit sexual activity in 1973 was no longer sufficient in 1978 (i.e., women with equally high levels of sex guilt were more likely to become sexually active in 1978 that in 1973). The mean sex guilt score for the *sexually active* women increased between 1973 and 1978 because more individuals with moderate and high sex guilt scores were sexually active in 1978.

Table 1. Mean Sex Guilt Scores by Year and Sexual Activity

Year	Mean for Year	Sexually Active	Sexually Inactive
1973–74	21.48	14.84	25.03
	(109)	(38)	(71)
1978–79	22.47	17.45	27.58
	(111)	(56)	(55)
1983–84	25.88	20.97	28.98
	(93)	(36)	(57)

Note: Number of subjects per cell is in parentheses.

These data provided an excellent opportunity to test the relationship hypothesized earlier in this chapter between a negative emotional orientation towards sex and contraceptive use. If sex guilt inhibits contraceptive use, even when it is not strong enough to inhibit sexual activity, then one could predict that the sexual revolution of the 1970s would be accompanied by a decrease in the use of effective methods of contraception. In other words, many of the moderate and high guilt women who were engaging in sexual intercourse in the late 1970s should have been inhibited from using effective methods of contraception. Two separate analyses provided support for this hypothesis. First, as reported in Gerrard (1982), there was a significant decrease in the use of effective methods of contraception between 1973 and 1978. The 1978 sexually active women in this study were less likely to report using the pill and IUD and more likely to report using less effective methods than were the 1973 sexually active women, X^2 $(df = 5) = 20.89$, $p < .0001$. Even more relevant to this issue, however, would be an examination of the contraceptive behavior of those moderate and high sex guilt women who were engaging in sexual intercourse in 1978 but would not have been sexually active if they had been part of the 1973 cohort. To determine whether this subgroup of women used poor contraception, the birth control methods utilized by sexually active women with sex guilt scores in the range of 13 to 23 (the sex guilt thresholds for sexual activity for 1973 and 1978, respectively) were compared with these methods used by sexually active women with sex guilt scores below 13. A Chi-square analysis of the methods used by these two subgroups was marginally significant (X^2 $[df = 4] = 8.94$, $p = .06$). This kind of inference, that is, using the threshold suggested by one cohort to define a subgroup in a second cohort, should be interpreted cautiously. It does, however, suggest that there is a group of moderate and high sex guilt women who were sexually active in 1978, but would presumably not have been sexually active if they had been part of the 1973–74 cohort. It also suggests that this group was using less effective methods of birth control than were the low sex guilt sexually active women. This analysis, then, supports the hypothesis that these women's sex guilt was not high enough to interfere with sexual activity, but it was high enough to inhibit effective contraception.

The 1983–84 Data

What happens, then, when we examine the 1983–1984 data? As can be seen in Table 1, sexual activity decreased between 1978 and 1983—from 51 percent reporting sexual activity in 1978 to 37 percent

in 1983 (partitioned X^2 [df = 1] = 6.41, p < .05).[5] Over the same
five-year period, the mean sex guilt score increased from 22.47 to
25.88 (F [1,202] = 5.09, p < .05). An examination of the probit
analysis conducted on these three samples reveals that although sex
guilt still predicts sexual activity, the maximum likelihood logistic
regression curve is significantly different in 1983 (G^2[4] = 12.7, p <
.05). The sex guilt threshold for sexual activity estimated by this
regression shifted from 23 in 1978 down to 18 in 1983. According
to the relationship I have hypothesized between sex guilt, sexual
activity, and contraceptive behavior, one would predict a return to
more effective methods of contraception in 1983 because fewer high
and moderate sex guilt women were engaging in intercourse. This
prediction is exactly what appears to have happened. As can be seen
in Table 2, the 1983 sexually active subjects were more likely to be
using effective methods of contraception than were the 1978 subjects.
A partitioned Chi-square test performed on the 1978 and 1983 data
reveals that this difference in methods was significant (X^2 [df = 4]
= 15.91, p < .01). There is clearly a trend back to the usage patterns
of 1973, with the pill once again becoming the method of preference
and the young women in the 1983 cohort relying much less on
ineffective methods such as rhythm, withdrawal, spermicides, or no
method at all. Moreover, these trends in contraceptive use are similar
to those reported in the 1982 National Survey of Family Growth
from the National Center for Health Statistics (Bachrach 1984).

One interpretation of these data, then, is that when sexual activity
increased in the mid-1970s, the increase was not accompanied by a
decrease in sex guilt. Women who became sexually active in the mid
to late 1970s, therefore, were more likely to have a disposition toward
sex that inhibited effective and consistent contraceptive use than were
sexually active women in the early 1970s. However, the trend toward
sexual activity among college students not only slowed in the early
1980s, but it actually reversed—sexual activity (at least on college
campuses) almost returned to levels of the early 1970s. Whether this
decrease was due to increased sex guilt among college women and/
or to the general tend toward more conservative political, economic,
and religious behavior remains to be seen. Clearly however, the
decrease in sexual activity was accompanied by a return to the use
of more effective methods of birth control, and there is good reason
to believe that the relatively better contraception reported in the
early 1980s resulted from the fact that fewer high and moderate sex
guilt women were engaging in sexual intercourse on a regular basis
than in 1978.[6]

This interpretation is also supported by data that indicate decreases
in fertility among young women over this same period of time

Table 2. Percentages of Sexually Active Women Using Specific Birth Control Methods in Each Year

	Pill	Barrier Methods	Spermicides	Rhythm, Withdrawal	No Method
1973–74	78.9	7.9	0.0	7.9	5.3
1978–79	36.5	9.6	13.5	23.1	17.3
1983–84	74.2	12.9	3.2	6.5	3.2

(O'Connell and Rogers 1984). This raises the possibility that the sexually permissive attitudes of the late 1970s and early 1980s were interpreted by many young women (and perhaps young men) as a sexual mandate—everyone was expected to be sexually active. This perception may then have contributed to many young women becoming sexually involved before they were emotionally (and contraceptively) prepared for intercourse. If so, what appears to have happened between 1978 and 1983 was a return (for whatever reasons) to a more conservative (and more typical) state of affairs, where young women were less likely to engage in sexual relationships. Women appear to have been more likely to wait until they were ready (both emotionally and contraceptively) for sexual intercourse.

Summary and Conclusions

The literature reviewed in this chapter on the emotional and cognitive barriers to effective contraception in women describes the female ineffective contraceptor as a person whose discomfort with sex influences her knowledge about birth control, her choice of methods, and her use of the methods she chooses. Furthermore, the literature supports an explanatory model suggesting that these negative attitudes toward sexuality interfere with women's abilities to process information about sex and contraception, to maintain internally consistent attitude and belief systems about contraception, and to take an active role in contraceptive decision making.

The research literature on male contraception supports the argument that most, but not all, of the dynamics of male contraception are similar to the dynamics of female contraceptive use. The one important difference between the sexes is that men with negative reactions have internally consistent and stable cognitions about sexual morality and contraception. In short, the literature on emotional and cognitive barriers to effective contraception for both men and women indicates that, though the dynamics are similar, men are less likely than women to be burdened with the confusion created by conflicting cognitions and thus are more likely to set the standards for sexual and contraceptive behavior. Whereas the female with negative attitudes is likely to be paralyzed by indecision and to follow her partner's lead, the male with similarly negative attitudes is likely to have definite ideas about the value and advisability of contraception. He will thus make the decisions for the couple, either consciously or unintentionally.

Some Speculations

The discussion now leads us to a consideration of couples' contraceptive behavior. Though it is always risky to speculate about how real people will behave in a given situation, I would like to hazard a guess (based on the literature reviewed in this chapter) about specific types of couples' contraceptive behavior. Let us consider four hypothetical couples: first, the couple that consists of an erotophobic male and an erotophobic female. To the extent that they are sexually active, this couple's behavior is predictable. Her confusion and passivity will more than likely augment his aversion to effective contraceptive methods, resulting in little or no initiation of effective birth control. When an erotophilic male is paired with an erotophilic female, the results are equally predictable. Both partners will be motivated to use effective contraception, have the knowledge necessary to do so, and not be inhibited in acquiring and utilizing an effective method.

But what about mixed couples—those couples whose emotional orientations toward sex are not congruent? First, let us examine a hypothetical couple where the male is erotophilic and the woman is erotophobic. Her erotophobia is likely to lead her to leave the decision making to him, and, being uninhibited by negative attitudes, he is likely to be motivated to avoid contraceptive risk. He will thus be inclined to prefer effective contraceptive methods, and she will be inclined to go along with his decision. The catch here is that the most effective nonsurgical method available to him (if she is truly passive) is the condom, not one of the most effective methods available. If she is not entirely passive and is willing to share some of the responsibility with him, they may attempt the IUD, sponge, diaphragm, or the pill. Research evidence suggests, however, that she will be inhibited from using these methods consistently and effectively. To have adequate protection, therefore, the erotophilic man with an erotophobic partner must be motivated enough to take the vast majority of the responsibility for both initiating and maintaining a contraceptive strategy. While I do not mean to imply that the woman in this hypothetical couple will actively sabotage her partner's efforts to avoid pregnancy, I am suggesting that her erotophobia will possibly make it difficult for her to be actively involved in the process, and thus may operate to undercut his efforts by inhibiting her conscientious cooperation in the strategy he has chosen (e.g., she may forget to take her pill daily).

Now for the last hypothetical couple, where the woman is erotophilic and the man is erotophobic. The woman in this couple will probably be motivated to adopt an effective method of contraception and will have the necessary information and commitment to do so. The man will more than likely be opposed to using effective methods of contraception and may actually argue against the use of the IUD, pill, or diaphragm. He will also probably be unprepared to use a condom. However, in this case, medical technology favors the woman—she can plan a strategy, take the steps necessary to implement it, and even practice effective contraception without her partner's knowledge, if need be. So though this particular hypothetical couple may experience the most overt conflict in joint decision making about contraception, the power to contracept lies in the woman's hands, and the result is likely to be effective contraception unless the woman is much less dominant than her partner.

As was noted earlier, speculation based on this body of literature is risky. It does, however, serve two important purposes. First, such speculation makes possible intervention strategies salient. The studies reviewed in this chapter suggest that men have a great deal of influence on couples' contraceptive behavior. They also suggest that men have greater attitude/behavior consistency than many women. Last, but not least, these studies demonstrate a very reliable relationship between contraception and emotional reactions to sex. All these conclusions have important implications for intervention strategies.

The second function of this type of review, and of speculation about the relationship between emotional/cognitive factors and couples' contraceptive behavior, is that they raise additional questions that future research can address. Obviously, many gaps exist in our knowledge of how emotions and cognitions affect female contraceptive behavior, in our knowledge of men's contraceptive behavior, and in our knowledge of the dynamics of couples' contraceptive behavior. All these areas are fertile ground for further investigation.

References

Ajzen, I., and Fishbein, M. (1980). *Understanding attitudes and predicting social behavior.* Englewood Cliffs, N.J.: Prentice-Hall.

Atkinson, L., Schearer, S. B., Harkavy, O., and Lincoln, R. (1980). Prospects for improved contraception. *Family Planning Perspectives, 12*, 173–192.

238   Meg Gerrard

238   Meg Gerrard

238 MEG GERRARD

238 — MEG GERRARD

Bachrach, C. A. (1984). Contraceptive practice among American Women, 1973–1982. *Family Planning Perspectives, 16,* 253–259.

Benditt, J. M. (1980). Current contraceptive research. *Family Planning Perspectives, 12,* 149–155.

Breda, C. R. (1985). *Sex guilt, moral reasoning, sexual activity and contraceptive practices among dating college couples.* Unpublished Masters thesis, University of Kansas, Lawrence, Kansas.

Cooperman, C., and Weinstein, S. A. (1978). Contraceptive counselor's dilemma: Safety of effectiveness? *Journal of Sex Research, 14,* 145–150.

D'Augelli, J. F., and Cross, H. (1975). Relationship of sex guilt and moral reasoning to premarital sex in college women and in couples. *Journal of Consulting and Clinical Psychology, 43,* 40–47.

Davidson, A. R., and Jaccard, J. J. (1975). Population psychology: A new look at an old problem. *Journal of Personality and Social Psychology, 31,* 1055–1073.

Fishbein, M. (1972). Toward an understanding of family planning behaviors. *Journal of Applied Social Psychology, 2,* 214–227.

Fishbein, M., and Ajzen, I. (1975). *Belief, attitude, intention and behavior: An introduction to theory and research.* Reading, Mass.: Addison-Wesley.

Fishbein, M., and Jaccard, J. J. (1973). Theoretical and methodological considerations in the prediction of family planning intentions and behavior. *Representative Research in Social Psychology, 4,* 37–51.

Fisher, W. A. (1980). Erotophobia-erotophilia and performance in a human sexuality course. Unpublished manuscript, University of Western Ontario.

Fisher, W. A. (1984). Predicting contraceptive behavior among university men: The role of emotions and behavior intentions. *Journal of Applied Social Psychology, 14,* 104–123.

Fisher, W. A., and Byrne, D. (1978). Individual differences in affective, evaluative, and behavioral responses to an erotic film. *Journal of Applied Social Psychology, 8,* 355–365.

Fisher, W. A., Byrne, D., Edmunds, M., Miller, C. T., Kelley, K., and White, L. A. (1979). Psychological and situation-specific correlates of contraceptive behavior among university women. *Journal of Sex Research, 15,* 38–55.

Fisher, W. A., Byrne, D., and White, L. H. (1983). Emotional barriers to contraception. In D. Byrne and W. A. Fisher (eds.), *Adolescents, sex, and contraception* (pp. 207–239). N. J.: Lawrence Erlbaum.

Fisher, W. A., Fisher, J. D., and Byrne, D. (1977). Consumer reactions to contraceptive purchasing. *Personality and Social Psychology Bulletin, 3,* 293–296.

Fisher, W. A., Miller, C. T., Byrne, D., and White, L. A. (1980). Talking dirty: Responses to communicating a sexual message as a function of situational and personality factors. *Basic and Applied Social Psychology, 1,* 115–126.

Galbraith, G. G., Hahn, K., and Lieberman, H. (1968). Personality correlates of free-associative sex responses to double-entendre words. *Journal of Consulting and Clinical Psychology, 32,* 193–197.

Galbraith, G. G., and Mosher, D. L. (1968). Associative sexual responses in relation to sexual arousal, guilt, and external approval contingencies. *Journal of Personality and Social Psychology, 10,* 142–147.

Geis, B. D. (1982). *College students' contraceptive behavior: A discriminant analysis of high, marginal, and low contraceptive effectiveness groups.* Unpublished Masters thesis, University of Kansas, Lawrence, Kansas.

Geis, B. D. (1984). *A covariance structure analysis of contraceptive behavior.* Unpublished Ph.D. dissertation, University of Kansas, Lawrence, Kansas.

Geis, B. D., and Gerrard, M. (1984). Predicting male and female contraceptive behavior: A discriminant analysis of groups high, moderate, and low in contraceptive effectiveness. *Journal of Personality and Social Psychology, 46,* 669–680.

Gerrard, M. (1977). Sex guilt in abortion patients. *Journal of Consulting and Clinical Psychology, 45,* 708.

Gerrard, M. (1982). Sex, sex guilt, and contraceptive use. *Journal of Personality and Social Psychology, 42,* 153–158.

Gerrard, M., and Gibbons, F. X. (1982). Sexual experience, sex guilt, and sexual moral reasoning. *Journal of Personality, 50,* 345–359.

Gerrard, M., McCann, I. L., and Fortini, M. (1983). Prevention of unwanted pregnancy. *American Journal of Community Psychology, 11,* 153–168.

Gerrard, M. (In press). Sex, sex guilt, and contraceptive use revisited: Trends in the 1980s. *Journal of Personality and social Psychology.*

Goldfarb, L. (1985). *Sex guilt, physiological arousal, and retention of contraceptive information.* Unpublished Ph.D. dissertation, University of Kansas, Lawrence, Kansas.

Goldsmith, S., Gabrielson, M., Gabrielson, I., Matthews, V., and Potts, L. (1972). Teenagers, sex, and contraception. *Family Planning Perspectives, 4,* 32–38.

Gough, H. G. (1973). A factor analysis of contraceptive preferences. *Journal of Psychology, 84,* 199–210.

Grimes, D. A. (1984). Second-trimester abortions in the United States. *Family Planning Perspectives, 16,* 260–266.

Harvey, A. L. (1976). Risky and safe contraceptors: Some personality factors. *Journal of Psychology, 92,* 109–112.

Henshaw, S. K., Forrest, J. G., and Blaine, E. (1984). Abortion services in the United States, 1981 and 1983. *Family Planning Perspectives, 16,* 119–127.

Horowitz, N. (1980). Contraceptive practices of young women with two adolescent pregnancies. In J. E. Bedger (ed.), *Teenage pregnancy: Research related to clients and services.* Springfield, Ill.: Charles C. Thomas.

Insko, C. A., Blake, R. R., Cialdini, R. B., and Mulaik, S. (1970). Attitudes toward birth control and cognitive consistency: Theoretical and practical implications of survey data. *Journal of Personality and Social Psychology, 16,* 228–237.

Jaccard, J. J., and Davidson, A. R. (1972). Toward an understanding of family planning behaviors: An initial investigation. *Journal of Applied Social Psychology, 2,* 228–235.

Jain, A. K. (1976). Cigarette smoking, use of oral contraceptives, and my-ocardial infarction. *American Journal of Obstetrics and Gynecology, 126,* 301.

Jain, A. K. (1977). Mortality risk associated with the use of oral contraceptives. *Studies in Family Planning, 8,* 50–54.

Janda, L. H., and O'Grady, K. E. (1980). Development of a sex anxiety inventory. *Journal of Consulting and Clinical Psychology, 48,* 169–175.

Keller, A. B., Sims, J. H., Henry, W. E., and Crawford T. J. (1970). Psychological sources of "resistance" to family planning. *Merrill-Palmer Quarterly of Behavior and Development, 16,* 286–302.

Kinnaird, K. (1985). *Attitudes about marriages, divorce, and premarital sexual activity among college women as a function of parent's marital status.* Unpublished Ph.D. dissertation, University of Kansas, Lawrence, Kansas.

Koenig, M. A., and Zelnick, M. (1982). The risk of premarital first pregnancy among metropolitan-area teenagers: 1976 and 1979. *Family Planning Perspectives, 14,* 239–247.

Kohlberg, L. (1964). Development of moral character and moral ideology. In M. L. Hoffman and L. W. Hoffman (eds.), *Review of child development research* (Vol. 1, pp. 383–432). New York: Russell Sage Foundation.

Langston, D. R. (1973). Sex guilt and sex behavior in college students. *Journal of Personality Assessment, 37,* 467–472.

Love, R. E., Sloan, L. R., and Schmidt, J. J. (1976). Viewing pornography and sex guilt: The priggish, the prudent, and the profligate. *Journal of Consulting and Clinical Psychology, 44,* 624–629.

Luker, K. (1975). *Taking chances: Abortion and the decision not to contracept.* Berkeley: University of California Press.

MacLeod, J., and Gold, R. A. (1953). The male factor in fertility and infertility: VI Semen quality and certain other factors in relation to ease of conception. *Fertility and Sterility, 4,* 10–33.

McCann, I.L. (1981). *Information only and cognitive restructuring interventions with contraceptive risk takers.* Unpublished Masters thesis, University of Kansas, Lawrence, Kansas.

Mendelsohn, M. J., and Mosher, D. L. (1979). Effects of sex guilt and premarital sexual permissiveness on role-played sex education and moral attitudes. *Journal of Sex Research, 15,* 174–183.

Mindick, B., Oskamp, S., and Berger, D. E. (1977). Prediction of success or failure in birth planning: An approach to prevention of individual and family stress. *American Journal of Community Psychology, 5,* 447–459.

Mindick, B., Oskamp, S., and Berger, D. E. (1978). *Prediction of adolescent contraceptive practice.* Paper presented at the American Psychological Association Annual Convention.

Mosher, D. L. (1966). The development and multitrait-multimethod matrix analysis of three measures of three aspects of guilt. *Journal of Consulting and Clinical Psychology, 30,* 25–29.

Mosher, D. L. (1968). Measurement of guilt in females by self-report inventories. *Journal of Consulting and Clinical Psychology, 32,* 690–695.

Mosher, D. L. (1973). Sex differences, sex experience, sex guilt, and explicitly sexual films. *Journal of Social Issues, 29,* 95–112.

Mosher, D. L. (1979). Sex guilt and sex myths in college men and women. *Journal of Sex Research, 15,* 224–234.

Mosher, D. L., and Cross, H. (1971). Sex guilt and premarital sexual experience of college students. *Journal of Consulting and Clinical Psychology, 36,* 27–32.

Mosher, D. L., and Greenberg, I. (1969). Females' affective responses to reading erotic literature. *Journal of Consulting and Clinical Psychology, 33,* 472–477.

O'Connell, M., and Rogers, C. C. (1984). Out-of-wedlock births, premarital pregnancies, and their effect on family formation and dissolution. *Family Planning Perspectives, 16,* 157–170.

Oskamp, S., Mindick, B., Hayden, M., and Pion, G. (1976). *Contraceptive attitudes and behavior of several groups of women.* Paper presented at the American Psychological Association Annual Convention.

Pratt, W. F., Mosher, W. D., Bachrach, C. A., and Horn, M. C. (1984). Understanding U.S. fertility: Findings from the National Survey of Family Growth, Cycle III. *Population Bulletin, 39,* 3–10.

Schwartz, S. (1973). Effects of sex guilt and sexual arousal on the retention of birth control information. *Journal of Consulting and Clinical Psychology, 41,* 61–64.

Seikel, P. (1985). *Contraceptive use in college women: A test of Lindemann's experiential model.* Unpublished Ph.D. dissertation, University of Kansas, Lawrence, Kansas.

Tanfer, K., and Horn, M. C. (1985). Contraceptive use, pregnancy and fertility patterns among single American women in their 20s. *Family Planning Perspectives, 17,* 10–19.

White, L. A., Fisher, W. A., Byrne, D., and Kingma, R. (1977). *Development and validation of a measure of affective orientation to erotica: The Sexual Opinion Survey.* Paper presented to the Midwestern Psychological Association Annual Convention.

Zelnick, M., and Kantner, J. E. (1979). Reasons for nonuse of contraception by sexually active women aged 15–19. *Family Planning Perspectives, 11,* 289.

Zelnick, M., and Kantner, J. E. (1980). Sexual activity, contraceptive use and pregnancy among metropolitan area teenagers: 1971–1979. *Family Planning Perspectives, 12,* 230–237.

Zelnick, M., Kim, Y. J., and Kantner, J. E. (1979). Probabilities of intercourse and contraception among U.S. teenage women, 1971–1976. *Family Planning Perspectives, 11,* 177–183.

Zelnick, M., and Shah, F. K. (1983). First intercourse among young Americans. *Family Planning Perspectives, 15,* 64–70.

NOTES

[1] Though this decline may be due in part to realistic concerns about the side effects of the pill and IUD (Atkinson, Schearer, Harkavy, and Lincoln 1980; Benditt 1980;

Cooperman and Weinstein 1978), much of the fear surrounding these methods can be attributed to a misinterpretation or overreaction to the health hazards associated with them. The pill is risky for female smokers over age 35, and up to 15 percent of the women who try IUDs cannot tolerate them. For young women, however, the medical risks associated with the use of both these methods still compare favorably with the medical risks involved in either abortion or pregnancy and delivery (Jain 1976, 1977).

² Throughout this chapter I will use the terms "attitudes toward sex" and "emotional orientation toward sex" interchangeably. These constructs are usually operationalized as the Sex Anxiety Inventory (Janda and O'Grady 1980), the Sex Guilt Inventory (Mosher 1966, 1968), and the Sexual Opinion Survey (White, Fisher, Byrne, and Kingma 1977). In an unpublished factor analysis of his thesis data, Geis (1982) found that these three measures formed a single factor with loadings ranging from .65 to .87. Fisher, Byrne, and White (1983) also report a correlation between the Mosher Sex Guilt Inventory and the Sexual Opinion Survey of .60.

³ Though one might question the generalizability of data collected at any one institution, such as the University of Texas, the contraceptive practices and sexual activity rates reported here are very consistent with those my students and I have found at the University of Kansas (Geis 1982, 1984; Goldfarb 1985; Kinnaird 1985; McCann 1981; Seikel 1985).

⁴ For a more complete report on the comparison of these first two samples, see Gerrard 1982.

⁵ This dramatic decrease in sexual activity among undergrduate women at the University of Texas has been replicated at the University of Kansas (Geis 1982, 1984; Goldfarb 1985; Kinnaird 1985; McCann 1981; Seikel 1985) and is consistent with national trends reported by Pratt, Mosher, Bachrach, and Horn (1984).

⁶ An alternative explanation for the shift away from the pill and IUD in the late 1970s is that these young women were influenced by publicity about these methods' medical side effects. While fear of these methods may explain some of the change, Gerrard, McCann, and Fortini (1983) provide evidence that high sex guilt women were more prone to attend to the medical risks associated with contraception than were low sex guilt women.

Appendix

Personal Description Scale

On the following pages are fifty-two statements. If a statement is highly characteristic of you, you would agree very strongly with it. If the statement is not at all characteristic of you, you would disagree very strongly with it. For each of the following, please respond with a letter *A* to *E* to express the degree to which a statement describes you. For each statement, use a pencil to indicate your answer on the computer answer sheet, starting with number one.

A response of *A* indicates either that the statement is highly characteristic of you or that you very strongly agree with it. A response of *E* indicates either that the statement is not at all characteristic of you or that you very strongly disagree with it. A response of *C* can indicate that you are not sure or have not decided, that the statement is a toss-up for you. Finally, a response of *B* would indicate somewhat more moderate agreement with the statement than an *A*; a response of *D* would indicate somewhat more moderate disagreement with the statement than an *E*. Remember:

A expresses *strongest agreement*
B expresses *moderate agreement*
C indicates you are *unsure* or *undecided*, or that it is a toss-up
D expresses *moderate disagreement*
E expresses *strongest disagreement*

I Strongly Agree : <u>*A* : : *B* : *C* : *D* : *E* :</u> I Strongly Disagree

(Items for male respondents)

1. Life can be pretty boring.
2. When I was a kid, I was suspended from school.
3. I usually eat breakfast.
4. I tend to defy people in authority.
5. I have done dangerous things just for the thrill of it.
6. I am the kind of person who would stand up on a roller coaster.

243

7. I do not believe in gambling.
8. I hate any kind of schedule or routine.
9. I usually meet deadlines with no trouble.
10. I insist on traveling safely rather than quickly.
11. I have my car serviced regularly.
12. Sometimes I don't seem to care what happens to me.
13. I like to play poker for high stakes.
14. I smoke over a pack of cigarettes a day.
15. I have frequently fallen in love with the wrong person.
16. I just don't know where my money goes.
17. Wearing a helmet ruins the fun of a motorcycle ride.
18. Lots of laws seem made to be broken.
19. I like jobs with an element of danger.
20. I often walk out in the middle of an argument.

I Strongly Agree $: A : B : C : D : E :$ I Strongly Disagree

I Strongly Agree $: A : B : C : D : E :$ I Strongly Disagree

21. Often I don't take very good care of myself.
22. I usually follow through on projects.
23. I've made positive contributions to my community.
24. I make promises that I don't keep.
25. An occasional fight makes a guy more of a man.
26. I usually call a doctor when I'm sure I'm becoming ill.
27. I sometimes forget important appointments I wanted to keep.
28. I drink two or fewer cups of coffee a day.
29. It's easy to get a raw deal from life.
30. I eat too much.
31. I often skip meals.
32. I don't usually lock my house or apartment door.
33. I know who to call in an emergency.
34. I can drink more alcohol than most of my friends.
35. The dangers from using contraceptives are greater than the dangers from not using them.
36. I seem to keep making the same mistakes.
37. I have my eyes examined at least once a year.
38. I lose often when I gamble for money.
39. I leave on an outdoor light when I know I'll be coming home late.

I Strongly Agree $: A : B : C : D : E :$ I Strongly Disagree

I Strongly Agree $: A : B : C : D : E :$ I Strongly Disagree

40. Using contraceptives is too much trouble.
41. I do things I know will turn out badly.
42. When I was in high school, I was considered a good student.
43. I have trouble keeping up with bills and paper work.
44. I rarely misplace even small sums of money.
45. I am frequently late for important things.

46. I frequently don't do boring things I'm supposed to do.
47. I feel really good when I'm drinking alcohol.
48. Sometimes when I don't have anything to drink, I think about how good some booze would taste.
49. It's really satisfying to inhale a cigarette.
50. I like to smoke.
51. I believe that saving money gives a person a real sense of accomplishment.
52. I like to exercise.

I Strongly Agree : *A* : *B* : *C* : *D* : *E* : I Strongly Disagree

Scoring Key for Chronic Self-Destructiveness for Male Respondents

Males: Add responses to items 3, 7, 9, 10, 11, 22, 23, 26, 28, 33, 37, 39, 42, 44, 51, 52.
Reverse score (1=5, 2=4, 3=3, 4=2, 5=1) and then add responses to items 1, 2, 4, 5, 6, 8, 12, 13, 14, 15, 16, 17, 18, 19, 20, 21, 24, 25, 27, 29, 30, 31, 32, 34, 35, 36, 38, 40, 41, 43, 45, 46, 47, 48, 49, 50.
Total = Chronic Self-Destructiveness Score

I Strongly Agree : *A* : *B* : *C* : *D* : *E* : I Strongly Disagree

(Items for female respondents)

1. I like to listen to music with the volume turned up as loud as possible.
2. Life can be pretty boring.
3. I do not stay late at social functions when I must get up early.
4. I use or have used street drugs.
5. I like to spend my free time "messing around."
6. As a rule, I do not put off doing chores.
7. Riding fast in a car is thrilling.
8. I tend to defy people in authority.
9. I have a complete physical examination once a year.
10. I have done dangerous things just for the thrill of it.
11. I find it necessary to plan my finances and keep a budget.
12. I let people take advantage of me.
13. I hate any kind of schedule or routine.
14. I usually meet deadlines with no trouble.
15. I am familiar with basic first-aid practices.
16. Even when I have to get up early, I like to stay up late.
17. I insist on traveling safely rather than quickly.
18. I have my car serviced regularly.

I Strongly Agree : *A* : *B* : *C* : *D* : *E* : I Strongly Disagree

I Strongly Agree : A : B : C : D : E : I Strongly Disagree

19. People tell me I am disorganized.
20. It is important to get revenge when someone does you wrong.
21. Sometimes I don't seem to care what happens to me.
22. I like to play poker for high stakes.
23. I have frequently fallen love with the wrong person.
24. I just don't know where my money goes.
25. Wearing a helmet ruins the fun of a motorcycle ride.
26. I take care to eat a balanced diet.
27. Lots of laws seem made to be broken.
28. I am almost always on time.
29. Often I don't take very good care of myself.
30. I rarely put things off.
31. I speak my mind even when it's not in my best interest.
32. I usually follow through on projects.
33. I've made positive contributions to my community.
34. I make promises that I don't keep.
35. I always do what my doctor or dentist recommends.
36. I know the various warning signs of cancer.
37. I usually call a doctor when I'm sure I'm becoming ill.
38. I maintain an up-to-date address/phone book.

I Strongly Agree : A : B : C : D : E : I Strongly Disagree

I Strongly Agree : A : B : C : D : E : I Strongly Disagree

39. I sometimes forget important appointments I wanted to keep.
40. It's easy to get a raw deal from life.
41. I know who to call in an emergency.
42. I can drink more alcohol than most of my friends.
43. I seem to keep making the same mistakes.
44. I lose often when I gamble for money.
45. Using contraceptives is too much trouble.
46. I often use non-prescription medicines (aspirin, laxatives, etc.).
47. I do things I know will turn out badly.
48. When I was in high school, I was considered a good student.
49. I have trouble keeping up with bills and paper work.
50. I am frequently late for important things.
51. I frequently don't do boring things I'm supposed to do.
52. Sometimes when I don't have anything to drink, I think about how good some booze would taste.

I Strongly Agree : A : B : C : D : E : I Strongly Disagree

Scoring Key for Chronic Self-Destructiveness for Female Respondents

Females: Add responses to items 3, 6, 9, 11, 14, 15, 17, 18, 26, 28, 30, 32, 33, 35, 36, 37, 38, 41, 48.

Reverse score (1=5, 2=4, 3=3, 4=2, 5=1) and then add responses
to items 1, 2, 4, 5, 7, 8, 10, 12, 13, 16, 19;, 20, 21, 22, 23, 24,
25, 27, 29, 31, 34, 39, 40, 42, 43, 44, 45, 46, 47, 49, 50, 51, 52.
Total = Chronic Self-Destructiveness Score

Name Index

Abbey, A., 74, *92*, 133, *137*, 160, *166*, 204, *207*
Abelson, H., 155, 163, *166*
Abel, G. G., 149, *166*
Ablanalp, J. M., 107, 117, 120, *120*
Abrahamsson, L., 108, *120*
Abrahams, D., 70, 74, *100*
Abraham, G. E., 105, 107, 108, 109, *120, 122*
Abramowitz, E. S., 111, *120*
Abramson, P. R., 6, *11*, 145, 147, 156, 158, *166, 171, 172*
Addison, R., 43, *54*
Addition, H., 43, *54*
Adler, J. D., 9, *11*
Adler, N., 19, *46, 56*
Agras, W. S., 144, *166*
Ajzen, I., 214, 215, *237*
Alan Guttmacher Institute, 151, *166*
Alcock, J., 61, 62, *92*
Alsum, P., 27, 31, *46, 54*
Alta, 175–176, *207*
Altman, I., 66, 76, *92*
Amoroso, D. M., 150, 154, 159, 162, *166, 167*
Andersch, B., 108, 109, *120*
Andersen, A. N., 107, 108, *120*
Anderson, B., 81, *94*
Andersson, M., 109, *120*
Arafat, I., 128, *137*
Arai, Y., 18, *46*
Armitage, C., 44, *54*
Arndt, W. B., 160, *166*
Arnold, A. P., 23, *48*
Aronson, L. R., 27, *55*
Aronson, V., 70, 74, *100*
Asano, Y., 111, *122*
Assael, M., 108, *123*
Asso, D., 104, *120*

Athamasion, R., 186, 207
Athanasiou, R., 131, *137*
Atkinson, L., 241, *237*
Austin, P., 43, *49*

Bachrach, C. A., 234, *238*, 241, 242
Backstrom, C. T., 118, *120*
Backstrom, T., 106, 107, 110, 113, 119, *120, 121, 125*
Bagnara, J. T., 14, *57*
Baird, D. T., 118, *120*
Baker, A. H., 111, *120*
Baker, R., 27, *53*
Baker, S. R., 36, *49*
Bakkestrom, E., 42, *58*
Balswick, J. O., 127, *138*
Balthazart, J., 19, *46*
Bambara, T. C., 191, 194, *207*
Bancroft, J., 38, 46, 81, 90, *92*, 106, 113, *120, 125*
Bandura, A., 91, *92*
Banikiotes, P. G., 77, *98*
Baral, R., 73, *95*
Barash, D. P., 60, 63, 65, 75, 80, *92*
Barclay, A. M., 144, 150, 160, *166*
Bardwick, J. M., 113, *123*
Barfield, R. J., 28, 32, *49, 56*
Barkley, M. S., *46*
Barlow, D., 144, 146, *172*
Barraclough, C. A., 17, *46*
Bartell, G. D., 136, *137*
Bart, P., 143, 155, *172*
Basu, B., 40, *51*
Bauer, K., 127, *138*
Bauman, K. E., 127, *137*
Baum, C., 184, *207*
Baum, M. J., 19, 22, 23, 27, *46, 47*
Beach, F. A., 13, 22, 26, 27, 31, 32, 45, *47, 52*, 70, 75, *94*, 142, 168, 178, *207*

Subject Index